Researc

Doing Educational Research in Rural Settings is a much-needed guide for educational researchers whose research interests are located outside metropolitan areas in places that are generally considered to be rural. This book is both timely and important, as it takes up the key question of how to conduct educational research within and for rural communities. It explores the impact of educational research in such contexts in terms of the lasting good of research and also those being researched.

The authorship is international and brings together researchers experienced in conducting educational inquiry in rural places from across European, Australian, American and Canadian contexts, allowing readers insight into national and regional challenges. It also draws on the research experiences and methodological challenges faced by senior figures in the field of rural educational research, as well as those in their early careers.

Key topics include:

- working with and within the rural
- the impact of educational globalisation and the problematisation of cultural difference in social research
- researcher subjectivities
- the position of education research in rural contexts
- the usefulness of research
- reciprocity and converging interest
- ethics and confidentiality.

This book is uniquely written with an eye to practicality and applicability, and will be an engaging guide for higher degree and doctoral students seeking to gain a stronger understanding of educational research in rural settings.

Simone White is Professor of Teacher Education at the Faculty of Education, Monash University, Victoria, Australia.

Michael Corbett is Professor at the School of Education, Acadia University, Nova Scotia, Canada.

Doing Educational Research in Rural Settings

Methodological issues, international perspectives and practical solutions

Edited by Simone White and Michael Corbett

Routledge
Taylor & Francis Group
LONDON AND NEW YORK

First published 2014
by Routledge
2 Park Square, Milton Park, Abingdon, Oxon OX14 4RN

and by Routledge
711 Third Avenue, New York, NY 10017

Routledge is an imprint of the Taylor & Francis Group, an informa business

British Library Cataloguing in Publication Data
A catalogue record for this book is available from the British Library

Library of Congress Cataloging-in-Publication Data
Doing educational research in rural settings: methodological issues,
international perspectives and practical solutions / edited by Simone
White, Michael Corbett.
pages cm Includes bibliographical references and index.
1. Education–Research. 2. Education–Research–Methodology.
3. Education–Research–Social aspects. 4. Education, Rural. I. White,
Simone. II. Corbett, Michael.
LB1028.D593 2014
370.72–dc23
2013042908

ISBN: 978-0-415-82350-0 (hbk)
ISBN: 978-0-415-82351-7 (pbk)
ISBN: 978-1-315-77844-0 (ebk)

Typeset in Galliard
by Cenveo Publisher Services

MIX
Paper from
responsible sources
FSC   FSC® C013056
www.fsc.org

Printed and bound in Great Britain by
TJ International Ltd, Padstow, Cornwall

We dedicate this book to all those who have shared their stories, experiences and challenges in living, learning and working in rural places with us. As researchers, we thank you and we hope that this book is used by future researchers to learn to tread more lightly when they need to; to consider the legacy they leave with the work they do and who will endeavour to give more than they receive.

Contents

About the contributors

Michelle Anderson has worked as a researcher in Australia and England. As a Principal Research Fellow at the Australian Council for Educational Research (ACER), much of her work involved research and evaluation projects in the areas of school leadership and school–community partnerships. This led to a strong research focus on philanthropy in education and the development of capacity-building initiatives for school leaders from regional, rural and urban settings. Through this work Michelle has connected with many interesting organisations, such as the Foundation for Rural and Regional Renewal. Complementing this work, Michelle is on the board of the not-for-profit organisation Schools Connect Australia. Previously in education, Michelle has worked as a teacher, executive across health and education and in the curriculum and welfare areas of the Victorian education department.

Pam Bartholomaeus is a Lecturer in the School of Education at Flinders University, located in Adelaide, South Australia. She teaches undergraduate and graduate-entry students in the middle and secondary school programme, with a focus on literacy education. She supervises doctoral students researching questions that have a focus on place, including seeking socially just educational outcomes for people with a close connection to their place. Her current research is focused on rural education, rural futures, rural sustainability, place-based education and theorising about place. She is also researching colonisation, particularly in relation to literacy education for rural students and their communities. Pam and her husband divide their time between working in Adelaide and managing a family farming property in rural South Australia, and so she is experiencing first-hand some of the changes happening in rural communities and primary industries. Her key objective is working for sustainability and exciting futures for rural communities and people living in non-metropolitan locations more generally.

Tanya Brann-Barrett is an Associate Professor in the Communication Department at Cape Breton University, Canada. Her research interests include social exclusion and rural community development education; issues of public engagement and citizenship as they relate to youth, young adults, gender, post-industrialism and class; health and family communication and visual ethnography and arts-based inquiry. She incorporates media and arts in her teaching and all aspects of her research from gathering insights to sharing what emerges from her work. Tanya's recent research examines ways youth living in small, post-industrial regions learn about, experience and perceive civic engagement. As the social, cultural and economic landscape of their communities shift, she focuses on the impact perceived local histories have on youth expectations of engagement and their sense of community connections both locally and globally. Envisioning communities as classroom, her intention is to inform educational practices that enable young people to interrogate the historical and contemporary condition that influence their sense of their small communities and their place therein.

Michael Corbett is Professor in the School of Education at Acadia University, Nova Scotia, Canada. His research interrogates contemporary and historical conceptions of the rural, and particularly the ways in which these conceptions have played into policy and discourse around education, schooling and literacies. This work has included studies of rural outmigration in Atlantic Canada, literacies in rural contexts, the viability of small rural schools and the use of film and video as a new literate medium in middle school. He has published widely in academic journals and in the popular press and has worked internationally in the United States, Finland, Norway, Australia, Korea and China. Michael has also supported a number of community groups in Nova Scotia and throughout Canada in struggles to protect small community-based schools. His most recent book is a collection entitled *Rethinking Rural Literacies: Transnational Perspectives*, co-edited with Bill Green and published by Palgrave Macmillan in 2013.

Kim Donehower's research on rural literacy began in her maternal Appalachian hometown, which had seen three waves of literacy interventions by outsiders. Since then, Kim has continued to investigate issues of rural literacy in a different region of the US, the Great Plains. She is an Associate Professor of English at the University of North Dakota, where her work focuses on the impact of literacy practices on the survival of rural communities. With Charlotte Hogg and Eileen E. Schell, Kim has co-authored *Rural Literacies* and co-edited *Reclaiming the Rural: Essays on Literacy, Rhetoric, and Pedagogy*. Her essays and book chapters have appeared in the *Journal of Appalachian Studies*, *Women and Literacy: Inquiries for a New Century*, and the forthcoming *Rethinking Rural Literacies: Literacy/Rurality/Education* and *Literacy, Economy, and Power: New Directions in Literacy Research*. She is currently at work on *Re-Reading Appalachia: Literacies of Resistance*, co-edited with Sara Webb-Sunderhaus.

Linda Farr Darling is the first Eleanor Rix Professor of Rural Teacher Education at the University of British Columbia (UBC) in Vancouver, British Columbia, Canada, a position she has held since 2009. Her work centres on preparing and recruiting elementary and secondary level teacher candidates for rural schools in the province, and supporting teachers who are already working in rural settings. She oversees a small UBC teacher preparation program in the interior of the province, mentors graduate students with rural research interests, and chairs a rural leadership group that advises the government on educational policy. She loves travelling to schools all over British Columbia, a geographically and culturally diverse province that covers an area over one and a half times the size of France, and reaches from the Rocky Mountains along the continental divide to the Pacific Ocean. Linda has ongoing partnerships with fifteen rural school districts, collaborating with teachers on classroom and school-wide projects that focus on inter-generational learning, community vitality, environmental issues and place-consciousness.

Bill Green is Emeritus Professor of Education at Charles Sturt University, Bathurst, New South Wales, Australia. He recently retired as Professor of Education. His ongoing research interests range across curriculum inquiry, literacy studies, English curriculum history and education for rural–regional sustainability. His most recent publications include *Literacy in 3D: An Integrated Perspective in Theory and Practice* (ACER, 2012), co-edited with Catherine Beavis, and *Rethinking Rural Literacies: Transnational Perspectives* (Palgrave Macmillan, 2013), co-edited with Michael Corbett, and he is completing *Body/Practice: The Body in Professional Practice, Learning and Education* (Springer, 2014/forthcoming), co-edited with Nick Hopwood.

Cath Gristy is a Lecturer in the Plymouth Institute of Education at Plymouth University, UK, and a schoolteacher working in the local community. Cath has a range of research interests in education, schools and teaching, which include social justice, inclusion and exclusion. A common thread that runs through these research engagements is the sense of rural place and space. Her research with young people in her local isolated, rural communities in the UK has led to a sustained engagement with research method and ethics in these places 'on the edge'. Cath is an active member of a pan-European research network of researchers working and writing about education and schooling in rural places.

John Halsey is the Sidney Myer Professor of Rural Education and Communities at Flinders University and a consultant in rural education through the Center for Relational Learning in Santa Fe, New Mexico. His doctoral research focused on how principals of rural schools construct their roles, and pre-service country teaching placements in Australia. John's research interests are predominantly in the areas of leadership formation, management and policy, with a particular focus on rural and remote contexts. John's research orientation is towards framing rural and remote education in non-deficit ways and innovative/ integrated policies and operations for sustainability. Prior to joining Flinders University, John was a teacher, a principal of two schools in South Australia, the Associate Director of the Senior Secondary Assessment Board of South Australia, an Executive Director in the South Australian Department of Education and

Children's Services and a Chief of Staff to a State Minister for Education and Children's Services. John has also worked as the Executive Officer of the Rural Education Forum, Australia.

Zane Hamm is a lecturer in Educational Policy Studies and Community Services-Learning at the University of Alberta in Edmonton, Alberta, Canada and teaches MBA courses with Cape Breton University and Northern Alberta Institute of Technology on community economic development and strengthening communities. She has an M.Ed. in International Education and specialization in Adult Education. Her doctoral research explored dialogue between generations to enhance rural education and community development. Her areas of research include rural education, community development, intergenerational learning, rural youth migration and mobility, apprenticeship and learning–work transitions, CSL pedagogy and how the CSL experience broadens opportunities to participate. Zane has worked with international experiential education programmes in Asia, Africa and Latin America. She is interested in instructional design, evaluation and how learners and instructors engage and reflect on their own learning. Zane grew up on a farm in rural Saskatchewan.

Linda Hargreaves is Reader in Classroom Learning and Pedagogy at the Faculty of Education, University of Cambridge, UK. She teaches master's and doctoral students in psychology and primary education. Her research centres on primary classroom processes, and typically involves systematic observation. She was an Associate Director of the Cambridge Primary Review, and is currently UK director of an ESRC UK–Hong Kong bilateral project on group work and primary mathematics. Her rural schools research began with her Ph.D, and has subsequently included curriculum implementation, rural schools' clustering, education for cultural diversity in England's most rural dioceses, and the status of teachers in rural and urban schools. In 1996, she set up Network 14, 'Communities, Families and Schooling in Educational Research', of the European Conference on Educational Research, with Rune Kvalsund and others. Network 14 has hosted European rural research papers ever since, and Linda has co-edited (with Rune Kvalsund) a Special Issue of the *International Journal of Educational Research* (vol. 48, issue 2) of rural research reviews in 2009.

Robyn Henderson is an Associate Professor (Literacies Education) in the Faculty of Business, Education, Law and Arts at the Toowoomba Campus of the University of Southern Queensland, Australia. She teaches both undergraduate and postgraduate students in courses about literacy curriculum and pedagogies, and she coordinates the doctoral programs in the discipline of education. Robyn researches in the fields of literacies, family mobility and its effects on schooling, and the student learning journey in higher education. She is interested in the nexus of literacy learning and student mobility in school contexts, especially in relation to itinerant farm workers' children. Robyn's research and teaching are closely linked. Themes related to pedagogies, diversity and capacity building run through her work. Robyn has published widely and she is the sole editor or co-editor of five books.

Aimee Howley is Professor of Educational Studies in the Patton College at Ohio University, where she currently serves as Senior Associate Dean for Research and Graduate Studies. She received a bachelor's degree in philosophy from Barnard College, a master's in special education from Marshall University, and a doctorate in educational leadership from West Virginia University. Aimee's research explores the intersection between social context and educational practice, and she has investigated a range of questions relating to rural education, educational policy and gifted education. She has co-authored five books, numerous book chapters, and more than fifty refereed journal articles.

Craig Howley holds a BA in English and Comparative Literature from Columbia College, an MA in Gifted Education from Marshall University Graduate College, and the Ed.D in Education Administration from West Virginia University. At present, Dr. Howley directs doctoral dissertations for the Educational Administration programme at Ohio University. His primary research interests include educational scale; rural education; intellect and talent development; mathematics education; and the relationship between culture, political economy and schooling. With Jerry Johnson and Aimee Howley, he is preparing a book on the dynamics of social class in rural schools. Previously he directed an ERIC clearing house and the research initiative of an NSF-funded centre that studied rural mathematics education.

Rune Kvalsund is Professor of Education at Volda University College in the North Western coastal part of Norway, the region of the fjords. One of the central fields of his educational research – longitudinal as well as cross-sectional – is rural schools and their communities, focusing on the different arenas of informal social learning in children's home environment. He has been a research advisor for the national association of rural schools in Norway based on his Ph.D research on comparative case studies of rural schools and international research reviews. Since 1996 he has been initiator and convenor of the European Educational Research Association (EERA) Network 14, Schooling, Families and Communities in Educational Research, together with Linda Hargreaves and others. The network has worked to encourage and support research on place-based sustainable education, comparisons of education in urban and rural communities, cooperation between families, parents, school and community – and research on schooling as life course transitions. In 2009 he and Linda Hargreaves co-edited a special issue of *International Journal of Educational Research* (vol. 48, issue 2), reviewing research on rural schools and their communities in Nordic and British countries.

Maija Lanas is currently a post-doctoral researcher in the University of Oulu, Finland. Maija completed her Ph.D in 2011 as a part of an Academy-funded project, 'Life in Place', conducting ethnography and living with her family in a reindeer herding village in Finnish Lapland. In her Ph.D, Maija studied how the meanings of misbehaviour are inscribed to student agency on a societal level. Maija is currently funded by the Academy of Finland, studying the production of discourse of exclusion and belonging in educational institutions. Maija is also a co-leader of March, an emerging collective of researchers based at the Faculty of Education in the University of Oulu, Finland. The members of March share an interest in poststructurally informed research in teacher education and the material-discursive ways in which teacher education produces childhood marginalisation in specific ways.

Sherilyn Lennon is currently a post-doctoral researcher and lecturer in Senior English at Griffith University, Australia. Prior to that she was a classroom teacher and Head of Department at a rural high school in western Queensland. Sherilyn is married to a farmer/grazier and divides her time between the city and the bush. Her research combines Freirean philosophy with a transformative agenda to communally problematise power relations and representations of gender. Sherilyn's research stretches the boundaries of qualitative research by merging critical, feminist, poststructural and social theories to suggest that research be considered a political act. Her approach positions the researcher as both transformative intellectual and vulnerable social activist. Embedded in a critical theoretical framework, Sherilyn's work is able to harvest new insights into how power, gender performances and educational phenomena are sustained in communities and how they might be interrupted.

Michele Lonsdale is an experienced researcher and spent twelve years periodically working with the Australian Council for Educational Research (ACER), including as a Principal Research Fellow. Much of Michele's research in recent years involved working with Aboriginal and Torres Strait Islander communities evaluating various (usually Commonwealth-funded) programmes. Another strong area of research interest has been in school–community partnerships. Michele has been fortunate enough to have experienced a rich range of research and community-related experiences, but among the most memorable is the time spent talking with and learning from Aboriginal Australians in remote communities. Michele has previously worked in education as a teacher and lecturer, and in the policy area with the Victorian government.

Pauliina Rautio is a post-doctoral research fellow at the Department of Teacher Education of the University of Helsinki in Finland. She works in a research project entitled 'Dwelling with the City – Children and Young People as Participating Residents' (2011–2015), funded by the Academy of Finland as part of its research programme 'The Future of Housing and Living'. This project is led by Sirpa Tani, Professor of Geography and Environmental Education. Pauliina is also a co-leader of March, an emerging collective of researchers based at the Faculty of Education in the University of Oulu, Finland. The members of March share an interest in poststructurally informed research of teacher education and the material-discursive ways in which teacher education produces childhood marginalisation in specific communities. Pauliina's research interests comprise everyday life, human–environment relations, posthumanism, new materialism, aesthetics, education and cultural geography. Pauliina is currently working with 5- to 7-year-old children, approaching child-matter intra-actions in children's everyday lives with a post-conventional theoretical and methodological framework.

Jo-Anne Reid is Professor of Education and Associate Dean, Teacher Education at Charles Sturt University, Bathurst, New South Wales, Australia. A past president of both the Australian Teacher Education Association (ATEA) and the Australian Association for Research in Education (AARE), she has worked as a literacy teacher educator in three rural universities (Ballarat, New England and Charles Sturt) and is committed to improving the preparation of teachers for schools in rural and remote locations. Her recent publications include *Literacies in Place: Teaching Environmental Communications* (Primary English Teaching Association, 2007), co-edited with Barbara Comber and Helen Nixon. She was Project Leader on the TERRAnova Project ('Teacher Education for Rural and Regional Australia'), a national study of rural teacher education in Australia (2008–2010).

Philip Roberts is an Assistant Professor in Curriculum and Pedagogy at the University of Canberra. Before joining the University of Canberra in July 2009 Philip taught in New South Wales Public schools for thirteen years, nine in rural and remote central schools and four in a regional high school. In addition to his teaching roles, Philip has worked as a union official and held representative roles on the curriculum board and teacher registration authority in New South Wales. Philip has completed major national research projects in the staffing of rural and remote schools and managed large-scale school-based research projects. His major ongoing research interest is how teachers situate the curriculum and how spatial theories are incorporated into educational thinking. Philip has an ongoing concern about quality and equity in education and works to disrupt the meta-narratives that have dominated, and hijacked, these import fields through the application of critical theory. His research demonstrates how pedagogy models, teaching standards and centralised curricula magnify disadvantage and deny situated knowledges when examined from a 'place-conscious' critical perspective.

Simone White is Professor of Teacher Education at Monash University and leads the Faculty of Education Teacher Education research group. Simone's publications, research and teaching are focused on the key question of how to best prepare teachers for diverse communities, in particular 'harder to staff' communities including low socioeconomic, high cultural and linguistic diversity and rural, regional and remote. She recently launched the Office of Learning and Teaching extended funded project known as RRRTEC (www.rrrtec.net.au) and its

accompanying online learning community at https://www.facebook.com/
rrrtec. This project has created particular resources, curriculum guidelines and
strategies that have been developed aimed at teacher educators (both school-
based and university-based) to make more 'visible' the ways in which preparation
for rural and regional communities staffing needs can be addressed. Simone is
currently President Elect for the Australian Teacher Education Association
(ATEA). She convenes the Rural Education SIG in the Australian Association for
Research in Education (AARE) and has recently been elected to serve as the
Secretary/Treasurer of the Rural Education SIG in the American Education
Research Association (AERA).

Acknowledgements

In 2011 some of the authors in this book attended the European Conference on Educational Research (ECER) in Berlin and gathered in a Network 14 research meeting – Communities, Families and Schooling in Educational Research. This meeting discussed what methodological issues and possibilities might need to be considered to increase the positive outcomes for those who live in rural communities. In turn, the ideas considered and the sharing of international rural research projects led to a joint symposium presentation titled 'Examining the Research "Footprint" in Rural Contexts: An International Discussion on Methodological Issues and Possibilities' (White et al., 2012) the following year. In our symposium proposal, we argued that a metro-centric approach to research meant that often the needs of rural students, their families and communities remained invisible and the impact of rural research methodologies unexplored. We felt it important and timely to highlight, unpack and critique various methodological issues and possibilities from the position of – and as they relate to – rural, regional and remote communities. One of the ideas posed in the symposium was the need to consider methodology in relation to a rural social space (Reid et al., 2010) and aspects such as ethics, anonymity, researcher position, power and impact. We raised the question 'What good is this research to those who are being researched in rural communities?' In short, 'What is the impact of the "research footprint" (White et al., 2012) in a rural place?'

This symposium then led to the development of this co-edited text with its diversity of international researchers as authors, both experienced and beginning, to further flesh out these questions and ideas in the chapters of this book.

We would like to acknowledge this journey of ideas and discussion from all involved in Network 14. We also wish to thank Dr. Graeme Hall for his speedy editorial support.

References

Reid, J., Green, B., Cooper, M., Hastings, W., Lock, G. & White, S. (2010). Regenerating rural social space? Teacher education for rural-regional sustainability. *Australian Journal of Education*, 54(3), 262–276.

White, S., Anderson, M., Kvalsund, R., Gristy, C., Corbett, M. & Hargreaves, L. (2012). Examining the Research 'Footprint' in Rural Contexts: An International Discussion on Methodological Issues and Possibilities. Symposium presented in Network 14, Communities, Families and Schooling in Educational Research, European Conference on Educational Research, 18–21 September, Cadiz, Spain.

Introduction

Why put the 'rural' in research?

Michael Corbett and Simone White

This book has been written for the most part with beginning researchers and their supervisors in mind. While there are many texts to support master and doctoral level researchers, we as co-editors found no such text that specifically focused on supporting those who research in rural locations. Some might say that conducting research is the same no matter where the research is located, but we strongly argue that 'place' and context do make a difference. Thus, we have invited a number of international researchers to help us uncover these differences and share with you their research stories. The chapters in this book collectively represent a study in place-based methodology and standpoint. While they are linked thematically and in terms of the international non-metropolitan geographies they represent, they are also independent research endeavours in themselves.

By adding the adjective 'rural' to research, we are explicitly differentiating research *in* and *for* rural communities and we are doing this deliberately. In our view, there is an urgent need to unpack the unexamined dominance of research methodologies as mainly metropolitan. We judge that this bias tends to position the rural in deficit rather than as different. As Atkin notes:

> Largely rural communities have seen an urban agenda . . . rolled out across the countryside, with issues of equity and access, rather than appropriateness, dominating the discourse. It is as if rural society is to be judged in terms of a deficit discourse (dominated by the desire to make them like us) rather than a diversity discourse (recognition and value of difference).
>
> (2003, p. 515)

We are therefore acutely conscious of the way that rurality has been constructed as a residual space which is often imagined: (1) outside the conceptual boundaries of modernity, (2) outside the geographic boundaries of the city which is increasingly understood as a distinctly modern or postmodern space and, (3) outside the temporal boundaries of a world which is supposed to be moving out of the country and into the metropolis. This conception of rurality is, for us, problematic in part because rural places remain resilient. At the same time, distinctions between the rural and the urban are increasingly difficult to make and rurality is often positioned as one side of a conceptual binary that imagines a teleological history and a one-dimensional transformation of space (Ching & Creed, 1997; Krause, 2013). In this book we centre the rural and particularly focus on conceptualisations and experiences of what rural education research is and what it might be.

This book takes the position that the idea of the rural remains important precisely because of the way it is both connected to and different from the burgeoning urbanising landscapes of the contemporary world. As Lefebvre (1992) has shown us, capitalism transforms space in ways that are complex, specific and dynamic. The rural was never a space apart from the mainstream of capitalisms; rather, it is intimately caught up in the way that people and place are defined, organised, exploited and moved. This is a book about educational research in rural contexts and it is clear that education has played, and continues to play, an essential role in rural development and underdevelopment. Indeed, rural education is not a sideshow on the margins of mainstream or urban education. We believe that our core understandings of education need to be spatialised (Gulson & Symes, 2007; Leander et al., 2010; Reid et al., 2010; Green, 2013), nuanced and scaled (Nespor, 2004) so that the particular educational problems that occur within a place or, as Pat Thomson (2000) puts it, in *this* particular place are more richly understood. It is our view that this way of conceiving of rurality needs serious unpacking through theoretically and methodologically sophisticated and careful research. We believe that this text offers both an international set of comparative examples of this kind of research along with a series of reflections or 'tales of the field' (Van Manen, 1988) offered by some leading scholars working in Australian, North American and European contexts.

We as co-editors come from literally opposite ends of the globe – Simone from Melbourne, Australia, and Mike from Wolfville, Nova Scotia, Canada – with different backgrounds and entries into our own rural research trajectories. But we came together in this project because we do believe that 'rural' matters when it comes to research. Thinking through research design, gathering data, analysing that data and, most importantly, disseminating research findings matter to a variety of audiences including those living in rural places. Research has impact and the authors argue throughout this book that this impact needs to be better understood and more carefully articulated by those who research in rural places. The point is to develop more theoretically attuned and methodologically careful and connected approaches to research in rural communities which are, it must be said, often communities of disadvantage which have not benefitted sufficiently from much social research. It is our hope that the diverse chapters in this book will help rural education researchers, both new and established, to find inspiration and stimulation as we all work toward better understandings of unique yet connected spaces and places of learning.

We both also work from a shared position that deeply values rural schooling, rural education and rural communities. We also come from a strong commitment to and ethic of social justice that has formed our separate research paths over many years. This is an invested research position which is echoed in the chapters that follow, and while it is not without problems (Coladarci, 2007) we believe that a strong, carefully conceived ethical framework only strengthens rural education research and it does so by acknowledging contemporary movements toward forms of social research that work toward strengthening a wide range of different rural communities that are faced by similar problems. While we acknowledge there are many questions connected to thinking about, developing and conducting rural research, we encourage as a predominant consideration the impact of our research in terms of the 'footprint' (White et al., 2012) we leave behind and what ways the outcome of the research might actually make a difference or improve the lives and places of those we research. It is our sense that if this were to become the very first question researchers reflect upon, there might be better and more profitable uptake of social research generally, but particularly in areas outside the metropolis. Indeed, as globalisation continues its current trajectory toward increasingly coordinated and invasive exploitation of marine, land-based and animal resources, the urgency and importance of high-quality rural research cannot be understated.

References

Atkin, C. (2003). Rural communities: Human and symbolic capital development. Fields Apart. *Compare, 33*(4), 507–518.

Ching, B. & Creed, G. W. (Eds.) (1997). *Knowing Your Place: Rural Identity and Cultural Hierarchy*. New York: Routledge.

Coladarci, T. (2007). Improving the yield of rural education research: An editor's swan song. *Journal of Research in Rural Education, 22*(3), 1–9.

Green, B. (2013). Literacy, rurality and education: A partial mapping. In B. Green & M. Corbett, *Rethinking rural literacies: Transnational perspectives*. New York: Palgrave Macmillan.

Gulson, K. N. & Symes, C. (eds) (2007). *Spatial Theories of Education: Policy and Geography Matters*. London and New York: Routledge.

Krause, M. (2013). The ruralization of the world. *Public Culture, 25*(2), 233–248.

Leander, K. M., Phillips, N. C. & Taylor, K. H. (2010). The changing social spaces of learning: Mapping new mobilities. *Review of Research in Education, 34*(1), 329–394.

Lefebvre, H. (1992). *The Production of Space*. London: Wiley-Blackwell.

Nespor, J. (2004). Educational scale-making. *Pedagogy, Culture & Society, 12*(3), 309–326.

Reid, J., Green, B., Cooper, M., Hastings, W., Lock, G. & White, S. (2010). Regenerating rural social space? Teacher education for rural-regional sustainability. *Australian Journal of Education, 54*(3), 262–276.

Thomson, P. (2000). 'Like schools', educational 'disadvantage' and 'thisness'. *Australian Educational Researcher, 27*(3), 157–172.

Van Manen, J. (1988). *Tales of the Field: On writing ethnography.* Chicago and London: University of Chicago Press.

White, S., Anderson, M., Kvalsund, R., Gristy, C., Corbett, M. & Hargreaves, L. (2012). Examining the Research 'Footprint' in Rural Contexts: An International Discussion on Methodological Issues and Possibilities. Symposium presented in Network 14, Communities, Families and Schooling in Educational Research, European Conference on Educational Research, 18–21 September, Cadiz, Spain.

Part I

Tales of the field

Working with/in the rural

Chapter 1

Making sense of rural education research

Art, transgression, and other acts of terroir

Craig Howley and Aimee Howley

We expect that many readers of this volume will be young scholars curious about doing rural education research, and we have already seen a new generation rising to do this work well. This rising generation of scholars may sometimes wonder what the experience of doing rural education and of researching the doing of rural education have been like for those of us who have done both for most of our career. Even for new scholars who are less inclined to look back to previous generations for inspiration or insight, we suspect the looming dangers of the present century may help sustain interest in and appreciation of the planetary importance of rural places and the education that takes place there (Howley, Showalter, Klein, Sturgill & Smith, 2013). Before we move to our substantive discussion – of where we stand based on where we've been – we want to give a brief glimpse of how we got there.

An act of terroir

Terroir (a term imported directly from French) refers to 'a sense of place' but also to the products of that place. The character of a particular wine or lentil, for instance, incorporates a unique set of characteristics reflecting a terroir. The more unique the characteristic of a place, the more likely is it to contribute to terroir. We like to imagine our own history as a move from placelessness in the nondescript suburbs of the nondescript cities of the United States to rootedness in Appalachia, notably West Virginia, notably west-central West Virginia, notably Reedy, West Virginia. There is no Reedy grape or lentil, but there is definitely terroir – the sense of place that our neighbours treated as a birthright and that we appreciated from our perspective as 'transplants' – refugees from what we increasingly saw as suburban complacence, cosmopolitan greed and internationalism gone awry as 'globalisation' (Davies & Guppy, 1997; Gilman, Goldhammer & Weber, 2011)

In coming to Appalachia in 1973 we were refugees of a sort, and we certainly did not expect to find a safe haven in the most despised part of America. To the contrary, we expected to find the machinations of big business (as with coal, oil and timber extraction) of vested interest in politics, and of struggle to make our own way. But we also, and more importantly, expected to find somewhat different ways of living and knowing. Engagement with rural pursuits connected us to the lives of our neighbours, although as introverts our actual engagement with neighbours was limited.

Nevertheless, our naïve decision to relocate remains among the most generative in our lengthening lives. Craig claims that his most meaningful education comes from what he's learned about gardening and farming, about plumbing and wiring, and from livestock (hogs, goats, cattle, horses, poultry) and from wood (cabinetmaking and construction, but also firewood cutting and burning). We still live in a rural place about 32 km (20 miles) from the university where we work; and we still garden, keep animals and heat with wood.

With this sort of history and outlook, we do not expect to find many like-minded people anywhere. We are, after all, refugees of multiple sorts, despite all this learning on home turf: internal refugees from our own nation, from the usual purposes of education (i.e. 'success') and most certainly from the standards of our chosen profession. That final alienation is deeply pertinent to our message here. It seems to us that some rural educators have been colonised by their professional training (in 'the [American] university') with its emphasis on 'one-best-ways' and narrow readings of education and its desirable outcomes. Our devotion to terroir, by contrast, has helped us appreciate rural alternatives and push-backs. As one thinks about doing rural education research anywhere in a still urbanising world, one ought to keep the role of rural places as sources of push-back *within the profession* but also *outside* it: a rich source of ideas and real-time practices for doing life differently from the capitalist or neoliberal template so widely advertised in schooling. The educative potential seems to us momentous, and momentously unrecognised by national governments and national ministries (Scott, 1998). That gap represents a potentiality akin to the negative and positive poles of electrical-magnetic force fields. The official disparagement and ignorance is part of the power inherent in the rural alternative. So we argue for, and we do, a kind of rural education research that actively privileges rural outlooks on the meaning of life.

Responses to claims about these alternatives and push-backs often come down to the question, 'Must one live rurally in order to do rural education research?' Our answer, which acknowledges the limits of our own experience as refugees, suggests that engagement with what is substantively rural requires direct experience with it. Indeed, the experience needs to be deep and extensive enough to produce a sense of appreciation. For those raised (as we were) on urban and suburban real estate, getting to an appreciative stance means relinquishing the sense of superiority tangled up with metro-centric economic and cultural privilege.

The difficulty of getting to such a stance is reflected in *mainstream* education research that impinges on rural schools and communities without ever engaging rural ways of being and living (what we call 'the substantive rural'). It proceeds *professionally* on two bases: (1) the presumption of rural inferiority and (2) the implied irrelevance of the substantive rural to both education and schooling. Such mainstream research often concerns curriculum and instruction (see, e.g.,

Howley, Howley & Huber, 2005), and its purpose is a haughty effort to 'improve' rural schools. The two positions constitute professional ignorance – they form it and they implement it. Referring to this viciousness, Craig once wrote, 'Rural school improvement is nobody's fault' (Howley, 1997, p. 132). Thus, without relevant experience of what is substantively rural, we cannot imagine how researchers might see beyond the ignorant reformist logic of the mainstream.[1]

Seeing beyond requires deep understanding of a world in which family trumps individual accomplishment, work calls itself into existence from the necessities of survival, and resistance looks a lot like failure to get with the programme. For us, seeing beyond has required four research commitments – to research as transgression, to research as art, to research as communication and to research as work at odds with the university. We turn attention to each.

Research as transgression: the rural education case in point

We start with the premise that social science research (including rural education research) will have value for action in the world to the extent it is transgressive. We hold this perspective not just for research subsumed under paradigms like critical theory or postmodernism, but for *all* social research (Howley & Howley, 2000; see also Portes, 2000). Two significant sites of transgression include what is studied and how it is studied. We explore these entry points for transgression using rural education research as an illustrative case.

We are, in a sense, using the term 'transgression' metaphorically by casting the shibboleths, conventions and quarries of normal social science (Kuhn, 1962) as the rules that the transgressor seeks to break. This perspective offers the possibility for researchers to push against the boundaries of prevailing paradigms, without waiting for those paradigms to disappoint. In fact, we argue that intentional limit testing in the realm of ideas is what scholars (as a case in point, rural education scholars) ought to be doing, because it produces sufficient ferment to inform dialogue in and across communities of potential agents – namely scholars themselves, community members and practitioners. Critique is transgressive in this sense (Howley, 2009).

At the same time, in a more literal sense and on behalf of that ferment, scholars' forays into the transgressive requires them to question what appear to be obvious and linear processes – not necessarily abandoning efforts to investigate surface appearances and self-evident patterns but also, and perhaps more importantly, imagining and finding ways to excavate and illuminate the 'hidden abode' below the surface (Marx, 1867/1990; Portes, 2000). This approach leads many scholars to speak out intentionally against inaction and domination. Edward Said (2004) said it well: 'dialectically, oppositionally … to challenge and defeat both an imposed silence and the normalized quiet of unseen power' (p. 135), to 'hypothesize a better situation from the known historical and social facts' (p. 140). Notably, however, the transgressive effort of scholars does not, according to us, require action in the world. For some, interrogating the dogma of their own disciplines is sufficiently disruptive and generative (Delborne, 2008).

What we study: the interpretive loop

Perhaps the most prevalent impulse in rural education research is to address the *problem* of rural schools, namely that they are deficient and need to be improved (e.g. Cubberley, 1922). Variations on this theme implicate the deficiencies of rural children (e.g. Henry, Cavanagh & Oetting, 2011), rural families (e.g. Reeves, 2012), rural teachers (e.g. American Council on Education, 1999), rural school facilities (Bowers, Metzger & Militello, 2010), rural culture (e.g. Graves, Haughton, Jahns, Fitzhugh & Jones, 2008), and so on.

Pushing against this usual impulse is a countervailing tendency to reclaim as valorous (or, in some cases, merely as valid or valuable) the practices of rural schools (e.g. Howley, Howley, Burgess & Pusateri, 2008), the character of rural people and their culture (e.g. Johnson, Baker & Bruer, 2007), the characteristics of rural children (e.g. Larson & Dearmont, 2002) and the potential of rural places (e.g. Budge, 2010; Howley et al., 2013; Reid, Green, Cooper, Hastings, Lock & White, 2010; White & Reid, 2008). One important commitment guiding this impulse to push back seeks virtue in those things that a corrupt system habitually vilifies (e.g. Giroux, 1992; Howley & Howley, 2000; Sleeter, 2012). This commitment encourages research that identifies the salutary practices of marginalised groups as well as scholarship that reclaims marginalised practices that conventional research has denounced. An example of the latter is Bickel, Tomasek and Eagle's (2000) demonstration of the cognitive complexity of the instructional discourse of science teachers who had been categorised as traditional, and therefore ineffective, by the staff of a US National Science Foundation (NSF) project. Examples of the former are theoretical and empirical writings supporting the practice of incorporating indigenous knowledge about the natural world into school curricula (e.g. Avery & Kassam, 2011; Le Grange, 2007). Even though these approaches to inquiry often deploy careful reasoning and rigorous methods, some critics dismiss them as 'romantic' and 'unrealistic' (e.g. Smith, 2002).

With the postmodern turn, additional subtlety complicates and enlightens the practice of sanctifying the marginalised. A deeper understanding of patterns and anomalies comes from efforts to problematise the location (both place location and social location) of subjects, showing simultaneously their agency as subjects and their restraint as dominated objects (e.g. Corbett, 2007). Where this line of inquiry also draws on ideas from Marxist and critical theory, it allows agency itself to embed contradictions, to be at once colonised and colonising (e.g. Greenwood, 2009; Naples, 1994), generative and regressive (e.g. Beech, 2004), local yet international (e.g. Carlone, Kimmel & Tschida, 2010).

This array of research concerns has no teleology. It neither points toward a less cluttered, better focused vantage nor offers an inclusive reframing that subsumes and surpasses the insights of any part of the scholarly picture. All parts of the picture are present, each offering a potential challenge to the others and each provoking alternative renderings of the small scale on the one hand (e.g. Burnell, 2003) and the large on the other (e.g. Berry, 1990; Scott, 1998). We imagine the array as providing substance for an interpretive loop in which representations of the social world inevitably are adjudicated in conversations among scholars (e.g. Habermas, 1984), hermeneutic dialogues (Freeman, 2011), debates among policy makers (e.g. Auriat, 1998; Burawoy, 2004) and sincere efforts to test use-value (e.g. Bell, 2008; Flyvbjerg, 2001). The ferment created by the interpretive loop suggests that a direct approach through the workings of social science alone does not (and perhaps cannot) lead to a clearer view of what is actually going on, let alone what should be done (e.g. Gieryn, 1999). We are not, then, particularly hopeful nor particularly chagrined. We believe that ordinary people do now and will in the future make their own sense. We expect our work will help them; that's all.

How we study: transgressive methodologies

As well as opening up new conceptions of the phenomena social researchers study, the transition to a postmodern sensibility has encouraged the proliferation of new methodologies, each promising to capture more complexity and reflect greater pluralism than is available through traditional methodologies (e.g. Barnett, 2009; Somerville, 2007). Among these methodologies, moreover, are reincarnations of traditional approaches, such as grounded theory, that researchers seek to invest with postmodern purpose (e.g. Clarke, 2003).

Whereas some scholars may judge postmodern methodologies to be too intricate and self-referential to be worth serious attention (e.g. Phillips, 2009), these methods do represent a critical response to an arrogant realism deployed in service of the neoliberal agenda (Baez & Boyles, 2009). At the same time, simplistic efforts to demonstrate the alignment between particular methods and particular ideological perspectives are, we find, misleading.

First, few researchers intend for their preconceptions to taint their research. Indeed, researchers working from a critical vantage often disclose or find ways to 'bracket' their preconceptions (Baez & Boyles, 2009). Revealing greater hubris, positivist researchers often assume that their methods are inherently neutral (Ross, 2008) – a stance that tends to ignore the ways in which the framing of a research question, the operationalisation of constructs, the contextualisation of the study within bodies of related literature and the interpretation of findings inevitably position a study to offer a particular perspective within an ongoing debate.

Second, many critical researchers accept methodological eclecticism as an opportunity, perhaps even a necessity, for exploration – with the obvious exception of some explicit attempts by postmodern researchers to view research method and research quarry as mutually constitutive.[2] Phillips (2009, p. 174) recalls two perspectives from the natural sciences – the first from physicist Percy Bridgman and the second from philosopher Paul Feyerabend – to characterise this view of social science research: 'the scientist has no other method than doing his damnedest' (Bridgman) and 'anything goes' (Feyerabend).[3]

Within the rural education literature, numerous studies use traditional methods to examine issues relevant to critical and postmodern discourses. For example, a recent study of teacher identity formation in a rural school with a very large population of Hispanic students coupled traditional ethnographic methods with two social constructionist theories of identity formation – *saberes docentes*[4] and situated learning – in order to offer insights about how social context intersects with teachers' life histories (Wenger, Dinsmore & Villagómez, 2012). Our own use of conventional regression methods to examine the differential impact of school size on achievement across socioeconomic status (SES) levels fits far more closely in intent with work in the domain of critical policy analysis than with positivist work using production functions, which its methods nevertheless closely resemble (e.g. Howley & Howley, 2004).

At the same time, studies that intentionally push against traditional methodologies also enrich discussion of issues facing rural schools and communities. For example, Jackson's (2010) use of a Foucauldian lens to examine the discursive construction of unified community identity discloses relations of race, gender, and power that limit school and community possibilities. Providing autoethnographic reflections on her engagement with indigenous knowledge in rural Japan, Mayuzumi (2009) reclaims her own agency and thereby offers warrant for the type of learning that occurs informally as part of rural community life. Eppley's (2010) critical content analysis of how picture books portray rural America opens up consideration of the rural meanings that such representations both disclose and misconstrue.

Common across these quite different approaches is the effort to illuminate what other methodologies tend to obscure. These researchers' intentional use of transgressive methodologies invites conflicting perspectives because it treats research as a basis for ferment rather than as an accumulation of stabilising truths (e.g. Farr-Darling, Chapter 10 this volume). This approach focuses not on rarifying the knowledge that research generates but rather on expanding the discursive field from which evidentiary claims might be drawn. For this reason, these and other transgressive research efforts can never properly offer prescriptions for action. Action, as Arendt (1958) aptly noted, requires freedom to pursue original conceptions of the world in consideration of the obligation to interpret that freedom within the realm of democratic pluralism. A view of action that presents it as an unfiltered application of expert knowledge to a field of human endeavour seriously constrains agency and therefore imposes unacceptable limitations on both freedom and community.

Research as art

Research is an art, and we think of ourselves as artists: as *writers*, above all else. Such a position remains uncommon among education researchers, but our research heroes, contemporary and classic, write with considerable clarity and grace and force. Their works comprise our model for how to write.

Good-to-excellent writing everywhere

Lacking good-to-excellent writing, research can barely exist: writing is what makes research, according to us. Writing is the path to a good-to-excellent idea for a study (conceptualisation), to a grasp of the relevant literature (literature review) and to specification of the way one will engage the data (methods). Surely, one needs familiarity with the good-to-excellent writing of others about all of these things, and well beyond them.

Writing thus powers systematic study, *especially* in an empirical mode. With systematic empirical inquiry one must marshal a range of thoughtful insights, strategies, sensibilities and speculations – sometimes sequentially, but often simultaneously. Writing is virtually the only way to do that within one's own mind, and it is the only way to do so publicly.

To write well, one must read and struggle with good-to-excellent works (Barzun, 2001), and this necessity is seemingly not imposed often on rising scholars in our business: otherwise, emerging educational research would exhibit far better writing than it does. Models of good-to-excellent writing are remarkably accessible in our world, but the nature of that world means that most people are blinded to the existence of these models – no matter how accessible they really are.

With rural education, as we have argued (e.g. Howley, 2009), one might access the meanings and commitments of the substantive rural, not only through lived experience, but also through reading good-to-excellent fiction about rural life. In recent years Paul Theobald has established the Rural Literature Rally[5] to promote the engagement of communities and teachers with the thousands of relevant works of fiction. Many of these works exhibit good-to-excellent writing and provide insights about the varied meanings and commitments that ordinary rural people prize.

In short, one cannot do rural education research well without such models of good-to-excellent writing everywhere. And one's own writing is the only hope for constituting good-to-excellent studies of one's own.

The quality of rural education research

The quality of rural education research might be judged by the precision of its methods, the usefulness of its findings or the clarity of its insights. In practice, judgements about the quality of studies in education fields have tended to address all three considerations, though to differing degrees.

For example, efforts to weight findings for inclusion in meta-analytic studies have spawned instruments that evaluate research designs and procedures (e.g. Wells & Littell, 2009). Relying on a more interpretative approach, critical reviews of primary research such as those published in journals like the *Review of Educational Research* often summarise well-established claims within an extant body of scholarship, identify pertinent topics of ongoing debate, and make judgements about the overall usefulness of findings. Other approaches include measures of popularity (such as the number of times a work is cited) or the researcher's prestige (Walters & Lareau, 2009).

Whereas these approaches tend to focus more on precision and usefulness than on clarity of insights, syntheses that address the value of theoretical contributions tend to implicate the latter through their interest in the coherence and generative force of theoretical claims (e.g. Marchand, 2012). These criteria might also be applied to empirical work, and Coladarci's (2007) discussion of what is inherently rural in rural education research offers an illustration of such an application. For Coladarci, attentiveness to a core set of rural meanings offers a central basis for establishing the coherence of research studies that claim to have salience for rural schools and the communities in which they are located.

The ostensible relevance of these evaluative lenses does not directly inform a technique for comparing the relative worth of different theories, lines of inquiry or studies. Arguably, such a quest is unnecessary and easily corrupted. By contrast, the reading of rural education scholarship might benefit from the systematic use of a set of filters for gauging precision, usefulness, and clarity. Indeed, with such filters in place we might be able to encourage some agreement about rural education scholarship with limited value on the one hand, and scholarship with extraordinary value on the other. On the middle ground between the poles, readers' personal experiences, inclination to favour method over substance (or vice versa) and something akin to 'taste' will inevitably sponsor arguments about quality.

As we have implied in earlier comments, however, conversations and debates about what research means and how important it is represent significant products of research and assist readers in making sense of the social world they encounter. This generative potential of research, in fact, offers justification for a lot of work on the middle ground.

Nevertheless, visits to the poles are instructive. For example, we have been working with a team of students to examine dissertations that explore the intersection between the domains of 'rurality' and 'curriculum and instruction'. The investigation has, as one might expect, surfaced a great deal of work that readers would agree lacks precision, offers limited utility and addresses rural issues tangentially. Arguably, dissertation research is not well positioned to do otherwise (Ponticell & Olivarez, 1997). Many published studies also suffer from these same limitations.

In contrast to rural education studies with little to commend them are some notable works that address crucial rural questions, incorporate rigorous methods and sponsor deliberations with practical import. On these grounds we often point to Alan Peshkin's book *The Imperfect Union* (1982) and Cynthia Duncan's collection of case studies, *Worlds Apart* (1999), when asked about quintessentially rural studies. For rural education history, we recommend Paul Theobald's studies (e.g. Theobald, 1997); for deep understanding of rural culture, Alan DeYoung's work (e.g. DeYoung, 1995); and, for an appreciation of the contradictions and complexities of rurality as a social and economic location, the work of Michael Corbett (e.g. Corbett, 2007).

Beyond a handful of studies – and therefore in much of what we read – we encounter work on the middle ground. For example, many studies that use sophisticated quantitative methodologies treat rurality simply as a geographic demarcation rather than as a complex cultural marker. And work that emphasises educational practices with unique applicability to rural places – for example, many studies of place-based education – tends to overlook the circumstances (e.g. the impositions of bad policy) that rural educators actually confront. An increasing body of theoretically freighted studies, moreover, offers appealing interpretative opportunities but neither undertakes nor even supports attempts at empirical verification.

We are not faulting the middle ground, but rather see it as part of the productive ferment that characterises the scholarly mission more generally. We do, however, take exception to certain tendencies in the research on rural education. Notably, we have concerns about efforts that: (1) view rural places and their schools as deficient, (2) treat rurality mostly as an opportunity to spin interesting theories or (3) offer recommendations for practice that require extraordinary effort or improbable levels of provisioning.

Research as conversation

Some researchers from our generation were 'trained' in the positivist tradition and, with the new regime of 'scientifically based' research, more are on the way. This tradition argues for a cumulative knowledge based on research – an aim that may be fine for natural science. But it's a questionable aim for social science where reality changes even as it is observed, described and explained – and changes, perhaps in some small measure and unanticipated ways, on account of the reported descriptions and explanations. Nonetheless, social science research does accumulate, perhaps also informing a growing communal wisdom. Circumspection requires that we entertain a less hopeful prospect, however.

This lesser aspiration imagines research as a sort of very well-considered, and perhaps very well-informed, conversation. A good conversation makes its own sort of progress, illuminating issues and puzzles – and durable dilemmas – of common concern. Over the years we have personally *accumulated* a group of research friends with whom we do, in an ordinary real-world sort of way, converse about these matters. It's a long trajectory, in a personal sense, and not by any means so focused as the different and similar *research work* that we do (sometimes jointly with these colleagues). This very chapter is something of a case in point. We'd been waiting to write it for perhaps ten years. Then we received an invitation.

Viewing research as part of an ongoing 'conversation' requires a broad and perhaps metaphorical use of the term. But the metaphor is not a long stretch if one sees *research as writing*.

Writing as a conversation with others

The view of good-to-excellent rural education research as a well-crafted written product suggests that it articulates something worth knowing about rural places and about the education and schooling appropriate to such places – and something worth making sure others come to know. Again, we refer to rural ways of being and knowing: 'the substantive rural'. This usage asserts a claim about a knowable and objective rural reality.[6] Indeed, as we enter the conversation with others through our writing we take on the role of 'public intellectual' – a role with two related obligations, objectivity and comprehensibility.

Because most people – about 80 per cent – in the Anglophone diaspora (we think particularly of North America, Canada, Australia and New Zealand) do *not* live rurally, they are generally uninformed about the meanings that inhere in 'the substantive rural'. They may doubt the continuing existence even of rural place itself. They don't know about mud, livestock, trees or deserts, or about hunting, heating with wood, gardening or preserving food. And they do not, therefore, see the relevance of such places and practices to education, much less schooling. Many do not themselves experience the readiness of neighbours to help one another ('community') or the local traditions of democratic engagement that some communities support.

Their profound ignorance threatens rural people and the thoughtful ways of engaging the world that (like anyone else) rural people experience and try to practise: what we insist on as the socially substantive rural reality. This realm implicates educational purpose, and a momentous one, especially given the prevailing ignorance. A thoroughly urban future is hardly guaranteed to the humans inhabiting the planet (e.g. Conkin, 2007).

Objectivity as a sharing of reality

For us, the first commitment in the role of public intellectual is to objectivity. One can appreciate the need: the rural *exists* – objectively, we argue. It is the ground of our research effort. Without it, we would have much less from which to fashion data and the meanings most significant to our work and, indeed, significant to us personally.

This reality of rural meanings, though, certainly is a *socially constructed* one, like all else in the social world. If the rural were, however, considered vague or undefinable or entirely subjective, the substance of the rural could not enter into play, since it wouldn't exist; that is, when the rurally ignorant dealt with 'the rural' they could not be expected to see or to credit the substance of the reality that *really is* already in play.

Objectivity as a methodological position (different from objective reality) can also help rural education research compel the rurally ignorant to pay attention.[7] Certainly, this forcing of evidence on others doesn't always work directly or quickly, and yet we have found no alternative as researchers. One needs to remember, we think, that *taking research public makes it political*. Such a statement means not only that 'objectivity' concerns us as researchers in the practice of 'doing our research', especially rural education research. Far more importantly, it means that what we and others make of 'objectivity' is *tied up with* the real-time human construction of rural reality, knowledge about such social reality, and the shared, reflective experience of it – including debates about it.

Comprehensibility and the rural political realm

At first we didn't ask ourselves why we ought to do rural education research: the reality provoking the engagement seemed to us obvious, rather like asking why one would research African-American or American-Indian education if one's skin were brown or red. The answer is political in those cases and in ours – politics writ very large, encompassing community, party politics, political economy (the economic base) and culture (the superstructure erected, according to Marx, on the economic base).

Because of its latent political motive, the second obligation of the writer as public intellectual is to make oneself understandable beyond the narrow realm of scholars. Such a view is compatible with the philosopher Jürgen Habermas's notion that 'communication' is the work (cf. Arendt, 1958) that language does (Habermas, 1987), but we have something very simple, and perhaps more accessible, in mind for this context. We don't ourselves imagine that public utterances can ever be produced in an ideal speech situation (Habermas, 1984); distortion and suppression are not just ubiquitous but permanent conditions in political action. That's why one needs to take further action: without our intrusion, our issues will almost certainly be ignored.

The first task after doing rural education research, or getting it going, is 'dissemination' in some research venue (conference, chapter, research journal article, in ascending order of presumptive respectability). But in rural education research per se, on the terms of the preceding discussion at least, this first task engages objectivity, but not comprehensibility as we mean it. Research articles are famously incomprehensible to anyone other than researchers – members of the public who *need* to understand what rural education researchers have to say in, about, and for rural places. These works must, indeed, be accessible to rural people – school practitioners, surely, but also ordinary rural people who are not 'professionals'.

Not only is it unreasonable to expect rural people (including rural teachers and principals) to read education research literature, the incomprehensibility of much of the writing that education researchers produce renders it inaccessible to other researchers. Although clarity of expression has lost favour in some education research circles, we believe the commitment to being a public intellectual requires it. We offer as two notable examples, the transformation from the abstruse to the accessible in the writings of Jürgen Habermas and Henry Giroux ... but remind yourself that the inaccessibility of educational research stems *far more* from bad writing than from the difficult discourse characteristic of brilliant original theorising. Most of us have less to offer than Habermas or Giroux – and even they learned to write more accessibly.

As noted above, however, research writing won't do for the wider audiences for whose benefit we attempt good-to-excellent rural education research. We owe them *more*, namely clear, simple descriptions of our claims and the evidence supporting (and challenging) them. Moreover, because practitioners in rural schools will often have been successfully colonised in ways that push *the substantive rural* out of the curriculum and, indeed, out of view (see, e.g., Ayalon, 2003; Theobald, 1997), we also owe them clear discussions of why the substantive rural is worth their attention and care.

Research at odds with the university

The rural is a realm of *locality* that puts it at odds with most of what 'the university' – at least in the US, and in our experience – is up to. We personally embrace this situation because rural education research is for us (not for everyone) *simultaneously* an oppositional project, a project of critique and a project of doubt and scepticism. The doubt and scepticism make it research, whereas the generative quality of rural experience sponsors a range of generative meanings and insights essential for doubt, scepticism and critique: for research that honours the substantive rural. Research conducted on such grounds had better understand the tensions of living within universities and simultaneously engaging the rural. Without such understanding, rural education researchers are prey to denial, frustration and intellectual corruption. In general, research needs to be perspicacious about its mission and principled as to methods. However real life, of course, is often different and such bad outcomes are commonplace in the academy and in life. Note, however, that the ways and means of rural education research argued here will enter the political arena of the university and that, though some universities might benefit, some will not and perhaps cannot.

The corruption of getting and spending

This insecure traditional home nonetheless offers one essential advantage for doing rural education research: the legacy *of academic freedom* (AAUP, 1940). It is a right, not a privilege, with teeth made of case-law, and it is not one that has been adequately asserted for teachers in K-12 schooling (Hightower, 2006). We can work with this right. We'd say more: one is obliged to. It's a rare chance for anything concerned with rural to proceed from the university (see Williams, 1973, for a related appreciation).

One's fortunate work is to write what one has to write (and what, in the happiest of conditions, one must write). Often colleagues seem unsure, however, if they can or if they have the right. The right is ensured, but developing the capacity is what constitutes the work. Alas, the justification of academic freedom lies in its use: use it or lose it – and academics are indeed losing it through neglect. We find, of course, that normal science (of the funded sort, for instance) is a principal culprit. Lacking a perspicacious mission of critique, research can be bought for the highest price: it's clearly a seller's market. We are perhaps *fortunate* that so few step up to buy rural education research.

We have, in fact, enjoyed remarkable grant support directly and indirectly relevant to our research, even at second- and third-rate universities in the US. Perhaps it was just the coincidence of our time with an affluent period, and a more pluralistic view of the project of research in the US than now prevails (see Phillips, 2006, for the reality and the pluralism). We avoided subversion of our mission – we hope we have – because we did *not* let the funders direct our work. One can apparently act contrary to funders' purposes if one has fully grasped one's own work. We were never in doubt, and we would have done our work anyway, and only a bit differently.

Rural education research does not require large sums, or even *any* (at least in the context of First World affluence). Despite our happily funded experience, we think it had better no*t require* such sums, at least. Legitimate questions, easy and cheap to study, abound if one can see the substantive rural (for our views, see Howley & Howley, 1999, 2007; Howley, 1997, 2009; see also Coladarci, 2007). The work thus accomplished is not just its own reward, though it is that – readers and thinkers will notice it, and they will seek out the author. Sometimes one will receive funding, but far, far more important are the colleagues drawn by the work, since they are also doing the work. We would say, as well, that doing good-to-excellent work is the priority: funding should follow the work, not lead it.

Job security as a distraction

In the early decades of the twentieth century, the motive for tenure in the US (a provision for job security) was to protect academic freedom (AAUP, 1940). Among other protections, academic freedom gave scholars the ability to exercise skepticism by investigating dangerous questions, reporting innovative or unpopular findings and offering relevant critique. Initially, the idea was that tenure (officially granted job security) would protect serious scholarship that offended powerful interests. (As elsewhere in the world, securing academic rank and position in the US is a long and somewhat arduous process of self-justification to the employing institution: 'tenure' is the shorthand sign for this peculiar practice.)

At some point, however, striving for tenure (and for advancement in rank) became the quest for job security for its own sake, rather than job security for the sake of edgy scholarly work, especially work offensive to, say, university trustees, captains of industry or politicians. With this perspective in mind, we offer a sceptical view of tenure (and its related forms of advancement in rank in many nations). In fact, only one of us has it, and neither of us regards it as very important. (We're not opposed to substantial job security for workers; but we understand university research work as *extremely privileged* work.)

Notably, we think that for rural education researchers, striving for tenure or advancement for its own sake is a distraction, because striving to do good-to-excellent rural education research is the priority. Tenure exists to protect that work and, if such work is not present, the tenure rituals are up to something else. If one does the work, one does need tenure because original scholarly work in rural education is likely to run afoul of vested interests – academic, corporate or governmental. As we've outlined the mission: that is its purpose.

What we're saying is itself unpopular with our colleagues who may see value in job security as a perk in an otherwise underpaid and undervalued career. But, despite some amount of sympathy for that perspective, we see it as wrongheaded. The quest for job security for its own sake is incompatible – in the present and in the durable climate of academe – with the nature of the work (Rinne, 2011; Taggart, 2011; Wood, 1993).

We know of some productive scholars who have not received tenure. This circumstance, painful as it may be, is evidence of a bad fit between a scholar and the employing department, college or university. It's a measure of the extent to which one's immediate colleagues do not understand one's work. So if, despite one's best efforts, those with whom one works don't understand, then one can leave a bad home productively and, eventually, happily.

This counsel is critical in this chapter because most junior faculty will have a hard time acknowledging that good work is not always rewarded (e.g. Verrier, 1992). In fact, our experience lends a reasonable amount of support to a slight adaptation of the old adage 'No good [scholarly] work goes unpunished.' Higher education is not an easy life, precisely because doing research – real scholarship – demands unusual devotion and sense of purpose.

The mainstream and a margin

The substantive rural – that wide variety of generative meanings, ways of being and ways of doing – is accessible to ever fewer humans. Most urbanites and all cosmopolitans (cf. Appiah, 2006, for one exception) deny rural any but a nostalgic significance to the rural margins. For perhaps 10,000 years (odd to think), the world has been urbanising: from the moment people adopted the settled life of (rural) agriculturalists, that development has sponsored cities, so that now in the US (as of 2010) just 15 per cent of people live rurally.

We are a left-over of 10,000 years of history, of prehistory itself. 'Marginalisation' is our fate as rural people, because we live in a real (physical, geographic) margin, not because we are unfairly excluded, silenced or oppressed (all of which we also suffer as a result of living in a cultural margin, too). For research, as well as for living, this sort of marginalisation is generative; to complain of it would be to deny our own strengths and purposes.

This point is apparently subtle and difficult. Some colleagues, as noted, find our position romantic or even reactionary. But they tend to accept the mainstream view of the substantive rural as deficient, and we have worked hard to disabuse them – with little success. We have come to accept the likelihood that what we oppose is deeply structured within the cosmopolitan culture and its dominant neoliberal ideology. Opposition is good work – if you can get it.

Notes

1 To those efforts and those researchers the very concept of 'rural meaning of life' does not make sense, and it has nothing to do with education. It's dismissed as conservative romanticism (see the discussion we had in 2005 with Arnold and colleagues in Howley, Theobald & Howley, 2005).

2 That is, some scholars find divisions between epistemological and ontological issues artificial, and they are more comfortable than others with the understanding that the fact of 'researching' some 'quarry' in a sense constitutes both ends of the work (e.g., Glesne, 2011).

3 The exact quote from Bridgman (1955, p. 535) is 'The scientific method, as far as it is a method, is nothing more than doing one's *damnedest* with one's mind, no holds barred." The controversial assertion made by Feyerabend first appeared in *Against Method* (1975/2010, p. 7).

4 According to the authors, 'the construct of *saberes docentes*, or teachers' pedagogical knowledge, [is] grounded and constructed in teachers' daily experiences with learners" (Wenger, Dinsmore & Villagómez, 2012, p. 2).

5 See http://rurallitrally.org

6 Rural ways of being, knowing, and loving do vary tremendously, of course. We are not arguing or endorsing any sort of single, essential 'ruralness'. On the contrary, we see an intriguing variety of engagements with family, land, nature, and community – of sorts and by means uncommon in suburban enclaves and urban neighbourhoods. Until 1800 or so, *rural* was the principal way to be human – with tremendous variety worldwide. The persistent variety is quite confusing if one wrongly thinks that the rural is outmoded. The rural *does exist* distinctively differently from 'the suburban" and 'the urban'. And it persists in this difference, not only in the variegated specifics, but in the generality.

7 For us, the politics of rural identity misses the point, because it turns what is objective and shared into a species of solipsism, for instance autoethnography, or perhaps arcane musings directed at researchers – like those on offer in this chapter. We are, however, addressing in the present venue a special audience of peculiar specialists.

References

AAUP. (1940). *Principles on Academic Freedom and Tenure*. Washington, DC: American Association of University Professors. Retrieved from http://www.aaup.org/file/1940-Statement-of-Principles-on-Academic-Freedom-and-Tenure.pdf

American Council on Education. (1999). *To Touch the Future: Transforming the way teachers are taught: An action agenda for college and university presidents*. Washington, DC: Author.

Appiah, K. (2006). *Cosmopolitanism: Ethics in a world of strangers*. New York and London: W. W. Norton.

Arendt, H. (1958). *The Human Condition*. Chicago: University of Chicago Press.

Arnold, M. L., Newman, J. H. & Gaddy, B. B. (2005). A look at the condition of rural education research: Setting a direction for future research. *Journal of Research in Rural Education, 20*(6). Retrieved from http://www.jrre.psu.edu/articles/20-6.pdf

Auriat, N. (1998). Social policy and social enquiry: Reopening debate. *International Social Science Journal, 50*(2), 275–287.

Avery, L. M. & Kassam, K. (2011). Phronesis: Children's local rural knowledge of science and engineering. *Journal of Research in Rural Education, 26*(2), 1–18.

Ayalon, A. (2003). Why is rural education missing from multicultural education textbooks? *Educational Forum, 68*, 24–31.

Baez, B. & Boyles, D. (2009). *The Politics of Inquiry: Education research and the 'culture of science'*. Albany: State University of New York Press.

Barnett, C. (2009). Towards a methodology of postmodern assemblage: Adolescent identity in the age of social networking. *Philosophical Studies in Education, 40*, 200–210.

Barzun, J. (2001). *Simple and Direct: A rhetoric for writers*, 4th ed. New York: Harper Perennial.

Beech, J. (2004). Redneck and hillbilly discourse in the writing classroom: Classifying critical pedagogies of whiteness. *College English, 67*(2), 172–209.

Bell, E. (2008). Great 21st century debates about the usefulness of research: Can they help rural research? *Rural Society, 18*(1), 3–16.

Berry, W. (1990). *What are People for?* San Francisco, CA: North Point Press.

Bickel, R., Tomasek, T. & Eagle, T.H. (2000). Top-down, routinized reform in low-income, rural schools: NSF's Appalachian Rural Systemic Initiative. *Education Policy Analysis Archives, 8*(12). Retrieved from http://epaa.asu.edu/ojs/article/view/403

Bowers, A. J., Metzger, S. & Militello, M. (2010). Knowing the odds: Parameters that predict passing or failing school district bonds. *Educational Policy, 24*(2), 398–420.

Bridgman, P. (1955). *Reflections of a Physicist*. New York: Philosophical Library.

Budge, K. M. (2010). Why shouldn't rural kids have it all? Place-conscious leadership in an era of extralocal reform policy. *Education Policy Analysis Archives, 18*(1), 1–23.

Burawoy, M. (2004). The critical turn to public sociology. In R. F. Levine (ed.), *Enriching the Sociological Imagination: How radical sociology changed the discipline* (pp. 309–322). Leiden, The Netherlands: Brill.

Burnell, B. A. (2003). The 'real world' aspirations of work-bound rural students. *Journal of Research in Rural Education, 18*(2), 104–113.

Carlone, H., Kimmel, S. & Tschida, C. (2010). A rural math, science, and technology elementary school tangled up in global networks of practice. *Cultural Studies of Science Education, 5*(2), 447–476. doi:10.1007/s11422-009-9233-2

Clarke, A. E. (2003). Situational analysis: Grounded theory mapping after the postmodern turn. *Symbolic Interaction, 26*(4), 553–576.

Coladarci, T. (2007). Improving the yield of rural education research: An editor's swan song. *Journal of Research in Rural Education, 22*, 1–9.

Conkin, P. (2007). *The State of the Earth*. Lexington: University of Kentucky Press.

Corbett, M. (2007). *Learning to Leave: The irony of schooling in a coastal community*. Black Point, NS: Fernwood.

Cubberley, E. P. (1922). *Rural Life and Education: A study of the rural-school problem as a phase of the rural-life problem*. Boston, MA: Houghton Mifflin.

Davies, S. & Guppy, N. (1997). Globalization and Educational Reforms in Anglo-American Democracies. *Comparative Education Review, 41*(4), 435–459.

Delborne, J.A. (2008). Transgenes and transgressions: Scientific dissent as heterogeneous practice. *Social Studies of Science, 38*(4), 509–541.

DeYoung, A. (1995). *The Life and Death of a Rural American High School: Farewell, Little Kanawha*. New York: Garland.

Duncan, C. M. (1999). *Worlds Apart: Why poverty persists in rural America*. New Haven, CT: Yale University Press.

Eppley, K. (2010). Picturing rural America: An analysis of the representation of contemporary rural America in picture books for children. *Rural Educator, 32*(1), 1–10.

Feyerabend, P. (2010). *Against method*, 4th ed. London: Verso. (Original work published 1975.)

Flyvbjerg, B. (2001). *Making Social Science Matter: Why social inquiry fails and how it can succeed again*, trans. S. Sampson. New York, NY: Cambridge University Press.

Freeman, M. (2011). Validity in dialogic encounters with hermeneutic truths. *Qualitative Inquiry, 17*(6), 543–551. doi:10.1177/1077800411409887

Gieryn, T. F. (1999). *Cultural Boundaries of Science: Credibility on the line*. Chicago, IL: University of Chicago Press.

Gilman, N., Goldhammer, J. & Weber, S. (ed.). (2011). *Deviant Globalization: Black market economy in the 21st century*. New York: Continuum.

Giroux, H.A. (1992). *Border Crossings: Cultural workers and the politics of education*. New York, NY: Routledge.

Glesne, C. (2011). *Becoming Qualitative Researchers: An introduction*. Boston: Pearson.

Graves, A., Haughton, B., Jahns, L., Fitzhugh, E. & Jones, S. J. (2008). Biscuits, sausage, gravy, milk, and orange juice: School breakfast environment in four rural Appalachian schools. *Journal of School Health, 78*(4), 197–202.

Greenwood, D. A. (2009). Place, survivance, and white remembrance: A decolonizing challenge to rural education in mobile modernity. *Journal of Research in Rural Education, 24*(10), 1–6.

Habermas, J. (1972). *Knowledge and human interest*, trans. J. J. Shapiro. London, England: Heinemann.

Habermas, J. (1984). *The Theory of Communicative Action*, Vol. 1, *Reason and the Rationalization of Society*, trans. T. McCarthy. Oxford, England: Polity Press.

Habermas, J. (1987). *Lifeworld and System: A critique of functionalist reason* (The Theory of Communicative Action, vol. 2). Boston: Beacon Press.

Henry, K., Cavanagh, T. & Oetting, E. (2011). Perceived parental investment in school as a mediator of the relationship between socio-economic indicators and educational outcomes in rural America. *Journal of Youth & Adolescence, 40*(9), 1164–1177.

Hightower, R. (2006). A review and analysis of academic freedom and public school teacher tenure. Doctoral dissertation, University of Georgia. Retrieved from http://getd.galib.uga.edu/public/hightower_tammy_j_200608_edd/hightower_tammy_j_200608_edd.pdf

Howley, A. & Howley, C. (1999). The transformative challenge of rural context. *Educational Foundations, 14*(4), 73–85.

Howley, A. & Howley, C. (2000). The transformative challenge of rural context. *Educational Foundations, 14*(4), 73–85.

Howley, A. & Howley, C. (2007). *Thinking about Schools: New theories and innovative practice*. Mahwah, NJ: Lawrence Erlbaum Associates.

Howley, A., Howley, C., Burgess, L. & Pusateri, D. (2008). Social class, Amish culture, and an egalitarian ethos: Case study from a rural school serving Amish children. *Journal of Research in Rural Education, 23*(3), 1–12.

Howley, C. (1997). How to make rural education research rural: An essay at practical advice. *Journal of Research in Rural Education, 13*(2), 131–138. Retrieved from http://jrre.psu.edu/articles/v13,n2,p131-138,Howley.pdf

Howley, C. (2009). Critique and fiction: Doing science right in rural education research. *Journal of Research in Rural Education, 24*. Retrieved from http://www.jrre.psu.edu/articles/24-15.pdf

Howley, C. & Howley, A. (2004). School size and the influence of socioeconomic status on student achievement: Confronting the threat of size bias in national data sets. *Education Policy Analysis Archives, 12*(52). Retrieved from http://epaa.asu.edu/epaa/v12n52/

Howley, C. & Howley, A. (2010). Poverty and school achievement in rural communities: A social-class interpretation. In A. Y. Jackson & K. A. Schafft (eds), *Rural Education for the 21st Century: Identity, place, and community in a globalizing world* (pp. 34–50). University Park, PA: Pennsylvania State University Press.

Howley, C. B., Howley, A. A. & Huber, D. S. (2005). Prescriptions for Rural Mathematics Instruction: Analysis of the Rhetorical Literature [computer file]. *Journal of Research in Rural Education (Online), 20*(7). Retrieved from http://www.jrre.psu.edu/articles/20-7.pdf

Howley, C. B., Showalter, D., Klein, R., Sturgill, D. J. & Smith, M. A. (2013). Rural math talent, now and then. *Roeper Review, 35*(2), 102–114.

Howley, C., Theobald, P. & Howley, A. (2005). What education research is of most worth? A reply to Arnold, Newman, Gaddy, and Dean. *Journal of Research in Rural Education, 20*, 18.

Jackson, A. Y. (2010). Fields of discourse: A Foucauldian analysis of schooling in a rural, US southern town. In A. Y. Jackson & K. A. Schafft (eds), *Rural Education for the Twenty-First Century: Identity, place, and community in a globalizing world* (pp. 72–94). University Park, PA: Pennsylvania State University Press.

Johnson, A., Baker, A. & Bruer, L. (2007). Interdependence, garbage dumping, and feral dogs: Exploring three lifeworld resources of young children in a rural school. *Early Childhood Education Journal, 34*(6), 371–377.

Kuhn, T.S. (1962). *The Structure of Scientific Revolutions.* Chicago, IL: University of Chicago Press.

Larson, N. C. & Dearmont, M. (2002). Strengths of farming communities in fostering resilience in children. *Child Welfare, 81*(5), 821–835.

Le Grange, L. (2007). Integrating Western and indigenous knowledge systems: The basis for effective science education in South Africa? *International Review of Education, 53*(5/6), 577–591.

Marchand, H. (2012). Contributions of Piagetian and post-Piagetian theories to education. *Educational Research Review, 7*(3), 165–176. doi:10.1016/j.edurev.2012.04.002

Marx, K. (1867/1990). *Capital: A critique of political economy,* trans. B. Fowkes. New York, NY: Penguin Books.

Mayuzumi, K. (2009). Unfolding possibilities through a decolonizing project: Indigenous knowledges and rural Japanese women. *International Journal of Qualitative Studies In Education (QSE), 22*(5), 507–526. doi:10.1080/09518390903048800

Naples, N. A. (1994). Contradictions in agrarian ideology: Restructuring gender, race-ethnicity, and class. *Rural Sociology, 59*, 110–135.

Peshkin, A. (1982). *The Imperfect Union: School consolidation and community conflict.* Chicago, IL: University of Chicago Press.

Phillips, D. C. (2009). A quixotic quest? Philosophical issues in assessing the quality of education research. In P. B. Walters, A. Lareau & S. H. Ranis (eds), *Education Research on Trial: Policy reform and the call for scientific rigor* (pp. 163–196). New York: Routledge.

Phillips, D. C. (2006). Muddying the waters: The many purposes of educational inquiry. In *The Sage Handbook for Research in Education: Engaging ideas and enriching inquiry* (pp. 7–22). Thousand Oaks, CA: Sage Publications.

Ponticell, J. A. & Olivarez, A. (1997). Dissertation quality and Kerlinger's methods myth. *Journal of Experimental Education, 65*(2), 113.

Portes, A. (2000). The hidden abode: Sociology as analysis of the unexpected. *American Sociological Review, 65*, 1–18.

Reeves, E. (2012). The effects of opportunity to learn, family socioeconomic status, and friends on the rural math achievement gap in high school. *American Behavioral Scientist, 56*(7), 887–907.

Reid, J., Green, B., Cooper, M., Hastings, W., Lock, G. & White, S. (2010). Regenerating rural social space? Teacher education for rural-regional sustainability. *Australian Journal of Education, 54*(3), 262–276.

Rinne, K. (2011). Independent scholars: A nomadic lot. *New York Times*, 11 February, p. BU8.

Ross, E.W. (2008). Social studies education. In D. Gabbard (ed.), *Knowledge and Power in the Global Economy: The effects of school reform in a neoliberal/neoconservative age,* 2nd ed. (pp. 367–376). New York: Routledge.

Said, E. (2004). *Humanism and Democratic Criticism.* New York: Columbia University Press.

Scott, J.C. (1998). *Seeing Like a State.* New Haven, CT: Yale University Press.

Sleeter, C. (2012). Confronting the marginalization of culturally responsive pedagogy. *Urban Education, 47*(3), 562–584.

Smith, P. (2002). 'It's déjà vu all over again: The rural school problem revisited. In D. Chalker (ed.), *Leadership for Rural Schools: Lessons for all educators* (pp. 25–62). Lanham, MD: Scarecrow Press.

Somerville, M. (2007). Postmodern emergence. *International Journal of Qualitative Studies in Education, 20,* 225–243.

Taggart, A. (2011). Can one lead a life of the mind in a post-patronage society? Retrieved from http://andrewjtaggart.com/2011/02/22/can-one-lead-a-life-of-the-mind-in-a-post-patronage-society

Theobald, P. (1997). *Teaching the Commons: Place, pride, and the renewal of community.* Boulder, CO: Westview.

Verrier, D. A. (1992). On becoming tenured: acquiring academic tenure at a research university. Presented at the Annual Meeting of the Association for the Study of Higher Education, Minneapolis, MN. Retrieved from http://www.eric.ed.gov/ERICWebPortal/detail?accno=ED352908

Walters, P. B. & Lareau, A. (2009). Education research that matters: Influence, scientific rigor, and policymaking. In P. B. Walters, A. Lareau & S. Ranis (eds), *Education Research on Trial: Policy Reform and the Call for Scientific Rigor* (pp. 197–220). New York and London: Routledge.

Wells, K. & Littell, J. H. (2009). Study quality assessment in systematic reviews of research on intervention effects. *Research on Social Work Practice, 19,* 52–62.

Wenger, K. J., Dinsmore, J. & Villagómez, A. (2012). Teacher identity in a multicultural rural school: Lessons learned at Vista Charter. *Journal of Research in Rural Education, 27*(5). Retrieved from http://jrre./psu.edu/articles/27-5.pdf

White, S. & Reid, J. (2008). Placing teachers? Sustaining rural schooling through place-consciousness in teacher education. *Journal of Research in Rural Education, 23*(7), 1–11.

Wood, J. (1993). The life of Thorstein Veblen and perspectives on this thought. London: Routledge.

Chapter 2

Social cartography and rural education

Researching space(s) and place(s)

Bill Green and Jo-Anne Reid

Introduction: researching the rural

Geography matters. This is manifestly so in a country such as Australia, with its vast open spaces and its relatively sparse population. But it is also the case in Finland or Norway, or in Newfoundland. In the latter, it tends to be terrain that is the key issue in separating places from each other so that some are marginalised because of their rurality, or difference from the urban norm, whereas in Australia it is more an issue of distance. Different geographies have different social effects. Yet Australia is also acknowledged to be one of the most urbanised countries in the world, with the majority of its population living along the coastal fringes – something that has been apparent for the best part of a century now, despite common perceptions of Australia as a 'wide brown land' that privileges its inland heart. What does this mean for rural education? That depends, of course, in part at least, on how rurality is understood. In our work, we have tended to see the rural as involving non-metropolitan life and livelihood – that, is, what counts as rural education for us are those forms of schooling and literacy occurring outside the Metropolis. In Australia, this means outside the capital cities in each of the States and Territories, in addition to a number of relatively large regional centres, or so-called 'second-tier' cities (Markusen, Lee & DiGiovanna, 1999), similarly often located near to, if not actually on, the coast. Beyond are the small towns and communities that make up the bulk of what is commonly identified as rural Australia. The 'outback' is something else again. Developing an informed geographical imagination goes hand in hand, then, with thinking socially and historically in researching rural education. And that means, perhaps above all else, attending to *place* and *space*, and also *scale* – indeed, to all three, as they interrelate in social-semiotic practice, in a dynamic manner (Green, 2013; see also Green, 2012).

In this chapter we focus on what is involved in researching place(s) and space(s), as especially significant in and for rural education research. We draw on our own work in rural (teacher) education and also in rural literacies, as well as that of other scholars. We see this as an opportunity to build on the increasing focus in rural education research on the significance of place, along with space, as a necessary consideration in best understanding and appreciating the circumstances and specificity of rural education and schooling. Halfacree (2006) has described the rural as "inherently spatial", and there is growing interest in rethinking geography as a major reference point in and for the field. This remains important *despite* the fact that, for some, recent developments in digital culture and new technologies promise to overcome many of the problems and challenges of geography, whether with regard to distance or terrain, or climate, etc.

How did we come to rural education research? It began, formally at least, when we moved to inland New South Wales (NSW), firstly in Armidale and then in Bathurst. Separately and collaboratively, we had always been committed to researching our own practice. This was initially as English teachers, caught up in the language-and-learning movement, and then as teacher educators, involved in various forms of action research and practitioner inquiry. Finding ourselves in inland NSW, we soon turned our attention to researching where we were and *from* where we were; that is, inquiry as a positioned practice. This quickly realised itself in a focus on teacher education for rural schools, and on what it meant, in particular, for English teaching and literacy education, in primary classrooms as much as in the high school.

We brought some prior practical experience of rural education to this work. Jo-Anne taught briefly in a small rural school prior to taking on the role, early in her career, of an 'English advisory teacher' for beginning teachers in rural schools over the whole of Western Australia. This meant that she learned much about the nature and situation of country towns, country schools, country teachers and country kids. Bill worked in several country high schools in Western Australia, always travelling back to the city on weekends. Other than that, we had little sustained practical knowledge or understanding of rural teaching per se. Rural schooling didn't figure much in our subsequent teacher education work at Murdoch University, and it was only when we moved to Victoria, when Jo-Anne was working at the University of Ballarat and Bill at Deakin University in the mid-1990s, that the matter emerged as something of potential interest and value.[1] However, this was only realised in substantive terms when we moved to inland NSW. We had longstanding interests in social justice, educational disadvantage and critical pedagogy, and this readily extended to rural contexts, linking up with Jo-Anne's continuing work in Aboriginal education and our new interests in environmental education. The work has been extremely generative, and deeply satisfying.

Foregrounding place, space and location in our thinking has emerged from these histories and geographies, and has been particularly informed by a growing awareness of Indigenous knowledge and emphasis on place, and relationship to Country. This is an all too often under-estimated and under-valued aspect of (re)thinking rurality. A key concept has been the notion of *rural social space* (Reid et al., 2010), which is linked in turn to another: rural-regional sustainability (Green & Reid, 2004). From the outset, in fact, we have been drawn to considerations of space, and also, relatedly, of place.[2] We became aware, early on, of much anecdotal reference to the significance of being located on the 'Other' side of the Great Dividing Range – the mountain chain extending down the eastern coast of Australia. This became a metaphor: 'West of the Mountains'. One project, the Rural (Teacher) Education Project (R[T]EP) (Green, 2008b), investigated the challenges and opportunities associated with rural (teacher) education in inland NSW, working with eleven School Districts located West of the Mountains: 'Its focus was on inland NSW, or those parts of the State that were on the "other", western side of the Great Dividing Range ... a vast, sparsely populated territory, estimated at the time as comprising more than three-quarters of the State's landmass, with just 13% of [its] population – and hence, representative in this regard of Australia more generally' (Green, 2008a, p. 387). We argue that the *experience of* 'space' and 'distance' and 'isolation', etc., in our lives and everyday work, is a matter of anecdote and imagery as much as rational or evidence-based knowledge. In effect, it produces something like Raymond Williams' sense of a 'structure of feeling'. This is important, we believe, because, as later explicitly emerged in our research, the rural must be understood as *both* real and imagined, or, after Henri Lefebvre (1991) and Edward Soja (1996), a 'real-and-imaginary' space. At issue here, fundamentally, is the relationship between geography and education, and it is this that we want to emphasise in this chapter.

We begin with a discussion of social cartography as a theoretical and methodological concept that allows us to deal adequately with relations of place and space and their effects on both the policy and practice of education. We then move to examine two instances from our research that highlight the sorts of productive tensions and opportunities that attention to place in rural education has produced for our work. Through this, we argue the importance of recognising that all knowledge and experience always produces a view from *somewhere*.

On social cartography

For our purposes here, a geographical perspective is organised around notions of place and space, along with scale, and takes in related concepts such as territory and region, boundary, inclusion/exclusion, and the patterning of population density and distribution. Rather than referring simply to the physical world, geography as we mobilise it encompasses social and cultural life in particular locales. It also takes account of maps, as texts and technologies, and of mapping as a social-semiotic knowledge practice.

There is, in fact, a growing interest in thinking geographically in rural education research, and indeed in educational research more generally (Gulson & Symes, 2007; Silvie & Zdenek, 2012; Taylor, 2009; Theim, 2009). This is directly associated with new and burgeoning interest in space (e.g. Usher, 2002) and place (e.g. Wyse et al., 2012) as key organising concepts and problematics, specifically for educational practice. Among others, Taylor (2009, p. 652) notes 'considerable and growing use of geographical ideas in education research', but suggests that there may well be some risk in approaching this in an 'undisciplined' way, without due acknowledgement of disciplinary frames and constraints. Nonetheless, there certainly seems to be value in drawing upon geographical ideas and techniques in educational research, albeit in a rigorously conceived interdisciplinary manner.

Paulston's (1996) concept of *social cartography* is immediately pertinent here, described as 'an alliance of education and geography' (p. xvi), as both a methodology and a practice involving heightened awareness of socio-spatial dynamics and the deployment of visual images as 'social maps'. Subsequently described as 'the reading and writing of maps addressing questions of location in the social milieu' (Paulston & Liebman, 1996, p. 7), this was taken as an organising principle in the NSW Rural (Teacher) Education Project (Green, 2008), and extended to include due consideration of mobility, of flows and trajectories as well as places and positionalities, networks as well as nodes (Castells, 1996). An account is provided below of R(T)EP's work in this regard. Such a heightened socio-spatial awareness seems eminently appropriate for thinking about, and re-thinking, rural education (Green & Letts, 2007). This is especially the case given contemporary understandings of rurality (e.g. Cloke, 2006) and rural space (Halfacree, 2006).

Social cartography as envisaged by Paulston and his colleagues was expressly conceived within a postmodern(ist) frame. This means working outside or at least sceptically with core principles and practices of modernity, notably those associated with representation and identity. Paulston (1996, xvii) refers to his early attempts to craft 'a ground-level social cartography project with critical potential ... build[ing] upon and extend[ing] earlier postmodern mapping contributions in geography, and also in feminist, literary and postcolonial studies'. He notes the view that social cartography, or 'social mapping', constitutes 'a new method to identify changing perceptions of values, ideologies and spatial relations' (Paulston, 1996, p. xix), and later describes it intriguingly as '... a ludic mapping practice' (p. xx). This implies, at the very least, a more flexible understanding of science and knowledge. We pick up, below, on the potentials of mapping in our research to help understand the social spaces of the present, in terms of both historical and geographical relations between people, place and social practice. Drawing directly on the definition of social cartography as 'the writing and reading of maps addressing questions of location in the social milieu', Mannion and Ivanič (2007, p. 18) observe that, while work along such lines 'involves the interpretation of objective reality and the representation of spatial relationships among different concepts and artefacts ... in social cartography the map itself can provoke further debate and is not seen as an effort to write a final truth'. The map is not simply instrumental, that is, nor is it neutral.

Yet that is precisely how it has tended to be deployed in rural education contexts and indeed in education more generally. This is perhaps understandable given the (social-scientific) character of education as a field of study linked to an institutional practice that functions as a central project of modernity. Maps have long played a significant role in science and its corollary, colonialism: mapping the world is a key technology of power/knowledge. Delineating and marking out territories is certainly a feature of Australian history, including its schooling, as it is in other countries. Maps and mapping are, moreover, instruments of bureaucracy, of organisation and control, and of governmentality in its various senses. But to think of them as merely 'tools' is misleading. They are always more productive and constitutive than that, even in their efficiency *as* tools. They seem 'real', or at least realistic – but this must be understood as yet another form of real*ism*, and another expression of the so-called 'modernism–postmodernism' debate, arguably still unfinished even though now clearly out of fashion.

A further consideration here is the increasing significance of new technologies in cartography and geography, and indeed in cultural and intellectual life more generally. Hugo (2001) sees an important role for what he calls spatial information in community and social planning, as an increasingly salient resource for social analysis and policy development. 'The significance of information technology in the global economy', he writes, 'can hardly be exaggerated' (Hugo, 2001, p. 269). His particular concern is with 'spatial information technology' or 'spatial information systems (SIS)' (p. 269). This is more commonly known as 'GIS' (Geographic Information Systems), and has become a matter of increasing interest and utility in social and educational research (e.g. Taylor, 2007). As Pickles (1999, p. 93) notes, this has 'become an exciting area of new mapping studies, particularly as digital mapping and the generalizing of technologies and practices of mapping to many more domains of social life create new forms and users of maps'. Hugo (2001, p. 273) explains the ability of these systems 'to act as an integrator of vastly different and complex spatially referenced data sets'. As he writes: 'One of the most fundamental of capacities of SIS is to depict spatial information graphically. Modern development in SIS allows us to take mapping to a new level of sophistication and impact' (Hugo, 2001, p. 276). Further: 'Overlaying two or more relevant coverages or several individual map layers allows all the dimensions of the concepts to be captured in a single new coverage' (p. 273). This means we can move beyond thinking about maps as singular, in their conventional two-dimensional character; rather, it is possible to work with them increasingly with regard to mobility and multiplicity, and indeed mutability, thereby allowing more dynamic representational work, and hence semiotic and cognitive complexity.

Paulston (2000, p. 318) expresses this well: 'In addition to its critical and demystification utility to make visible ideas and relations that otherwise might remain hidden, social cartography will also be useful to convert increasing flows of data into visual images.' That is, there are two key reasons for the use of what might be called educational cartography: firstly, working with maps is a distinctive and highly effective way of portraying spaces and place, locations and territories, and their interrelationships; and secondly, it provides a good basis for moving beyond conventional forms of representation and communication, particularly in academic work. Further to this, there is opportunity here to bring together not simply the humanities and social sciences but also the arts and sciences, in ways that greatly enrich (rural) educational research. At the very least, social and educational cartography provides a way of working across the qualitative/ quantitative divide, and hence might even be framed within a revitalised 'mixed-method' perspective on research.

In summary: While arguably little utilised or understood in educational policy or practice, outside of a more conventional mathematico-statistical framework, there is considerable potential value in drawing on more hermeneutically and textually oriented visual and spatial forms of inquiry and data (and its display) with regard to educational phenomena. Indeed, there are signs of increasing engagement on the part of educational theory and research with cartographic work, with cartography perhaps rather ironically described recently as 'largely uncharted territory in educational theory' (Ruitenberg, 2007, p. 8). Maps are more than instrumental in such work. They are as much interventions as descriptions, 'never merely represent[ing] the world, but always also produc[ing] or constitut[ing] it'. Hence they open up 'the possibilities of ... social, critical and tactical [uses of] cartography in educational theory' (Ruitenberg, 2007, p. 9) – and quite likely in educational practice and policy as well.

Working with maps

We have sought to draw on maps and mapping, literally and metaphorically, in a number of our projects over the past decade or so. As noted already, cartography figured significantly in the R(T)EP study of rural (teacher) education in New South Wales. That project addressed the relationship between rural schooling and teacher education in what was more than three-quarters of one of Australia's largest states – an ambitious, even quixotic undertaking, as it now seems. Partly what was, and remains, at issue here was *centre-periphery* dynamics – the relationship between centre(s) and periphery(ies), given that this is always to be conceived in a scalar-dynamic fashion, that is, as a matter of multiple centres, realised at different scales. A further, related consideration is what we have called metro-centricity, or metro-centric normativity, which, while certainly a general feature of modernity, is also a register of Australia's particular demographic and settlement profile. How is all this to be represented?

A major hypothesis of R(T)EP was that the spatial dimension of educational policy and practice is too often overlooked or ignored, and that this has particular implications for rural (teacher) education. This hypothesis was extended to a focus on geography more generally, rethought through contemporary interdisciplinary developments and debates, building on a new spatial turn in social and educational research. Notions such as 'isolation', or remoteness and accessibility, and the effects of distance, are usefully reconsidered in this light. We began literally with what maps there were available, starting with one of the State itself and various spatial depictions of the public education system. At that time, the 'District' was the organising principle for the Department, as a distinctive spatial-administrative unit. Over the project's course there was a major administrative shift from the 'District' to the 'Region', with the latter then subdivided into still smaller spatial units. The original eleven Districts were, among other things, the sites at which assessment and accountability were organised, and school and student performance monitored, then relayed to Head Office. The research team worked at the level of the District (or its later equivalent), both for ethnographic fieldwork and to analyse the relation among location, educational achievement and quality teaching.

As we found early on, each District had its own map of the territory, indicating where the schools within its ambit were located and delineating a boundary. This was expressly and strictly instrumental, and meant, for instance, that communities which played in the same football tournaments on the weekends might travel to quite different locations for school events. However, somewhat to the bemusement of our Departmental colleagues, we began to work with these maps as *texts*, signifiers of educational space and its associated social meaning. It was particularly useful to look at these maps *comparatively*, to see what patterns might emerge as features of interest, and then to speculate on matters such as movement through these territories by educational consultants and the like, as well as teachers, students and their families. This latter point became particularly significant in relation to Aboriginal student achievement, and the lifestyle mobility of some Aboriginal groups, for instance, up and down the Darling River. Student mobility created problems for schools, with their characteristically fixed locations, and for systems more geared to quantitative measures of similarly fixed populations and territories (Nespor, 2004).

All up, over 300 maps were produced, drawing on the resources of the Spatial Data Analysis Network, Charles Sturt University (CSU), and working where possible with digital technologies. While it was originally intended that R(T)EP would produce or at least contribute to a social cartography of rural education in (inland) NSW, or even a social atlas of rural education and schooling, this proved beyond the expertise and capacity of the research team at the time. It was envisaged as literally mapping the provision and practice of rural education, taking into account both the range and distribution of schools across NSW and the system of distance education with its associated forms of networking and exchange, as well as various forms and patterns of mobility among consultants, teachers and students. This was ideally to be cross-referenced with and mapped onto available sociological, staffing and student achievement data. Further, this 'scientific' mapping was to be complemented by more metaphorical and narrative forms of mapping, emerging through interviews and stories.[3] A huge undertaking, as we have already acknowledged, it is only in retrospect that its scope and ambition can be apprehended and appreciated. It involved working with *both* qualitative and quantitative research methodologies, in an informed pluralist spirit – something we increasingly see as being particularly apposite for rural education research.

What we also recognise now is that this is a good example of what might be called *emerging methodology* – that is, a perspective not yet entrenched and fully developed, and not yet duly or properly authorised, but which is becoming more and more compelling as a productive and appropriate way of conducting research, particularly in rural and other non-metrocentric education. There is much further thinking to do in this regard. Hopefully, however, we have provided here a sense of what is possible, and why it is worth pursuing. The point is: Space matters, and therefore how is it to be taken into account in rural education research?

Addressing place

However, it is *place* as a concept that seems more congenial to, and increasingly of interest in, rural studies. This is partly under the influence of 'place-based' or 'place-conscious' education (Gruenewald, 1993a, 1993b; Gruenewald & Smith, 2008), in literacy, environmental, Indigenous and rural education. Steadily growing in significance over the past decade or so, it has increasingly figured in our own work as well (e.g. Comber, Nixon & Reid, 2007; Cormack, Green & Reid, 2008; White & Reid, 2008), along with that of many others (e.g. Eppley, 2011; Somerville & Rennie, 2012). More recently there has been a developing critique in this regard (McInerney, Smyth & Down, 2011; Nespor, 2009) – productively so, in our view. This is because of a rather disturbing trend towards romanticism and humanism in some of the work appearing on the scene, which needs to be guarded against. When place is evoked simply because it seems to affirm or defend un(der)-theorised notions of community and proximity, localism, or certain metaphysical values of presence and natural-ness, it becomes a problem. As Nespor (2008, p. 480) put it, pungently, in such work it all too often seems as if

> [r]edemption ... can be found through emphasizing place, becoming more conscious of it, digging in, working and living on a more localized scale, and, in regards to schooling, grounding pedagogy and curriculum in the notion of place-as-community.

While there is rich possibility in theoretically and politically sensitive and informed place-conscious work in rural education, and some indication that this is indeed happening in the field, it is insufficient to simply reassert the power of the local, of place as proximity and propinquity, of place-*as*-the-local. More is needed to make place really matter as an organising principle for social justice and environmental agency.

There are a number of issues needing to be taken into account in such work. One certainly has to do with thinking through the implications and challenges of what might, admittedly somewhat provocatively, be called 'place-as-identity'. A focus on place would seem to be congruent with what has been described as 'thisness' (Thomson, 2000), posited as a rhetorical and conceptual resource for social justice initiatives in education at a time when school reform movements characteristically emphasise standardisation, quantification and populational rationalism. As Nespor (2004, p. 320) elsewhere observes, '[t]here are ... powerful processes at work to produce totalising maps that allow distant students and teachers to be plotted with respect to one another'. To focus, rather, on what happens in *this* school, or *that* one, in *this* place or *that* one, is to insist on specificity, on the particularity and complexity of situated practice(s). An understanding of the specificity of place displaces the metro-normative assumption of a unitary rural 'Other'. A further consideration concerns the metro-normative use of large-scale standardised testing as a measure of quality teaching and learning. But this acknowledgement of difference raises a dilemma: how *not* to identify and name these schools and, more to the point here, these places. Yet that runs counter to much standard practice in educational research, methodologically and ethically, as Nespor (2000, p. 547) argues: 'It is, after all, a methodological axiom in some fields that researchers should withhold the real names and locations of the settings and participants they study.'

This has been a constant issue in our own projects, and a matter of on-the-ground professional learning, as we have worked through some of the practical challenges and political dilemmas as well as the theory itself. Working with maps otherwise freely available in the public realm can be problematic in this regard. Consider for instance a map of New South Wales, indicating among other things where particular towns are located. Given that in many instances these are themselves relatively small, and schools are commonly located in them, or in their environs, how is it possible *not* to identify them, in discussions about education staffing, administration or student outcomes? How is it desirable to do this? In the TERRAnova project (i.e. Teacher Education for Rural and Regional Australia) (Reid et al., 2010, 2012), where we were deliberately focused on what was working well in terms of attracting and retaining teachers, especially newly graduated teachers, there was good reason to celebrate the success of the particular sites in question. Moreover, the project team was concerned to take into account and represent 'an *affective* sense of place' (Reid et al., 2013, p. 58), drawing on a comprehensive range of data, including the visual. Photographs were used therefore as resources, as reminders as well as texts in themselves, and as 'markers of location, of history, and of connectedness to place'. What is immediately significant when collecting data though photographing places is that questions of anonymity become moot. This was important to us, methodologically. Following the work of Nespor (2000), we argue that anonymisation of place in qualitative research washes out the specificities of geography, environment, history and social relations that have produced the particular form of rural social space that forms the actual object of our inquiry. In this way, we saw it as inappropriate to erase from a research report the things that create what Thomson (2000) calls 'thisness' in relation to place, and which are directly associated with the thing we wanted to know: How did *this* school successfully retain its teachers? As Nespor (2000, p. 552) writes:

> If one knows exactly where and what its setting was, for example, one could ask if the processes described in the [setting] studied would play out in the same way in a suburb with a different political economy, with students of

different ethnicities, at some other period in history, at a larger or smaller school, at a school with a different curriculum, and so on.

The taken-for-granted ethical requirements of 'anonymisation' in qualitative research, and the almost *de rigueur* 'disclaimer' about generalisability that must therefore accompany a representation of 'someplace', reflect the metro-normativity of educational research, and fail to acknowledge that the material and affective dimensions of place cannot be factored out of any understanding of it. As Nespor (2000, p. 561) notes in relation to his point above, this raises different issues for research integrity: '[a]nother reason there are relatively few identifications of anonymised qualitative studies may be that researchers and other readers *prefer* to have these pseudogeneral accounts; we do not *want* to deal with the spatial and temporal situatedness of the events and processes described' (our emphases). Certainly attention to real places in research is complex and difficult. It is 'harder', requiring perhaps more overtly rigorous member-checking and confirmation of researcher interpretation – not as fact, but as a legitimate interpretation of the information at hand.

The politics of public educational systems granting access to schools for social inquiry are well known; however, even in circumstances where there were clearly issues and problems regarding the nature and quality of education in certain rural settings, we still ask whether there is *necessarily* value in insisting on anonymity and confidentiality. Educational outcomes, like life experiences, always come from somewhere, and it can be helpful to include social cartography to understand the rural social spaces that produce different forms of educational outcomes for certain students and communities. Our work in TERRAnova confirms this, as it is clear that the schools identified as successful, and studied as cases in our research, could be seen as similar in two main ways.

First, they had similar *spatial* characteristics that became identifiable on maps of their location. The schools that were successful in retaining staff appeared to be located far enough away from larger regional hubs to make it more convenient for teachers to live in the community rather than commute, but not so far that their isolation produced difficulties in accessing the amenities focused in the metro-centre. Most of these communities had access to road or air transport directly linking them with the amenities needed for health, welfare and culture (Reid et al., 2012). This is crucially important for educational planning, as, although it does not relieve the management of these schools and communities from the task of professional and social support for their staff, it enables discourses of deficiency around rural communities, related to their failure to retain staff, to be recast. Working with this information as indicative of the specificity of rural education, rather than measuring rural schools against a generalised norm, means that discourses of enablement must be introduced to support those schools whose spatial location requires the use of distributive justice for equity.

Second, there were aspects of the rural social space that had developed in each of these locations that were difficult to talk about and that were noted as silences in our analysis of the maps, images and other ethnographic data collected in the case studies.

Little of the interview data in the communities we visited, for instance, indicated high numbers of Indigenous children in these schools. Yet most of the maps we consulted and produced for the study retained traces of the Indigenous custodians of the land, on which settlement had re-inscribed and mapped a colonial culture.[4] The names of rivers, landforms, streets and suburbs often tell a different story than the accounts of teachers, farmers, business owners and local government officials in these communities, and suggest the complex histories that have produced particular forms of rural social space in the present. Raising these issues, along with others like rural poverty and environmental degradation, always remains an ethical issue for researchers in relation to the specificities of place.

Conclusion

Educational cartography as we have sought to describe it here is still very much a work in progress. For us, it is particularly generative in and for researching rural education. Whatever else it is, rural education raises a range of questions relating to space and place, the dialectical relationship between which is always to be understood at scale. Working with maps and mapping, both those already available in one form or another or those one generates oneself, is potentially extremely productive, and an important supplement to more established research practices and perspectives in the field. This is because spatiality is always inextricable from social and political considerations, but is also significant with regard to praxis and pedagogy, in ways still to be fully appreciated. Much work still remains to be done, of course. In drawing this chapter to a close, we want to briefly outline some of the possibilities we see opening up in this regard, before making some final observations about what this all means for research(er) development.

Clearly cartography as a research practice involves both highly sophisticated digital technologies and techniques and well-established disciplinary conventions. It also must be understood both literally and metaphorically, and indeed this is entirely appropriate given the view that the rural is real-and-imaginary. Reference was made earlier to Paulston's (1996, p. x) view of social cartography as 'a ludic mapping practice', framed as it is for him within a postmodern(ist) sensibility. We have sought to draw deliberately on a mix of the modern and the postmodern in rethinking the concept. This has involved, in particular, approaching 'the map as research method' (Powell, 2010, p. 539), with the proviso that this always be viewed flexibly, and bearing in mind that '[as] a visual genre, maps cross disciplinary boundaries of art, creative writing, geography, and cartography as they link with larger social, cultural, and political issues' (Powell, 2010, p. 540). This means accounting for the 'performative' aspect of mapping (Del Casino & Hanna, 2006), with '[m]aps, like other representations ... open to interpretation, contested, and mutable' (Del Casino & Hanna, 2006, p. 39). This is demonstrated very clearly in innovative work by scholar-practitioners such as Somerville (e.g. Somerville, 2013; Somerville & Perkins, 2010), drawing on Indigenous ways of knowing, and also Powell, working with notions of collage, reinscription and 'palimsestuous reading' (Powell, 2010, p. 541), and a range of digital and artistic resources. Such work offers exciting possibilities in terms of both theory and method. As Ferrare and Apple (2010, p. 216) note: 'In order to examine spatial processes in education, we not only need these "new" theories, but we also need to employ methodological tools that "think" spatially.' This includes re-assessing the use-value of quantitative research resources and perspectives as well as those of a more qualitative orientation, which clearly has implications and challenges for research training and development, including the value of working with/in multi-disciplinary research teams. The opportunity is there, however, and rural education research has much to gain in exploring the cartographic imagination more fully.

Notes

1 As noted in Green and Corbett (2013), the idea of developing a rural education and literacies research network ('REAL') was first mooted in the mid-1990s, with specific reference to rural-regional Victoria.
2 We see these terms as conceptually and analytically distinct, although they are clearly related – to some extent, it is *scale* that determines their pragmatic usage, in particular circumstances. See Agnew (2005) for an excellent discussion.
3 Our early efforts in this regard were rather rudimentary and, at best, speculative and exploratory – a matter of combining available technical expertise with a sense of what might be possible ('what if ...'). It is hoped that more fully and better articulating what is involved here, methodologically, will be taken up elsewhere, in part building on this chapter. We're mindful here also of *not* including actual maps and the like – a decision partly arising from word length constraints, although a further and important consideration has been the very challenge of working with visual and spatial data, taking into account presentational matters such as colour, etc.
4 In this regard, see Somerville and Perkins (2010), especially their concept of 'deep mapping' (pp. 176–186).

References

Agnew, J. (2005). Space: Place. In P. Cloke & R. Johnston (eds), *Spaces of Geographical Thought: Deconstructing human geography's binaries*. London: SAGE Publications, pp. 81–96.

Castells, M. (1996). *The Rise of the Network Society*. Oxford: Blackwell.

Cloke, P. (2006). Conceptualizing rurality. In P. Cloke, T. Marsden & P. Mooney (eds), *Handbook of Rural Studies*. London: Sage, pp. 18–28.

Comber, B., Nixon, H. & Reid, J. (eds) (2007). *Literacies in Place: Teaching Environmental Communications*. Sydney: Primary English Teachers Association (PETA).

Cormack, P., Green, B. & Reid, J. (2008). Writing Place: Discursive constructions of the environment in children's writing and artwork about the Murray–Darling Basin. In F. Vanclay, J. Malpas, M. Higgins & A. Blackshaw (eds), *Making Sense of Place: Exploring concepts and expressions of place through different senses and lenses.* Canberra: National Museum of Australia, pp. 57–75.

Del Casino, Jr., Vincent, J. & Hanna, S.P. (2006). Beyond the 'Binaries': A methodological intervention for interrogating maps as representational practices. *ACME: An International E-Journal for Critical Geographies, 41,* 34–56.

Eppley, K. (2011). Teaching rural place: Pre-service language and literacy students consider place-conscious literacy. *Pedagogies: An International Journal, 6*(2), 87–103.

Ferrare, J. J. & Apple, M. W. (2010). Spatializing Critical Education: Progress and cautions. *Critical Studies in Education, 51*(2), 209–221.

Green, B. (2008). Conclusion(s), implications, challenges. In B. Green (ed.), *Spaces and Places: The NSW Rural (Teacher) Education Project.* Wagga Wagga: Centre for Information Studies, Charles Sturt University, pp. 387–406.

Green, B. (2012). Literacy, place and the digital world. *Language and Education, 26*(4), 377–382.

Green, B. (ed.) (2008b). *Spaces and Places: The NSW Rural (Teacher) Education Project.* Wagga Wagga: Centre for Information Studies, Charles Sturt University.

Green, B. (2013). Literacy, rurality, education: A partial mapping. In B. Green & M. Corbett (eds), *Rethinking Rural Literacies: Transnational perspectives.* New York: Palgrave Macmillan, pp. 17–34.

Green, B. & Corbett, M. (2013). Rural education and literacies: An introduction. In B. Green & M. Corbett (eds), *Rethinking Rural Literacies: Transnational perspectives.* New York: Palgrave Macmillan, pp. 1–13.

Green, B. & Letts, W. (2007). 'Space, equity and rural education: A 'trialectical' account. In K. N. Gulson & C. Symes (eds), *Spatial Theories of Education: Policy and geography matter.* New York & London: Routledge, pp. 57–76.

Green, B. & Reid, J. (2004). Teacher education for rural-regional sustainability: Changing agendas, challenging futures, chasing chimeras? *Asia-Pacific Journal of Teacher Education, 32*(3), 255–273.

Gruenewald, D. (2003a). The best of both worlds: A critical pedagogy of place. *Educational Researcher, 32*(4), 3–12.

Gruenewald, D. (2003b). Foundations of place: A multidisciplinary framework for place-conscious education. *American Educational Research Journal, 40,* 619–654.

Gruenewald, D. A. & Smith, G. A. (eds) (2008). *Place-Based Education in the Global Age: Local diversity.* New York & London: Lawrence Erlbaum Associates.

Gulson, K. N. & Symes, C. (eds) (2007). *Spatial Theories of Education: Policy and geography matter.* New York & London: Routledge.

Halfacree, K. (2006). Rural space: Constructing a three-fold architecture. In P. Cloke, T. Marsden & P. Mooney (eds), *Handbook of Rural Studies.* Sage, London, pp. 44–62.

Hugo, G. (2001). Addressing social and community planning issues with spatial information. *Australian Geographer, 32*(3), 269–293.

Kučerova, S. and Zdeněk, K. (2012). Changes in the spatial distribution of elementary schools and their impact on rural communities in Czechia in the second half of the 20th century. *Journal of Research in Rural Education, 27*(11), 1–17.

Lefebvre, H. (1991). *The Production of Space.* Oxford: Blackwell.

Mannion, G. & Ivanič, R. (2007). Mapping literacy practices: Theory, methodology, methods. *International Journal of Qualitative Studies in Education, 20*(1), 15–30.

Markusen, A., Lee, Y.-S. & DiGiovanna, S. (eds) (1999). *Second Tier Cities: Rapid growth beyond the metropolis.* Minnesota: University of Minnesota Press.

McInerney, P., Smyth, J. & Down, B. (2011). 'Coming to a *place* near you?' The politics and possibilities of a critical pedagogy of place-based education. *Asia-Pacific Journal of Teacher Education, 39*(1), 3–16.

Nespor, J. (2000). Anonymity and place in qualitative inquiry. *Qualitative Inquiry, 6*(4), 546–569.

Nespor, J. (2004). Educational scale-making. *Pedagogy, Culture and Society, 12*(3), 309–326.

Nespor, J. (2008). Education and place: A review essay. *Educational Theory, 58*(4), 475–489.

Paulston, R. G. (2000). A spatial turn in comparative education? Constructing a social cartography of difference. In J. Schriewer (ed.), *Discourse Formation in Comparative Education.* New York: Pete Lang, pp. 297–354.

Paulston, R. G. (ed.) (1996). *Social Cartography: Mapping ways of seeing social and educational change.* New York & London: Garland Publishing, Inc.

Paulston, R. G. & Liebman, M. (1996). Social cartography: A new metaphor/tool for comparative studies. In R. G. Paulston (ed.), *Social Cartography: Mapping ways of seeing social and educational change.* New York & London: Garland Publishing, Inc., pp. 7–28.

Pickles, J. (1999). Social and cultural cartographies and the spatial turn in social theory. *Journal of Historical Geography, 25*(1), 93–98.

Powell, K. (2010). 'Making sense of place: Mapping as a multisensory research method. *Qualitative Inquiry, 16*(7), 539–555.

Reid, J., Green, B., Cooper, M., Hastings, W., Lock, G. & White, S. (2010). Regenerating rural social space? Teacher education for rural-regional sustainability. *Australian Journal of Education, 54*(3), 262–276.

Reid, J., White, S., Green, B., Lock, G., Cooper, M. & Hastings, W. (2012). *TERRAnova: Renewing teacher education for rural and regional Australia,* vol. 2, Case-Study Reports. Wagga: CSU Print.

Reid, J., White, S., Green, B., Lock, G., Cooper, M. & Hastings, W. (2013). *TERRAnova: Renewing teacher education for rural and regional Australia,* vol. 1, Draft Project Report. Wagga: CSU Print.

Ruitenberg, C. W. (2007). Here be dragons: Exploring cartography in educational theory and research. *Complicity: An International Journal of Complexity and Education, 4*(1), 7–24.

Soja, E. W. (1996). *Thirdspace: Journeys to Los Angeles and real-and-imagined places.* Oxford: Blackwell.

Somerville, M. (2013). *Water in a Dry Land: Place-learning through art and story.* New York and London: Routledge.

Somerville, M. & Perkins, T. (2010). *Singing the Coast.* Canberra: Aboriginal Studies Press.

Somerville, M. & Rennie, J. (2012). Mobilising community? Place, identity formation and new teachers' learning. *Discourse: Studies in the Cultural Politics of Education, 33*(2), 193–206.

Taylor, C. (2007). Geographical Information Systems (GIS) and school choice: The use of spatial research tools in studying educational policy. In K. N. Gulson & C. Symes (eds), *Spatial Theories of Education: Policy and geography matter.* New York & London: Routledge, pp. 77–94.

Taylor, C. (2009). Towards a geography of education. *Oxford Review of Education, 35*(5), 651–669.

Theim, C. H. (2009). Thinking through education: The geographies of contemporary educational restructuring. *Progress in Human Geography, 33*(2), 154–173.

Thomson, P. (2000). 'Like schools', educational 'disadvantage'' and 'thisness'. *Australian Educational Researcher, 27*(3), 151–166.

Usher, R. (2002). Putting space back on the map: Globalisation, place and identity. *Educational Philosophy and Theory, 34*(1), 41–55.

White, S. & Reid, J. (2008). Placing teachers? Sustaining rural schooling through place-consciousness in teacher education. *Journal of Research in Rural Education, 23*(7), 1–11.

Wyse, D., Nikolajeva, M., Charlton, E., Cliff Hodges, G., Pointon, P. & Taylor, L. (2012). Place-related identity, texts, and transcultural meanings. *British Educational Research Journal, 38*(6), 1019–1039.

Chapter 3

Theory as the source of 'research footprint'[1] in rural settings

Rune Kvalsund and Linda Hargreaves

In this chapter we explore the questions raised for rural researchers by the globalist position. First we own up to our own 'research footprints' (White et al., 2012) in rural settings, and explain what we mean by this concept. Later, we present an overview of social science theory ranging from the general and abstract to the explanatory and empirical, and exemplify our argument with reference to Giddens' (1984) theory of contemporary society, and Elder and Giele's (1998) theoretical principles of life course development. These theories for us represent the abstract and empirical respectively. The methodological implications of assuming one or another position (amongst several) are intrinsic to our comparison of the two approaches, and, we suggest, critical in the formation of the research footprint (White et al., 2012).

Globalisation is said to render the cultural world a smaller place and subsume local into global space. We question the generalisations that flow from this view. We argue that social theory derived from the globalist perspective is of limited value for research in rural settings, and suggest that empirically grounded theory that recognises time, place and their connectedness is more likely to leave a research footprint (White et al., 2012) that is transparent, authentic, ethical and open to locally meaningful interpretation. In rural settings, however defined, failure to address this eventual footprint could wreak unjustified but damaging impact on everyday lives. One immediate, tangible, concern in this respect is the closure of rural schools, and the ensuing consequences.

Aspects of legitimation: some questions

The message of globalisation is that instant media and synchronous intercontinental communication have devalued the fundamentals of everyday life, supplanting the significance of local place by the importance of global space (Castells, 1996; Giddens, 1991). Is this conveyed by normative theories or underpinned by empirical documentation? Is it a kind of silent informal sense-making, or is it explicit ideology? In the globalist perspective, individualism and free choice are said to have grown, but what kind of theory of education, schooling and community underlies this view? Does the dominance of the global perspective undermine the relevance of place-related concepts in the theoretical vocabulary of educational research? Are social scientists still neglecting school and community as a research field? And, most critically, are educational researchers aware of the indirect normative and ideological position they occupy by neglecting the school–community dimension over time? Our key question, however, is which theories and concepts are most relevant to research in rural settings?[2]

Our first footprints

Both of us began rural research in the 1980s: Kvalsund in Volda, Norway, Hargreaves in Leicester, England. Kvalsund carried out comparative research on rural schools, jointly funded by the Norwegian Research Council (NRC) and Organisation of Norwegian Municipalities. The project, 'School Localisation, Educational, Sociological and Economical Aspects', included a strategically selected sample of 20 schools. Kvalsund was responsible for the educational part of the project that traced informal and formal social learning in and out of classrooms. Because this was a national research project, local actors initially suspected the researchers' intention was a disguised attempt to influence small rural school closure. Convinced, however, by the fact that the project would do comparative analysis of smaller and larger schools with the possibility of small schools documenting their qualities: local parents, teachers and children, in the end, decided to take part despite their initial doubt. The radical differences Kvalsund found in social learning between smaller and larger rural primary schools led the researcher to pursue this focus using a longitudinal design across the transition from primary to lower secondary school (Kvalsund, 2004).

The project compared coastal communities with communities in the valleys, in the north, south, east and west of Norway, and developed new, empirically grounded knowledge on community– and home–school cooperation and on social learning in small rural and bigger urban-like schools. Complete network data were analysed for the pupils of each school based on interaction during lessons, breaks and spare time after the school day. The research also focused on children's voices about their lessons, recesses and informal learning. The research found no evidence of low quality of informal social learning in rural schools compared with the larger urban ones – it was rather on the contrary. Local parents, children and teachers still use this research in their campaigns to retain their schools. The results also led to an argument for the establishment of an arms-length national database to monitor the development of rural schools (e.g. Kvalsund, 1994, 2004; Kvalsund & Hargreaves, 2009a, 2009b).

Hargreaves' first footprint was part of a UK government-funded observational survey of curriculum provision in small primary schools (PRISMS) (Galton & Patrick, 1990). Alongside systematic classroom observation, teacher interviews and attainment tests, she developed a context-based assessment package of study skills in a nationwide sample of 68 small, majority rural, primary schools (Hargreaves, 1990; Patrick & Hargreaves, 1990). This pragmatic, mixed methods study, found that educational provision in small schools was essentially the same as that in larger urban schools, and that pupil attainment was equivalent or better. The teachers were equally well qualified, had as broad experience and the same opportunities for professional development as their urban school colleagues. Typically the teachers in small rural schools taught smaller classes with wider age ranges, and had more responsibilities. The rural schools were more likely to have links with other schools than did large urban schools, and to have community volunteers. Teachers extolled the positive ethos and collegiality that they experienced compared with their prior work in large schools. In short, there was no evidence of any 'rural deficit'. Regardless of these findings, the government recommended that 9- to 11-year-olds should be taught by curriculum specialists and that 'pupil numbers should not fall below the level at which three teachers are justified [except in] isolated rural areas [where village school resources might be augmented] to give pupils a good education' (Department for Education and Science (DES), 1985, p. 14). Subsequently, a government grant for curriculum development in rural schools was announced and evaluated (Galton et al., 1991, 1998). It revealed curricular breadth and depth, especially where small rural schools were working in voluntary clusters (Hargreaves et al., 1996). Thus, while Hargreaves' footprint may have been from 'outside and above', the PRISMS research refuted government presumption of a rural deficit in teacher quality and pupil performance, a presumption subsequently refuted also by the Inspectorate (OfSTED, 1999).

What do we mean by 'research footprint'?

A research footprint (White et al., 2012) can be thought of as not only the disturbance created by the presence of the researcher and her questions and measures, but also the lasting ripples and repercussions of that researcher–community relationship. These repercussions ('footprints') might be great or small, and beneficial or disadvantageous to the rural place and its people. The research designs, however, could have been very different. Both studies could merely have imposed centrally administered 'at a distance' measures (attainment tests and questionnaires) on the rural settings taking part and drawn conclusions from those data without ever seeing the day to day lives of the children and teachers. Kvalsund rejected the opportunity to develop attainment tests for wide distribution in favour of studying children's social learning networks by asking children in specific rural locations. He subsequently extended his research well beyond the primary school, to examine the influence of earlier experience on the children's later lives in the project 'Vulnerable Youth – Transition to Adult Life' (Kvalsund & Bele, 2010a, 2010b).

The PRISMS project involving Hargreaves, could simply have administered standardised tests and questionnaire surveys, but instead worked with local teachers to devise, trial and apply the observation schedule (showing a radical degree of user-engagement in the 1980s). These researcher-teachers knew the local areas and their educational mores. Here, too, the standard measures and common observation system revealed educational inequalities that needed redress. Thus, in both Kvalsund's and Hargreaves' studies, the intended *stamp* of a preconceived and uninformed government footprint on the rural settings was mitigated, and unforeseen strengths were discovered. The need to be explicit about potential 'research footprints' (White et al., 2012) stands up between governmental expectations of research associated with the implementation of change and the research imperative to ask questions that other actors do not ask.

Why theory?

All empirical researchers will leave a 'research footprint' (White et al., 2012) but its form, content and impact will depend on several aspects of the local situation, including the researchers' understanding of theory, and of its wider and longer term implications for the settings in question. It will depend on the answers to decisions about the sample: whose voices are heard – those of the majority, the bureaucrats and vote-seeking politicians, or the local people, the children, the minority, vulnerable or marginalised citizens? Is there conflict, complacency, inequality or unemployment in the community, motivating some participants to speak louder than others, leading to a warped view of the place? Do the research methods allow for local meanings and cultural values to be found? How far should the researcher aim to become immersed in and/or seek to be invisible in the local 'crowd'? These questions constitute not only methodological but also ethical dilemmas. We need to ask whether the potential footprint is fair and acceptable from the community's perspective, and to recognise the educational researcher's responsibility to investigate disadvantage, injustice and inequality. Thus, the role of 'the etic', the view from 'outside and above', must be recognised alongside the 'emic' (Headland et al., 1989). The researcher must be not only friend and stranger but 'theoretical' friend and 'understanding' stranger (Powdermaker, 1966).

Theory will inform research questions, the nature of sample, the selection of methods and the interpretation of the data. As educational researchers we are subject to biases of confirmation from the prejudices that influence our first impressions. Understanding the role of theory in research design can help to reduce such threats to validity from both our personal beliefs (e.g. that 'rural is good'; 'my village has looked like this since the 16th century') and common administrative assumptions ('rural services are unsustainable'; 'we need to adapt to the accelerating global pace of change'). While many of the points raised above will be specific to place, the factor of time, both historical and ongoing, must also be taken into account. As Kvalsund and Hargreaves (2009a) recommended, the rural research footprint (White et al., 2012) may be lessened by longitudinal research that recognises their significance.

Theory in perspective

Theory is 'the glasses' through which we look into the actual research field and a tool for the interpretation and explanation of research data. Theory is a more or less comprehensive set of statements that describes and analyses different aspects of some phenomenon or that explains by combining concepts in the *relationship* between two or more variables (Berg & Lune, 2012; Silverman, 2006). The *abstract–concrete* dimension concerning whether or not a theory is testable using concrete empirical data, or whether it operates in the abstract, at a distance from observable or measurable phenomena, is central in our discussion of theory as a source of research footprint. Accordingly theory is organised in two broad categories – *general (descriptive) theory* versus *specific explanatory theory* (Aakvaag, 2008; Danermark et al., 2006; Layder, 1993; Sayer, 2010).

'General theory' covers abstract subcategories of social ontology, epistemology and methodology, clarifying the basic presumptions of research, what we cannot know (Elder-Vass, 2012), as well as providing a theory (diagnosis) of contemporary society. General theory has an ambition of mediating wholeness and unity of social interaction in society and culture (see, for example, Baumann, 2000; Beck, 1992; Giddens, 1984; Hargreaves, 1998). Are they empirically valid descriptions of contemporary society?

On the other hand, the '*specific explanatory theory*' intends to explain more restricted social phenomena within or across disciplines of social science. This is theory which, according to Flyvbjerg (2001; Flyvbjerg et al., 2012), might have normative aspects as well as descriptive – what he terms 'practical phronesis'. Theories are composed by selected specific relevant variables and concepts for the properties, structures, internal relations and mechanisms with restricted range of validity specifying how specific social phenomena are interpreted and explained. Theory at this level is challenged by questions of how to address and act on social problems in a particular context including issues of power, interests and values. This theory has to be sensitive to its application in specific settings and follow a new standard for an acceptable research methodology that is context sensitive, pointing to the use of case studies, narratives and datasets that help social actors to learn the complexities of social interaction to create alternative ways of change. The perspective might be relevant for rural researchers meeting the challenge of theories based on concepts of placeless society.

Theoretical concepts influence what researchers observe and the meaning they find in their observations, but it is their ethical responsibility to make these presumptions and concepts (or the lack thereof) explicit because this is how researchers and participants can gauge the eventual footprint. To show this more clearly below, we shall analyse and compare two different theoretical perspectives – Giddens' *diagnosis of contemporary society* to exemplify general theory and Elder and Giele's *theoretical orientation of the life course* to exemplify empirically founded, explanatory theory.

Reviewing research literature on rural schools and their communities, Kvalsund and Hargreaves (2009b, p. 142) identified three generic main positions. First is the atheoretical position, in which the researcher collects and analyses data, and offers findings in the form of answers to interview questions, and tables of results, but neglects the researcher's duty to help us understand and explain the results.

In the *second* position researchers may signal an allegiance to a particular theory such as Bourdieu or Vygotsky as a way of seeing, but do not use this as an analytical tool. In the *third* position, however, the theoretical choices are not only stated but theoretical concepts are developed and used in the analysis and interpretation of the data. This position affords the researcher the possibility of seeing beyond the observed phenomena and gaining insights into them, as well as developing the theory itself. Just as a house is more than a heap of bricks, and a rural school is more than a collection of children and teachers, so research is more than the compilation of data and social facts: theory enables these to achieve a conceptually organised unity.

In our review (cited above), we found that Nordic and British rural schools research was often under-theorised (and policy-driven; see Hargreaves, 2009). Secondly, educational researchers often looked inside the school without looking out, while social researchers tended to stay outside the school, without looking in. The challenge is whether the scope of theory includes an extended perspective, such as the relationship between school and local community. Thirdly, we suggested then, as now, that there is a case for more longitudinal, longer-term research both on the unfolding of educational processes and on the influence of education on people's lives (Kvalsund & Hargreaves, 2009a). What are the short- and long-term consequences at individual and community level when its school closes? Examples of research that emphasises the neglected time and place perspectives include Corbett's (2007) study of the effects of schooling in a coastal fishing community; Gillies' (2013) analysis of how education and employment influenced people's leaving, staying or returning in the 1901–2000 period on the Scottish Hebridean island of Raasay; and Bagley and Hillyard's (2011) ethnographies of the role of school in community in two contrasting English villages over time. We reiterate here that doing research in rural schools and their communities needs theoretical perspectives, concepts and data susceptible and sensitive to time, as well as place-based analyses.

The theoretical orientation of life course research

One aspect of temporality in educational research is to attempt to understand the trajectory of individual lives. Elder and Giele trace the emergence of what they call the *life course paradigm* from the 1960s and 'the sudden appearance of "major longitudinal studies" of the life course after years of survey research' (2009, p. 2). In contrast to cross-sectional surveys which describe some aspect of a large sample of people at one particular time, long-term longitudinal research enables researchers to *retrospectively* 'look back in time' or preferably *prospectively* follow persons over time to see how past events both within individual lives, and in the world around them, might explain those individuals' current situations. The *context*, in time and place, of lived events is of critical interest for life course researchers. This enables them to see a rich spectrum of transitions in several areas of life that can be studied to reveal a more complete picture of how, for example, children adapt to school and community (see Elder, Johnson & Crosnoe, 2003, pp. 3–5). We suggest that the life course approach is especially relevant for research in rural settings because it requires the researcher to record people's lived experiences, for example in childhood, and examine the influence of the *rural context* on their later lives.

Life course research encourages the collection of both quantitative and qualitative data (Belli et al., 2009) so that comparative analyses can be made of *cumulative* advantage and disadvantage in people's lives from childhood through adulthood to old age. In this way, researchers can trace, for example, how earlier school experiences influence behaviour, action and adaptation in different communities – urban or rural – later in life, by comparing data gathered before and after each transition (George, 1993).

Elder and Giele (2009, p. 11) identified a 'fourfold paradigm' of mutually influential layers for the conduct of life course research. The first layer, enveloping the other three, is that of the *historical time and place*, or *cultural background*. Since social and educational research is reconstructive and concerned with events that have already happened, both the individual's age when transitions take place and the historical events that surround them are critical variables. In rural settings, this principle guides the researcher away from age-specific cross-sectional studies towards recognition of the individual, while still recognising the influence of context on life choices. Importantly, it ensures that the research is grounded in people's everyday lives, in physically located places, at particular times in their lives, and in the passage of time. In particular it focuses on transitions in a child's life between levels of schooling and between small rural elementary schools or in moving to a larger high school in a more urban area. Such transitions are often accompanied by a change in status or identity expressed in new roles. The sequence of transitions and subsequent roles constitutes the life trajectory or the unified whole which is the person's life course (Elder et al., 2003, p. 8).

The next layer in the combined model is that of '*linked lives*', or the phenomenon of *social integration*. This principle refers to the social ties in our lives that link us to others with whom we live and interact interdependently. For the rural researcher, the effects of the closure of a local industry, for example, such as a small fishery in coastal Norway, may have a negative effect on children's learning in school because parents are depressed by lack of employment. An educational researcher who looks only on the inside of the school, insensitive to such local events, may interpret poor performance as a feature of the school and potentially leave an even more devastating footprint if the school is also fighting for survival. On the other hand, Kvalsund (2004) left a constructive footprint in his study of social networks and social learning in small rural primary schools in Norway. Here he found that social networks were more socially integrated in the small rural as compared with the larger urban schools, which could be described as socially segregated. Then, after their transition to the local secondary school, the rural school pupils extended their social networks, while those from the larger urban schools simply reinforced restricted segregated networks.

The third life course principle is that of *human agency* or *individual goal orientation* (Elder & Giele, 2009, p. 13) concerning the individual's ability to influence their life trajectory, to make decisions and take action to change. In Corbett's (2007) study of schooling in coastal Nova Scotia, young men's decisions to leave school to work in the fisheries rather than stay in school aiming to achieve a higher educational level and 'escape' to a wider range of opportunities represent personal choices to get off the expected educational trajectory, and join the wider world of work. Decisions to make transitions such as this refute the local socially embedded norms or expectations about when certain transitions ought to begin or end. However, the transitions are at the same time results from social change – for example, changes in the content of schooling – making this a possible alternative. If an individual does not conform to these expectations at the expected time, individuals' social networks will change, and they will develop new social relations with people on similar, but individual, trajectories – or be marginalised. However, they have to face the challenge of myth and reality about youth and the emerging adults (Arnett, 2007; Dwyer & Wyn, 2001).

The fourth principle is *timing – location of transitions in time* – or the strategic adaptation *or* timing of key life events such as leaving school to start work, changing jobs or having children. All these elements of the life course have to go through the 'timing funnel', where they are strategically balanced through the person's adaptation to concrete events and situations in life (Elder & Giele, 2009, pp. 10–11). It is important to recognise, however, that such strategic choices are often heavily influenced by opportunity and chance.

Taken together, these principles of life course theory give the researcher an overall picture of the life course of the relevant persons rather than an overall picture of society. This theoretical perspective therefore enables the researcher to follow living persons through long periods of their lives, and to address the system and the context as potentially problem-producing. In this perspective there is no pre-formulated social or psychological theory. Life course theory is in this sense deeply empirically grounded and sensitive to the concrete rural situation.

Theory and diagnosis of contemporary society – researching placeless society?

We turn now to Giddens' theory of contemporary society as an example of a general and abstract theory, because its *ontological assumptions* cannot be refuted on empirical grounds. The theory builds on others' concepts and studies rather than empirical research evidence, and it is left to the researchers to develop concrete theories in pursuing empirical research. Giddens' principle of individualisation, for example, has been discussed and criticised for its lack of empirical grounding (e.g. Aakvaag, 2008; Furlong & Cartmel, 1997; Harvey, 1989; Krange, 2004; Krange & Øia, 2006).

The run-away world and the loss of place

Giddens' description of contemporary society contrasts modern and pre-modern societies. He argues that the increasing pace of change in society as electronic media, information technology and easy mobility eclipse the reality of the relationship between time and place, leads to a dynamic 'run-away world': [in which] not only is the *pace* of social change much faster than in any prior system, so also is its *scope* and the *profoundness* with which it affects pre-existing social practices and modes of behavior (Giddens, 1991, p. 16, original emphases). Giddens postulates three basic structural characteristics underlying the radical dynamic of change: (i) the separation of time and space from place; (ii) the lifting out or disembedding of traditional social activity and knowledge; and (iii) institutional reflexivity. The first of these is critical for the rural researcher. Giddens continues: 'There is no society in which individuals do not have a sense of future, present and past. Every culture has some form of spatial markers which designate a special awareness of place. In pre-modern settings, however, time and space were connected *through* the situatedness of place' (ibid). In late modernity, time becomes disconnected from the local context of events and actions. As Giddens (1991, p. 17) says, our acceptance of globally standardised time zones and a universal date system, makes today's world 'socially and experientially different from all pre-modern eras'. Consequently, a specific place has no privilege over any place – they are simply map locations in the 'run-away-world'.

Why does this matter for the rural researcher? Giddens explains that the time–space separation does not render time and space as alien aspects of social activity. They *can* be recombined, but without reference to place: 'the "when" of our actions is directly connected to the "where", but not, as in pre-modern epochs, via the mediation of place' (p. 17). In other words, in Giddens' dynamic modern world, the uniqueness or nature of any particular place, such as an isolated rural settlement, is immaterial: its isolation is eroded by the means to communicate easily with people in other places. Yet, the original determinants of its 'isolation' (mountains, rivers, deserts) still affect the daily lives of the inhabitants, as do the face-to face interactions in families, schools and other local institutions. Primary production, such as forestry, farming and fishing, must be place-based, however, erstwhile everyday actions such as making tools, daily work, education, and social care become 'lifted out' from homes and local communities, mass-produced by specialists, or 'expert systems', and paid for with 'symbolic tokens' such as money. They are now taken over by a huge process of institutionalisation with separate organisations, including schools and hospitals, covering the whole life course based on knowledge from faceless expert systems.

Thus, parents raising their young children increasingly depend on advice from child care experts rather than grandparents. This process of deskilling creates the need for people to trust these expert systems in an ever-changing globalised world. Meanwhile the expert systems, the child care experts, professional nurses and school teachers, reflexively evaluate and improve their services making themselves more indispensible to relatively deskilled lay people. Such expert systems include rural schools, of course, where expert teachers teach a common 'national' curriculum with supposed universal validity, aimed at success in the so-called 'world class tests', essential, we are told, for competition in the global race (but see Alexander, 2011; Nichols & Berliner, 2007).

Giddens (1991, p. 32) sees the processes of globalisation and self-identity development as opposite poles of the local–global dialectic neglecting the collective aspects of identity development. In the face of institutional disembedding and reflexivity, where once local needs and activities would have shaped individual identities within a communal place-identity, now the individual must determine their own identity, by choosing a role and a lifestyle. Thus, the development of self-identity becomes a project, creating a narrative of the self. The actor has four structural resources at their disposal – *material objects* (allocative resources), *social power* (authoritative resources), *norms* telling the actor what to do and *interpretative rules* telling them the pattern of meaning in social situations and settings, for example, in the daily life of rural schools and communities. The structures are virtual, that is, they exist only when they are part of the actors' thinking (Giddens, 1984, pp. 18–24).

Choosing how to act becomes a challenge. Personal decisions associated with transitions, events and actions in the person's life provide answers to the question 'Who am I?' and produce what Giddens (1991) refers to as *authentic life styles*. Personal strategic calculation of individual benefit of relationships with other people ('What is in it for me?') is what Giddens (1991, pp. 6–7, 87–89, 185–187) refers to as *the pure relation*. Individualisation is directly connected to the logic of producing things in global markets, now dominating welfare services so that even teaching and learning in schools become commodities. Giddens' theory of structuration concerning the relationship and mutual influence between self and social structures is therefore compatible with the globalising disembedding mechanisms that transform self-identity and reflexivity, rendering the individual alone responsible for developing and sustaining self-identity through choices and personal decisions.

How are local communities and rural actors conceived as seen through the 'glasses' of Giddens' diagnosis of societies of high modernity? These concepts seem relevant for describing and analysing the social practices of the actors at schools, local communities and specific places. For the rural researcher, such questions, and the project of the self-as-researcher identity, present a moral dilemma: What kind of researcher would I be, and which theoretical perspective will leave the least injurious research footprint? How could this theoretical perspective of society be used in analysis of rural schools and communities?

Comparison and discussion of two theoretical perspectives as sources of 'research footprint'

What are the possible contours of the research footprint (White et al., 2012) in local communities if Giddens' urban concept of place is adopted when doing research on schooling in rural communities? What are the consequences when using life course theory as a source for theoretical orientation in research on rural settings? And which theory better enables researchers to anticipate the transparency, authenticity, interpretation and ethic of wellbeing of their research footprint?

The core concepts of Giddens' diagnosis of contemporary society – agent, structure, structuration and power, locale, time–space separation, disembedding mechanisms – have ontological flexibility in the sense that a wide variety of social practice can be developed from them – schooling in rural communities included. Giddens' theory does not accept the existence of external structural reality – explanatory mechanisms – and is restricted to interpretative explanations (Giddens, 1984, pp. 212–213, 329, 333). On the other hand, life course theory accepts external structural explanatory mechanisms as well as socially constructed explanations, agency and chance and is open for a variety of research methods, i.e. multi-method research within the time perspective (Tashakkori & Teddlie, 2003).

In life course theory, research is oriented towards the study of concrete lived life, human development and ageing. The focus of research is living persons, in places at specific points and periods of time; they grow up and live in places – not in society, not in space, global or local. Society is conceived to be an abstraction. Seen from a life course perspective, places exist, urban as well as rural. In fact, this might develop into an important diversity to be studied and compared in most countries. Places – urban or rural – possess three essential features: geographic location, a material form or culture, and meaning and value for the inhabitants. This notion of place gives meaning to the study of people's life trajectories, where, for example, schools are closed down. Even though Elder et al. (2003, pp. 5–7, 12) refer to the rapidity of present social change, there is no normative preconception of place as in Giddens' diagnosis of contemporary society. Persons, lives, ageing, transitions, trajectories, time and place are empirical phenomena and to be recognised by the researcher within this perspective. In fact, this perspective insists on doing comparative research on people's lives in rural and urban contexts just because they are different, reflecting variation in the contexts of life-producing diversity at an individual level as well. These empirical concepts contribute to the transparency of the life course approach, which might help to reduce the eventual footprint.

In Giddens' diagnosis, the traditional concept of *place* is given the meaning of a material environment in which a huge variation of social normative action or conduct occurs. Giddens sees the concept of place in social theory as a parallel flaw to defining psychology in purely behavioristic terms. He replaces the concrete concept of place with the flexible concept of *locale* (Giddens, 1984, pp. 118–119) which may range from a room in a house, street corner, a shop floor of a factory, towns, cities to the territorially demarcated areas occupied by nation-states. But locales are not places. Social units, such as local community and rural places, with closure across space and time, have no room in Giddens' diagnosis of contemporary societies.

For Giddens, an external world system (joint forces of government, bureaucracy, capitalist finance and production) invades and dissolves local communities, and this is 'normal' and to be accepted as a basic social fact before research starts. In general, Giddens' interests are said to be about urban social life and schooling in advanced urban societies, a perspective in which rural places and their inhabitants become invisible. This is documented again and again when small rural schools are judged by politicians as well as educational researchers as deviant cases of larger urban schools – 'the rural deficit' notion of schools – and not as cases with qualities in their own right. We observe many signs that a parallel mechanism lies behind selective migration where young women from rural communities migrate to the cities. Life course principles, on the other hand, require the participation of the people themselves and recognition of their social connections, their linked lives, thus incorporating greater possibilities of the authenticity of the data, thereby potentially decreasing the footprint.

Applying Giddens' diagnosis in this way when studying rural places, researchers take on the role as world teachers for rural places telling us all – 'place dismissed'! Analyses and interpretations based on Giddens' theory will come to overlook local variations of rural social practice, and so incur serious risk to the validity and authenticity of the work, and increasing the destructive potential of their research footprint. Further, by saying little or nothing about the known uneven distribution of structuring resources (and rules) in society, and the differences in the creative and transformative capacity of social agents, especially in local places and communities, Giddens makes it virtually *impossible to do comparative analysis of school and community in rural and urban contexts*. This raises the question of interpretation in rural research, as the researcher has privileged knowledge, withheld from the participants. Furthermore, structuration theory as well as the diagnosis of contemporary society, is clearly oriented towards the individual actor and closely associated with individual instrumental action rather than collective and altruistic action. Such assumptions challenge the ethic of care in the rural research footprint, where, in comparison, Elder and Giele's life course approach accommodates social structures and the role of community, as well as actors' ingenuity, together with the influence of chance on our lives.

Giddens' theory, in weighting the individual and the collective, clearly shares strategic and competitive individualisation as the basic value in self-centred life projects – a kind of coercive new liberality: self-identity based on inevitable individual choices. Reflecting the concept of 'pure relations', an anxiety for social commitment and stable relations seems to be embedded in this theory. In addition, the theory does not discuss the possible burden of continuous change, being in movement, reconsidering, choosing all the time – the consequences of which could be erosion of the self and personal fatigue. Embedded in the theory seems to be an illusion about the actor's nearly complete freedom of choice and limitless capacity to strategically create and recreate self-identity within a core arena of freedom in capitalist society, the market. Caring altruistic human beings seem to be far outside the concepts of Giddens' theories. The theory is in this sense one-eyed, and it is ontologically grounded in its own presumptions.

Individualisation, however, does not preclude gender, class and geographical location as structural aspects still affecting outcomes of, for example, education.

Following principles of life course research, agency and making strategic judgements of timing represents a quite different kind of individual strategic decision-making with room for values of individual needs and interests as well as altruism and values of community responsibility. Within life course theory these are empirical questions related to historical time and place, and would seem more likely to be sensitive to local interpretations of phenomena.

Giddens' theory of contemporary society therefore seems to have a special understanding of the concept of self-identity. According to Mead (1936) identity has an address based on encounters with other persons in historical time and place. By its basic self-reflexive, contemporary and strategic aspects, *future* and identity in Giddens' diagnosis is something quite different; meeting mainly himself in the self-reflexive process here and now, future becomes 'anonymous' to the person – reinforcing the burden of continuous individual choices. The theory seems to have considerable challenges of validity at this point as well. However, as we have presented above, there are alternatives.

Concluding reflections

In the introduction to this chapter we referred to the research interest of leaving a research footprint (White et al., 2012) that is transparent, authentic, ethical and open to locally meaningful interpretation. We have compared these aspects in two theories and argued that they have different implications for the rural research footprint. Following Krange and Øia (2006), we have suggested that the empirical grounding and basic concepts of Giddens' theory of the diagnosis of contemporary society are rather weak. The theory moves from analysing 'what is' to deciding 'what ought to be' even before there are data to consider. The theory transforms concepts for the critical analysis of schooling and place-based education into a sociological ideological rhetoric for globalised urban life. It dissolves rural place and local community into faceless social units, whose people are trapped under an undemocratic horizon of understanding, where they are left wide open to strongly imposed external change factors. Consequently, and critically for the rural research footprint, it places the local people in a very *asymmetrical* relationship with the researcher who represents an external expert system and a (mis-)leading theoretical perspective under-communicating the burdens of individualisation.

Elder and Giele's life course paradigm, on the other hand, sees local democracy as part of everyday life, providing the data not only to describe 'what is' but also, over time, to explain 'what happened'. Here the people–researcher relationship strives for greater symmetry, taking an *emic* perspective (within and from below), in contrast to the researcher's *etic* position (from outside and above) dominant in Giddens' theories. Its aim is to construct actor meaning by developing categories, typologies and related concepts (i.e. theory) which are typically neglected as far as people from rural places are concerned, but made explicit for urban contexts. This does not mean that external structural mechanisms or historical changes as well as chance are not parts of life course theory. In addition, it might be complemented by Flyvbjerg's practical phronesis to be more precise on specific rural settings, contexts and alternative measures. Thus, Giddens-led researchers may conceptualise rural places as 'non-existent' (as seen through urban glasses), whose local people have become disembodied and disempowered members of 'the global village' where urban social space erases physical and cultural rural place.

This brings us finally to an ethical concern. Is it ethically defensible for social scientists to speak of schools in 'the global village' in terms of Giddens' concept of disembedding expert systems? A basic research ethical dilemma here lies in judging the researcher's *need to know* against place-based informants '*right to remain unknown*'. If the educational researcher adopts the individualistic global concepts of Giddens' theory of contemporary society as their analytical tool, thereby distorting local rural social reality and rendering silent local voices, the local people must assert their right to remain unknown – and not consent to data collection. Educational research on rural schools and communities would become seriously distorted within Giddens' perspective. Life course theory, and practical phronesis emphasising place-based narratives and case studies, however, asks the researcher to discover the beliefs, attitudes, acts, knowledge and *reflexivity* of the individuals, and of their 'linked lives' in the rural community, and how these sit within and interact with the local and more distant social structures. Rural people's agency in this process is central here, and reveals not the dissolution but the distinctiveness of each rural place. An important ethical norm is that research should not work to the detriment of the informant. In this way the researcher's rural footprint has a better prospect of being valid, ethical and empirically grounded.

Notes

1   As outlined in the Acknowledgements in this book, this term was first used in the symposium presented in Network 14, Communities, families and schooling in educational research, European Conference on Educational Research, 18–21 September, Cadiz, Spain (see White et al. 2012).
2   Experienced researchers will know that many points raised here have significant academic longevity and roots that reach into less well-known and less visited corners of the field. Novice researchers should also be aware that little here, or in social science, is 'new'. Unfortunately space precludes us from presenting these research histories, but we would be happy to share them with readers who wish to go beyond the present text.

References

Aakvaag, G. C. (2008). *Moderne sosiologisk teori [Modern sociological theory]*. Oslo: Abstrakt forlag.

Alexander, R. (2011). Evidence, rhetoric and collateral damage: the problematic pursuit of 'world class' standards. *Cambridge Journal of Education*, 41(3): 265–286.

Arnett, J. J. (2007). Suffering, Selfish, Slackers? Myths and realities about emerging adults. *Journal of Youth Adolescence*, 36: 23–29.

Bagley, C. & Hillyard, S. (2011). Village schools in England: at the heart of their community? *Australian Journal of Education*, 55(1): 37–49.

Baumann, Z. (2000). *Liquid modernity*. Cambridge: Polity Press.

Beck, U. (1992). *Risk society. Towards a new modernity*. London: Sage.

Belli, R. F., Stafford, F. P. & Alwin, D.F. (2009). *Calendar and time diary methods in life course research*. London: Sage.

Berg, B. & Lune, H. (2012). *Qualitative methods for the social sciences*. Boston: Pearson.

Castells, M. (1996) *The rise of the network society*. Oxford: Blackwell.

Corbett, M. (2007). *Learning to leave. The irony of schooling in coastal community*. Canada: Fernwood Publishing.

Danermark, B., Ekström, M., Jacobsen, L. & Karlsson, J. C. (2006). *Explaining society. Critical realism in the social sciences*. London: Routledge.

Department for Education and Science (DES) (1985). *Better schools – a summary*. Cmnd, 9469, London: Her Majesty's Stationery Office. Available at http://www.educationengland. org.uk/documents/des/betterschools.html (accessed 16 May 2013).

Dwyer, P. & Wyn, J. (2001). *Youth, education and risk. Facing the future*. London: Routledge Falmer.

Elder, G. H. & Giele, J. Z. (1998). Life course research: development of a field. In G. H. Elder & J. Z. Giele (eds) *Methods of life course research. Qualitative and quantitative approaches*. London: Sage.

—— (2009). Life course studies: an evolving field. In G. H. Elder, Jr. & J. Z. Giele (eds) *The craft of life course research*. New York: Guilford Press.

Elder, G. H., Johnson, M. K. & Crosnoe, R. (2003). The emergence and development of life course theory. In J. T. Mortimer & M. J. Shanahan (eds) *Handbook of the life course*. New York: Springer.

Elder-Vass, D. (2012). *The reality of social construction*. Cambridge: Cambridge University Press.

Flyvbjerg, B. (2001). *Making social science matter: why social science fails and how it can succeed again*. Cambridge: Cambridge University Press.

Flyvbjerg, B., Landman, T. & Schram, S. (eds) (2012). *Real social science: applied phronesis*. Cambridge: Cambridge University Press.

Furlong, A. & Cartmel, F. (1997). *Young people and social change: individualization and risk in late modernity*. Buckingham: Open University Press.

Galton, M. & Patrick, H. (eds) (1990). *Curriculum provision in the small primary school*. London: Routledge.

Galton, M., Fogelman, K., Hargreaves, L. & Cavendish, S. (1991). *The Rural Schools Curriculum Enhancement (SCENE) project final report*. London: Department of Education and Science. Available from L. Hargreaves, and the British Library http:// hdl.handle.net/10068/467214 (accessed 3 October 2013).

Galton, M., Hargreaves, L. & Comber, C. (1998). Classroom practice and the National Curriculum in small rural primary schools. *British Educational Research Journal*, 24(1): 43–61. Available at http://hdl.handle.net/10068/467214 (accessed 3 October 2013).

George, L. K. (1993). Sociological perspectives on life transitions. *Annual Review of Sociology*, 19: 352–373.

Giddens, A. (1984). *The constitution of society*. London: Sage.

—— (1991). *Modernity and self identity: self and society in late modern age*. London: Polity Press.

Gillies, D. (2013). Learning and leaving: education and depopulation in an island community. *Cambridge Journal of Education* (published online). doi:10.1080/03057 64X.2013.837865 (accessed 2 October 2013).

Hargreaves, D.H. (1998). *Creative professionalism: the role of teachers in the knowledge society*. London: Demos.

Hargreaves, L. (1990). Context-based assessment of study skills at primary level. Unpublished Ph.D thesis, University of Leicester, UK.

—— (2009). Respect and responsibility: review of research in small rural schools in England. *International Journal of Educational Research*, 48(2): 117–128.

Hargreaves, L., Comber, C. & Galton, M. (1996). The National Curriculum: can small schools deliver? Confidence and competence levels of teachers in small rural primary schools. *British Educational Research Journal*, 22(1): 89–99. Also available at http:// onlinelibrary.wiley.com/doi/10.1080/0141192960220106/abstract (accessed 3 October 2013).

Harvey, D. (1989). *The condition of postmodernity*. Oxford: Basil Blackwell.

Headland, T. N., Pike, K. L. & Harris, M. (1989) *Emics and etics: the insider/outsider debate*. Beverly Hills, CA: Sage.

Krange, O. (2004). *Grenser for individualisering: ungdom mellom ny og gammel modernitet [Limits to individualization: Youth between new and old modernity]*. Unpublished Ph.D thesis, NOVA Report 4, 2004.

Krange, O. & Øia, T. (2006). *Den nye modernitete: ungdom, individualisering, identitet og mening [The new modernity: youth, individualisation, identity and meaning]*. Oslo: Cappelen Academisk forlag.

Kvalsund, R. (1994). *Elevrelasjonar og uformell læring-Kompareative kasusstudiar av fådelte og fulldelte bygdeskular [Pupil relations and informal learning. Comparative case studies of smaller and larger rural schools]*. Unpublished Ph.D. thesis, University of Trondheim.

—— (2004). Schools as environments for social learning-shaping mechanisms? Comparisons of smaller and larger rural schools in Norway. *Scandinavian Journal of Educational Research*, 48(4): 347–370.

Kvalsund, R. & Bele, I. (2010a). Adaptive situations and social marginalization in early adult life: students with special educational needs. *Scandinavian Journal of Disability Research*, 12(1): 59–76.

—— (2010b). Students with special educational needs – social inclusion or marginalisation? Factors of risk and resilience in the transition between school and early adult life. *Scandinavian Journal of Educational Research*, 54(1): 15–35.

Kvalsund, R. & Hargreaves, L. (2009a). Reviews of research on rural schools and their communities in British and Nordic countries. *International Journal of Educational Research*, 48(2): 79–150.

—— (2009b). Reviews of research in rural schools and their communities: analytical perspectives and a new agenda. *International Journal of Educational Research*, 48(2): 140–149.

Layder, D. (1993). *New strategies in social research*. Cambridge: Polity Press.

Mead, G. H. (1936). The problem of society – how we become selves. In M. H. Moore (ed.) *Movements in Thought of the Nineteenth Century*. Chicago: University Press.

Nichols, S. N. & Berliner, D. (2007). *Collateral damage: the effects of high stakes testing on America's schools*. Cambridge, MA: Harvard Education Press.

OfSTED (Office for Standards in Education) (1999). *A review of primary schools in England 1994–1998*. Available at www.officialdocuments.co.uk/document/ofsted/ ped/ped-it.htm (accessed 17 August 2001).

Patrick, H. & Hargreaves, L. (1990). Small and large schools: some comparisons. In M. Galton and H. Patrick (eds) *Curriculum provision in the small primary school*. London: Routledge.

Powdermaker, H. (1966). *Stranger and friend: the way of an anthropologist*. New York: W. W. Norton.

Sayer, A. (2010). *Method in social science. A realist approach*. London: Routledge.

Silverman, D. (2006). *Interpreting qualitative data*. Thousand Oaks, CA: Sage.

Tashakkori, A. & Teddlie, C. (Eds.) (2003). *Handbook of mixed methods in social and behavioral research*. London: Sage.

White, S., Anderson, M., Kvalsund, R., Gristy, C., Corbett, M., & Hargreaves, L. (2012). Examining the research 'footprint' in rural contexts: an international discussion on methodological issues and possibilities. Symposium presented in Network 14, Communities, Families and Schooling in Educational Research, European Conference on Educational Research, 18–21 September, Cadiz, Spain.

Chapter 4

A trialogue about method in rural education

Experiential perspectives

Pamela Bartholomaeus, John Halsey and Michael Corbett

Introduction

This three-way conversation or 'trialogue' demonstrates that people come to research in rural education in a variety of ways, with the personal journey of the researcher impacting on research questions, how the research is conceptualised and the importance ascribed to research problems. Mike and John became committed to rural education through their first appointments as teachers, while Pam's commitment comes from being a lifelong rural resident. We each continue to participate in our rural communities and have concerns about policies for education in rural communities and for the future wellbeing of rural communities. In what we have called a 'trialogue', we reflect on how we became researchers of/in rural education and share some of our research priorities and then move to discussion about our individual and collective understanding of researcher objectivity. We conclude with an exchange about rural education research in an era of globalization, including measures of educational outcomes, the importance of understanding and foregrounding the complexity of rural education and taking 'radical hope' into rural education.

We have decided to use this 'trialogue' approach as a tool both to help us make explicit the views that underpin and shape our research, and to stimulate those interested in learning more about rural research.

Mike: There are a number of methodological issues connected to educational research in rural places that I would like to take up in this trialogue. Each of us, I believe, comes out of a particular 'embeddings' in community, school systems, and our respective positions in and out of the academy. I have always thought of my work as straddling various fields: the field of teacher education and professional practice, the theoretical locations that I work from (Marxism, pragmatism and poststructuralism in dynamic tension) and academic disciplinary fields (sociology, literacy studies and rural studies). I would like to start by thinking about my location in the rural as a person who has spent most of the last 30 years working and living in small rural places. This rural standpoint I think is important to articulate in the research act. I am not going to argue that it is impossible or inappropriate to do research in rural education if you live in a city, but rather that one's particular location as a researcher should be acknowledged and accounted for in the research. So, for me, location becomes a methodological issue. But it is more than that. It is also where I live, amongst all of the crosscurrents, complexities, settlement patterns and histories and geographies. The idea that the rural is some kind of simpler place compared to the urban is a crucial error that obscures the contested and complex nature of rural living and making sense of the role education could play in rural development.

The research questions which have interested me have arisen from dilemmas I faced as a teacher in communities that were faced by multiple challenges. I started teaching in an Aboriginal community in Western Canada, where I came face to face with problems such as student resistance to the agenda of schooling, the challenges of English as a second language and the cultural 'hidden curriculum' of knowledge practices which had a limited footing in the traditional life practices of the community. Questions of positionality were among the most difficult I had to answer as a young teacher. It was the failure of the system to reproduce a certain kind of modern person that both troubled and engaged me. I came to think that this modern person was a mobile person who would leave the community and integrate into an urban and European-dominated world.

I became a qualitative researcher when I was a teacher, gathering a kind of 'action research' data about the community. I did this because the methodology of teaching to which I was introduced failed miserably. As I have written, I think I was lucky to have had an undergraduate degree in the social sciences to fall back upon (Corbett, 2010). Teaching in this remote community and in other rural contexts convinced me of the importance of strong and receptive (as opposed to transmissive) qualitative research methodology as the foundation of a professional teaching engagement. I have always lived in or very near the communities in which I taught. So, qualitative data gathering and analysis have become a bit of a way of life. I remember being at a party where a neighbour told me that he ought to be careful what he said to me for fear that it would turn up in an article. My life and my research are entwined in ways that are pretty deep, and I do try to be reflective and aware of this entanglement in my writing and analysis.

John: Like you Mike, I think it is important to acknowledge and render visible, personal connections with rural places, spaces, and people, when thinking about and doing research in and about rural communities. There are two main reasons for this stance. Firstly, it can help to situate and ground yourself as a researcher, and to bring into the foreground issues, challenges and opportunities which characterise doing research in rural contexts compared with, for example, research in urban locations. In terms of Australia, obvious 'reminders' are distance and overall low population density, and how these play into the design of research and the resources required for that research.

Secondly, and perhaps more importantly, I have consistently found that doing research in rural areas is enabled when a researcher can establish some rural background experience or connection. This is not meant to imply that researchers with no rural experience/roots cannot or should not do rural research – quite the opposite. However, rural background, rural experiences and rural stories that resonate with potential research respondents, in my experience, help build relationships and bridges. They also help to diminish a sense of rural people and their communities having research done *on* them rather than *with* them and *for* them. The point can perhaps be better illustrated by a comment made when I was in a remote Aboriginal community: 'We're sick of being researched. You fellas get a Ph.D. and we get nothing.' For researchers who have no firsthand rural experience or stories to draw on to help them enter into rural contexts and build relationships, I advise reading local newspapers and consulting peak body websites such as the Primary Industries Education Foundation and Australian Women in Agriculture (as Australian examples). These are sources that can help an enquirer gain a sense of what is going on, and what seem to be current issues. In my experience, entering a broad acre grain-farming community as a researcher, knowing recent rainfall patterns and last year's harvest data 'signals' a sense of connection with the local community and conveys your valuing of what is valued by them.

In providing 'practical advice' about entering into research contexts, I am not advocating a feigned or forced interest in the subject(s) to offset some of the difficult questions or issues that may emerge from being a rural researcher. Rather, what I am advocating is some genuine engagement with 'what might matter' in a particular context before entering and commencing data collection. What I would also caution from experience is phoniness and pretence. These are often readily detectable, and therefore it is best to enter research sites 'fresh and naïve', rather than trying to put something on which betrays authenticity.

My work as a rural researcher also straddles various fields and is partly framed and 'captured' by 47 years as an educator. Ten years of this time I lived and worked in rural communities as a teacher and then a principal. A further 20 years were spent as a principal of an urban school and then in senior executive positions responsible for policy, statewide rural field operations and political advice. These employment experiences have been formative in my evolution as a rural researcher and have disposed me towards designing and undertaking research which is framed by an informing voice. Jonathon Lear's words from *Radical Hope* are a way of describing the challenging character of the voice: 'to find an appropriate way to behave in circumstances in which it is possible to do too much or too little' (Lear, 2006, p. 17). Academic fields and theoretical lenses also influence how I locate myself as a rural researcher and what I focus upon. These include teacher and leadership formation, globalisation, sustainability, organisation theory and relationships. I am particularly interested in how rural schools and communities might become locations for disturbing and disrupting 'accepted conventions', and for pushing back against the privileging of metro-centricity.

Pam: The development of my interest in research in rural contexts and rural education differs from Mike's and John's. I have lived in the same rural location all my life, with life circumstances at some stages requiring me to live part-time in another location. My husband and I own his family's farm in the valley where I grew up. I am the fourth generation of my family to have lived in this valley. My roots in rural South Australia are deep.

From the beginning of secondary schooling I had doubts about the education I was receiving. I entered our local high school with expectations about the literature I would study in English and the sorts of studies I could experience in other classes and became sure my peers attending private schools in Adelaide, the capital city of South Australia, were receiving a different and superior education. This impression was not diminished when I commenced studies at university in Adelaide. My new friends had attended private and government schools in the city and seemed to transition to tertiary studies more easily than I did. My theory, that students attending rural schools were disadvantaged, gained impetus.

I began my teaching career at the secondary school I had attended as a student. Many of my teaching colleagues had come to the school during the four years I had been away. I found it disturbing being surrounded by their negative talk about the students, who were often identified as having low levels of ability, being disinterested in school, or having no ambition apart from 'going home on the farm' or joining the family business. At times this talk developed into deficit views of students' families and the community as a whole.

I needed to resign from this teaching position when I had young children and there was no child care available in the community. Employment for female teachers in rural South Australia, particularly for women who are local residents, has been difficult for many years (Poiner, 1990). So, as an underemployed teacher I commenced postgraduate and then doctoral studies in education, returning to my questions about disadvantage for rural students. My studies led to employment at Flinders University, located in Adelaide, and I can now pursue my questions about rural communities and rural education from within the academy. I believe it is important to acknowledge my position as a rural person and the nature of the rural background I bring to my research. There are frameworks and positions I draw on as a qualitative researcher who works in the fields of rural education, place-based education and literacy education. My research is shaped by poststructuralism, feminism, rural ideology, colonisation theory and sociocultural theories. I work in the disciplinary fields of rural sociology and literacy studies.

I have mentioned my concerns about objectivity in rural research and wonder what each of you thinks.

John: Pam, the concern you pose on objectivity is particularly important for a researcher who is deeply embedded in a rural context or associated with one where they are known in other ways, for example as a farmer, a mother, a spouse and, say, an elected member of a local governing body. One issue people have raised with me while doing research in a rural context is my bias or, if you like, my ability, even willingness, to 'be objective'. I think in part this concern arises because, as well as identifying myself as researcher I am also very explicit about being an advocate for rural spaces, places and people. Frequently in papers I have presented and had published, as well as in media commentary, I make my standpoint clear. I intentionally take the position of shifting the location of privileging by, for example, foregrounding rural in discussions relating to policy. In so doing I recognise my approach has inbuilt limitations. I cannot and do not claim to speak for *all* rural groups or rural circumstances; rather, what I strive to do is make *rural* visible by bringing it into the foreground of discussions and considerations and so open spaces for discussions and problematising that might otherwise remain closed.

A critical issue for a rural researcher, indeed a researcher per se, is being aware of the importance and role of objectivity and, perhaps more importantly, acknowledging it upfront rather than trying to disguise or ignore it. I also assume that readers of research have agency and capacities to make judgements about research and research outcomes, and that coming to terms with and weighting/factoring in a researcher's objectivity is 'part and parcel' of their reading.

Chilisa, in *Indigenous Research Methodologies*, has some helpful things to say about objectivity. She locates her discussion in the positivism/post-positivism paradigm, commencing with Aristotle and the philosophy of realism which 'assumes an actual external reality that can be objectively investigated' (2012, p. 26). Chilisa draws upon the seminal work of Bacon and Locke to highlight the influence of empiricism in defining what constitutes research, that 'genuine knowledge is based on sense experience and can be advanced only by means of observation and measurement' (Chilisa, 2012, p. 27). The 'flaw', in this stance, the inability or unwillingness to embrace so-called objective measures that may not actually measure phenomena under investigation, led to the recognition that observations may be fallible; to overcome fallibility or to reduce the likelihood of measures not measuring what was intended, using multiple sources of data around a specific phenomenon emerged 'to get closer to what is happening in reality' (Chilisa, 2012, p. 27).

Considering the issue of rural researcher objectivity through ontological, epistemological and axiological lenses helps to progress discussions further and in a more nuanced way. A post-positivist ontological
lens 'reveals' that reality is never fully capable of being known, for there
is always more, and an important part of the 'mission' of research is to
continue to engage in the investigation of this 'moreness'. Consistent
with this, a post-positivist epistemological lens posits that 'perfect objectivity cannot be achieved but is approachable' (Chilisa, 2012, p. 28). This
is not 'near enough is good enough'. This is recognition of the complexity (impossibility?) of controlling for every conceivable factor likely to
impact on a piece of research and a researcher. Axiologically speaking, a
post-positivist lens helps to make explicit what a researcher brings to
doing research and how this may impact on what is under investigation
compared with the generation of the outcomes of research. Research is
always about values and therefore is always about choices, particularly
choices about how to use finite resources, time and so on.

Mike: For me the question of objectivity is, in one sense, a non-issue and in
another sense the most crucial issue we face as social/educational researchers. It is a non-question because very few people who do social research
any longer believe that they are neutral objective observers of phenomena
that are separate from them. On the other hand, though, there is a great
deal of pressure on all of us to produce what the Americans have been
calling science-based, evidence-based or data-driven educational research
which mimics the imagined objectivity of the natural sciences. Funding
has been caught up in this ideology of objective science, which has made
it very difficult for critical and qualitative researchers, in the USA particularly (see Howley & Howley, Chapter 1 in this volume). Patti Lather
(2004) and others (e.g. Biesta, 2007) have critiqued this impetus for
some years now. I think there is what Raymond Williams (1965) called a
'long revolution' going on in social research, and the residual elements of
a type of social science that aspired to neutral objectivity sits alongside
emerging understandings that are more epistemologically sophisticated
and complex. We are only just coming to understand that educational
problems are so enormously complex, so located and so nuanced that our
research designs really have to become methodologically richer rather
than narrower and focused on providing simple answers to equally simple
questions. A case in point here is Phillip Jackson's (2011) exploration of
John Dewey's challenge to teachers to spend their careers investigating
the most basic question of all: 'What is education?'

Dewey and Jackson's points are that education is not a singularity.
Neither is rural. It is interesting too how each of us positions ourselves
inside the rural in different ways. We may also mean different things
when we use the term 'rural'. Our positioning speaks to questions of
equity in which rurality is seen as a problem space for education. Rurality

is consistently positioned as a space of educational disadvantage and the idea of difference seems important. On the one hand, we celebrate the differences rurality represents, and on the other hand, we bemoan the way this difference often ends up in disadvantage. We also speak to a certain particular authenticity and locatedness that is somehow thought to be missing in urban spaces. While there are problems here, no doubt, what is often missing from a great deal of educational research is attention to emotional geographies (Kenway & Youdell, 2011), or the sense of a researcher's affective relationship to a place. In a sense there is a question here that concerns not only what research 'subjects' feel about a place, but also what the researcher feels as well. Rather than bury love for a place in some methodological whitewashing, or explaining away people's emotional attachments to place and to the networks they represent as nostalgia, how can we account for the richness of relationships to the human and non-human dimensions of places that are defined as rural? How, too, does rurality as a definitional category that is imposed on a person, or as a claimed identity position, matter in education?

There is also in this way of thinking about the rural a sense of responsibility for preservation and stewardship (Berry, 1977), which can lead to a kind of conservatism that has at its root the idea of conservation (Bowers, 2003). This is what I was trying to say in my introduction. I thought I saw a difference between the education I received which was a set-up for mobility, and the education that most of my students and their parents in rural and remote and Aboriginal communities were receiving. The goal was leaving, but most students were not escaping, which was constructed as the key educational problem in schools. But it seemed there was something going on in the community that was partly about the restricted mobility of my students, but also about stewardship and a deep connection to local place. I wanted to see if I could gain a better and perhaps more complex picture of this phenomenon, which posed the methodological challenge of honouring attachment to place, engaging the voices of people in the community and seeking to avoid being nostalgic about place.

As you point out, John, the way schools end up looking is powerfully influenced by what we might call policy-scapes. Policy is generated for the most part in metro locations, depending on the level of centralisation in the particular national or state/provincial system. I think we need better international comparative work exploring the ways educational governance operates. John, your work both in the rural and bureaucracy, and in rural activist groups, positions you well to do this both nationally and internationally.

Back to Pam's question about 'objectivity', that is the way in which globalisation of/in education (Ball, 2012; Rizvi & Lingard, 2010; Spring, 2008) has catapulted our work on to a much larger stage. The way that allegedly objective measures of educational performance have taken off in the last 20 years is remarkable. It is the big story of education in the 21st century that 'objectively' positions rural places along with other geographies of economic disadvantage. In my Canadian context, for instance, we get regular updates from various standardised tests and skills assessments which demonstrate not only that parental income and education are the best predictors of children's achievement, but also that the uneven economic and social geography of the country has a rural/urban dimension. And of course, what gets buried here are real people struggling against both corporate capitalism and the mobility imperative embedded in formal schooling to live in places they care about. This is the emotional geography that is effaced in the fog of numbers.

We need to work to understand the complexity of this simplified picture represented by a kind of reporting that boils the educational performance of a country, state, province, district or school down to a couple of easily digestible numbers. This level of analysis obscures what is distinctive and what is really going on in particular places. It is for me a cartographic question relating to scale (Nespor, 2004). Educational discourse has been scaled up to the national and global levels and the allegedly objective methodologies of transnational comparative research based on standardised testing is positioned as the gold standard for the production of educational knowledge about all places and subsequently about particular places that are evaluated. This leaves us scrambling to justify funding for rural research, which tends to be particular and located as well as for research that proceeds in a qualitative fashion.

The ideologically motivated call for objectivity in educational research, or for an education science that would outline, for example, how to teach the generic child to read with a standardised programme, must be strenuously resisted. Rural children and youth are the losers in this shift from place and culturally sensitive education to standardised and often scripted pedagogies and mass comparative assessment. Qualitative methodologies are important tools for complexifying the drift toward dangerous and insensitive educational policy.

Pam: Some interesting questions and tensions for research in rural locations have been raised. I shall tackle objectivity in research first. I think it is important the researcher understands and is sensitive to the experiences of the subjects of the research and how they interpret their world. There are advantages and disadvantages for the researcher who is closely connected to the research subjects. Therefore it is important that the researcher is conscious of their position, acknowledging why they are conducting the research, and their stance in relation to the research question (Corbin Dwyer & Buckle, 2009), remembering no researcher is neutral (Janesick, 2000; Lincoln & Denzin, 2000). People who consider themselves insiders, in the way I do with my rural community, are liable to be accused of bias. Van Heugten (2004) suggests if the pros and cons of being an insider are considered and acknowledged at all stages of planning, data collection and analysis of the project, then the reliability and validity of the research will be evident.

The point about equality in educational outcomes for rural students is important and complex for a few reasons. Firstly, the concept of social justice is under-defined. Starr (1991) highlighted this by differentiating between the conservative (equal opportunity), liberal (equal access) and socialist (equal worth/equal power) views of social justice. A socialist view of social justice calls for rural students (and their rural community) to be equipped to be self-determining, which aligns with my vision for rural communities. Secondly, Sher and Sher (1994) point out rural schools need to prepare students for either a future based in a rural community, in an urban location or for movement between rural and urban locations; a more complex mission than that asked of schools in urban locations. In addition, rural students bring to school a diversity of cultural capital and literacy experiences that do not necessarily equip them for effective literacy learning through all stages of their primary school education (Gee, 2012). The literacy education of young rural students continues to be generic rather than reflecting the cultural practices of the community or patterns of students' interests and experiences (Breen et al., 1994). For Australian students, this trend appears set to continue, with standardised testing beginning before the middle of their fourth year of school. The standardised tests are identical for Indigenous students, for whom Standard Australian English may be the third or fourth language, and the mainstream urban student. As a result it is easy to view students in rural and remote locations as deficient and disadvantaged, with publication of schools' standardised test results on the MySchool website doing further violence (Bourdieu, 1991).

Mike, as you say, it is important that statistics and standardised test results are read critically and we should encourage beginning researchers to keep this in mind as they do their research reading. A simple literal reading of data that compares rural and urban students can be very misleading. Yet too often policy and discussion in the Australian press and the public arena are based on literal readings of the data. In Australia, even school retention data is unreliable, as there is no mechanism for tracking rural students. If a rural student transfers to a school in an urban location, they contribute to the poor retention of rural students to the end of secondary schooling and add to the higher levels of school retention of urban schools. Until there is more careful collecting of statistics, we will not know what is really happening to our rural students or what they are achieving.

Mike: The direction of the discussion leads me to want to think about questions that often get framed these days under the umbrella of knowledge transfer or the way that research is now supposed to matter in a concrete way to some audience outside the academy. We are supposed somehow to 'contribute' and be 'relevant', which of course assumes that educational researchers have not been doing this all along. As usual, there is a lot that can be said here in a critical vein. The idea is that rural education research has not been sufficiently useful to either policy makers, educational practitioners or to rural people themselves.

I like to think about these kinds of questions in terms of how we conceptualise hope in relation to thinking about future rural research projects and why the term 'hope' has entered the conversation. For me hope flows out of the sense that we operate in a context where we have some real choice that is consequential. My greatest source of hope comes out of working with aspiring teachers. The pre-service teachers often come to my Educational Foundations course, which is a kind of 'Cook's tour' of educational theory, both with a reluctance to engage with material that is not considered 'practical' and classroom-ready, and they also don't see themselves as having much curricular or pedagogical agency. Many of these students come out of rural communities in Nova Scotia and I feel these communities particularly need engaged teachers and not technocrats who conceive of curriculum as a metro-centric or generic script. I want them to see curriculum as an invitation. So I begin my courses with a TED talk video by an American teacher named John Hunter (2011). Hunter tells the story of how he was hired for his first teaching job and when he asked the Superintendent who hired him what he should do as a teacher, the Superintendent responded, 'What do you want to do?' Hunter decided that he wanted to achieve world peace and developed a wonderful game that he uses in his elementary school's classes to help his students understand global politics, economics, diplomacy, trade and culture. It is a remarkable achievement. He has spent his career answering that simple question which is not unlike Dewey's question I mentioned earlier.

This is the question I pose to my students at the beginning of the course. Forget the outcomes, the tests, the norms of the school – what everybody else tells you that you should be doing as a teacher – and focus on what it is that you want to accomplish. What is your passion as a teacher? I think it is important to read curriculum as a set of possibilities that can be read differently in different contexts by different readers. This is what Cormack (2013) and Comber (Comber, 2011) and her collaborators (Comber et al., 2007) have been doing for some years. Look for the openings and the ways that curriculum can be read through a place-based, ecological, project-based lens, for example, rather than simply using it as an excuse to reproduce deficit pedagogies and approaches that disembody knowledge. I think a lot of the resistance that teachers see in rural students, particularly those who come from working-class families, is rooted in the way that school knowledge is made unnecessarily foreign and abstracted.

Pam: Thinking about hope, for me it is important that teachers avoid using deficit discourses, particularly in rural or low socioeconomic status schools, that is, phrases beginning 'They can't ...', 'They don't ...' or 'They just ...' (Bhabha, 1996). Using 'they talk' or 'gap talk', accompanied by a focus on educating students to become members of mainstream society, is to colonise them. When researching literacy education in rural locations, Gee's work (2012) is useful. Gee defines a literate person as one who is fluent in the forms of communicating, behaving and understanding of at least one social community other than the one they were socialised into as a child. That is, teachers need to be actively inducting students to become successful participants in classrooms, understanding and valuing what the students bring to the classroom, and building on that foundation to equip them to achieve their aspirations and those of their families and rural community. In my view teachers need to value rural students for the young people they are. As a researcher of literacy, particularly in rural contexts, it is important to understand the values and communication practices of the study population. There is hope for all rural students when teachers value what students bring to the classroom and then work to prepare them well for their future.

Mike: I think it is also important to remember the critical action research tradition which originated in Australia with the work of Carr and Kemmis (1986). To teach well is to be a researcher and, as I have argued, good rural teaching is a particularly rich opportunity to conceptualise teaching as research (Corbett, 2010).

John: Before outlining a few thoughts on sources of hope and doing rural research, I think Mike's brief observation, that (at least for some commentators) researchers are not doing so well in relation to impacting 'properly' on rural education, merits a couple of comments.

Mike: I'm actually glad that you are not comfortable to leave that on the table unchallenged, John.

John: Bacchi (2000), in her paper on discourse and the uses to which it is put in relation to policy analysis, makes several pertinent points that shed some light on whether rural researchers are doing well or not. Let's presume that doing well at least in part is 'measured' by the extent to which a piece of research impacts on policy or something which visibly manifests itself on the ground. A specific example may help here. As a consequence of research on accessing education, a school board decides to abolish free school bus transport. With reference to Bacchi and the locus of meaning making in terms of 'what the research is saying needs to be done', there are readers and writers of text. Or in her words, there are those 'involved in the creation of text [researchers?] and those involved in the reading of the text [policy makers?]' (Bacchi, 2000, p. 46). Bacchi makes a further point through reference to Michalowski (1993) that '[m]eanings are bound to historical conditions' (Bacchi, 2000, p. 47).

In relation to the wellness or otherwise of rural research, it is important to recognise there are many players who determine the performance and relevance of research. There are always context, timing and timeliness, historical conditions and scenario speculation. Currently neoliberal assumptions and standpoints have consequences for the value ascribed to a piece of research. In specific terms, user pays is in vogue; for example, 'What if the policy decision was to maintain free transport?' This statement and question embody a critical role of research and policy, namely, to inform and press the case that there is *always other*. While policy makers might prefer alignment with the dominant/prevailing political ideology, researchers should aim to nurture the generation of fertile questions characterised by being 'open, ... undermining ... rich ... connected, ... charged, ... practical' (Harpaz, 2005, p. 146).

I have not associated hope with research before, but after reflecting on Mike's challenge on how I think about and understand hope, it has something to contribute towards research and being a researcher. An intrinsic motivation for undertaking research is discovery. Zournazi (2002) interviewed a diverse group of people about hope. For me, she unearthed some insights that resonate with why rural research is critical. Specifically, 'hope ... [is] a space opened for something else to begin ... hope lies in the rhythms and the sounds that come to mind when you hear a word or a phrase – it's the possibilities offered' (Zournazi, 2002, pp. 30, 79).

For me hope is imbued with energy; while it may be constrained by past failures or a sense of unfulfilment, it nevertheless is forward-looking and frames what might become of something in an expectant way. Hope is other than just optimism, which generally refers to a goal or line of action and the probability of an outcome. Hope is less a goal and more of a companion quality. This does not diminish the intellectual rigour, stamina and tenacity required to undertake high-quality rural research, especially in very isolated locations, nor is it intended to romanticise research. What it is intended to do is to suggest that hope is a resource for researchers and researching, as well as a potential research focus.

Pam: John and Mike, thanks for this trialogue, which has reiterated for me the importance of educational research for rural schools and communities. Mike, your point about the increasing attention paid to objective statistical measurement of educational outcomes on a global scale and the deficit messages this is giving about rural education is important. Research showing the how and why of rural educational outcomes is needed if we are to convey a rich and nuanced understanding of rural schools and their students that shows the quality of what is happening in these settings and the challenges faced in an era of increasing forces of standardisation of education.

Our trialogue demonstrates how research is closely linked to personal experiences, and for each of us is linked, at least initially, to our experiences as teachers in rural locations. We are agreed that as researchers we need to make our connections to rural places visible, which is a part of establishing the reliability of our qualitative research. As researchers in the field of rural education it is necessary to acknowledge the extent and nature of the rural understanding held, revealing whether it is recent or lifelong, based on a desire to research questions about the rural, or a result of residence and participation in a rural community/communities. From this disclosure the researcher gains credibility, with research subjects, sponsors of research projects, and the resultant research is seen as having increased reliability. With connections to rural place clarified, the researcher is better placed to pose questions and concerns about rural education, and claim the space to be as creative and innovative as their vision for rural education calls for, whether that be seeking hope for the future, social and economic sustainability for rural communities, increasing understanding of rural education in an era of globalisation or pursuing a goal for rural education.

It has been an interesting trialogue. Thank you.

References

Bacchi, C. (2000). 'Policy as discourse: What does it mean? Where does it get us?' *Discourse: Studies in the Cultural Politics of Education*, 21(1), 45–57.

Ball, S. J. (2012). *Global Education Inc: New Policy Networks and the Neo-liberal Imaginary*. New York: Taylor & Francis Group.

Berry, W. (1977). *The Unsettling of America: Culture and Agriculture*. San Francisco, CA: Sierra Club Books.

Bhabha, H. (1996). 'The other question', in P. Mongia (ed.), *Contemporary Postcolonial Theory*, pp. 27–54. London, UK: Arnold.

Biesta, G. (2007). 'Why "what works" won't work: Evidence-based practice and the democratic deficit in educational research'. *Educational Theory*, 57(1), 1–22.

Bourdieu, P. (1991). *Language and Symbolic Power*. Cambridge, UK: Polity Press.

Bowers, C. A. (2003). *Mindful Conservatism: Re-thinking the Ideological and Educational Basis of an Ecologically Sustainable Future*. Lanham, MD: Rowman & Littlefield Publishers.

Breen, M. P., Louden, W., Barrat-Pugh, C., Rivalland, J., Rhydwen, M., Lloyd, S. & Carr, T. (1994). *Literacy in its Place: An Investigation of Literacy Practices in Urban and Rural Communities – Overview and Interpretations*. Canberra, ACT: Language and Literacy Branch, Department of Employment, Education and Training.

Carr, W. & Kemmis, S. (1986). *Becoming Critical: Education Knowledge and Action Research*. New York: Routledge.

Chilisa, B. (2012). *Indigenous Research Methodologies*. Thousand Oaks, CA: SAGE Publications.

Comber, B. (2011). 'Making space for place-making pedagogies: Stretching normative mandated literacy curriculum (response to Lenny Sánchez)'. *Contemporary Issues in Early Childhood*, 12, 343–348. Available at http://dx.doi.org/10.2304/ciec.2011.12.4.343 (accessed 4 June 2013).

Comber, B., Nixon, H. & Reid, J. (eds) (2007). *Literacies in Place: Teaching Environmental Communications*. Newtown, NSW: Primary English Teaching Association.

Corbett, M. (2010). 'Backing the right horse: Teacher education, sociocultural analysis and literacy in rural education'. *Teaching and Teacher Education*, 26(1), 82–86.

Corbin Dwyer, S. & Buckle, J. L. (2009). 'The space between: On being an insider outsider in qualitative research'. *International Journal of Qualitative Methods*, 8(1), 55–63.

Cormack, P. (2013). 'Exploring rurality, teaching literacy: How teachers manage a curricular relation to place', in B. Green & M. Corbett (eds), *Rethinking Rural Literacies: Transnational Perspectives*. New York: Palgrave Macmillan.

Gee, J. P. (2012). *Social Linguistics and Literacies: Ideology in Discourses*, 4th edition. Abingdon, UK: Routledge.

Harpaz, Y. (2005). 'Teaching in a community of thinking'. *Journal of Curriculum and Supervision*, 20(2), 136–157.

Hunter, J. (2011). *John Hunter: Teaching with the World Peace Game*, TED talk. Available at http://www.youtube.com/watch?v=0_UTgoPUTLQ (accessed 22 March 2013).

Jackson, P. W. (2011). *What Is Education?* Chicago, IL: University of Chicago Press.

Janesick, V. (2000). 'The choreography qualitative research design: Minuets, improvisations and crystallization', in N. K. Denzin & Y. S. Lincoln (eds), *Handbook of Qualitative Research*, 2nd edition. Thousand Oaks, CA: Sage Publications.

Kenway, J. & Youdell, D. (2011). 'The emotional geographies of education: Beginning a conversation'. *Emotion, Space and Society*, 4(3), 131–136.

Lather, P. (2004). 'This is your father's paradigm: Government intrusion and the case of qualitative research in education'. *Qualitative Inquiry*, 10, 15–34.

Lear, J. (2006). *Radical Hope: Ethics in the Face of Cultural Devastation*. Cambridge, MA: Harvard University Press.

Lincoln, Y. S. & Denzin, N. K. (2000). 'The seventh moment: Out of the past', in N. K. Denzin & Y. S. Lincoln (eds), *Handbook of Qualitative Research*, 2nd edition. Thousand Oaks, CA: Sage Publications.

Nespor, J. (2004). 'Educational scale-making'. *Pedagogy, Culture and Society*, 12, 300–326.

Poiner, G. (1990). *The Good Old Rule: Gender and Other Power Relationships in a Rural Community*. South Melbourne, Vic: Oxford University Press.

Rizvi, F. & Lingard, B. (2010). *Globalizing Education Policy*. Abingdon, UK & New York, NY: Routledge.

Sher, J. P. & Sher, K. R. (1994). 'Beyond the conventional wisdom: Rural development as if Australia's rural people and communities really mattered'. *Journal of Research in Rural Education*, 10(1), 2–43. Available at www.jrre.psu.edu/articles/v10,n1, p2-43,Sher.pdf (accessed 5 June 2013).

Spring, J. (2008). *Globalization of Education: An Introduction*. New York, NY: Routledge.

Starr, K. (1991). 'What is social justice?' *Curriculum Perspectives* (newsletter edition), September, 20–24.

van Heugten, K. (2004). 'Managing insider research: Learning from experience'. *Qualitative Social Work*, 3, 203–219. doi:10.1177/1473325004043386

Williams, R. (1965). *The Long Revolution*. London, UK: Broadview Press.

Zournazi, M. (2002). *Hope: New Philosophies for Change*. Annandale, NSW: Pluto Press.

Part II

Reflexivity and standpoint

Chapter 5

Understanding 'the community' in rural community research

Tanya Brann-Barrett

The work of researchers is best rooted in the communities they aim to serve. These words, informed by the teachings of Pierre Bourdieu, find their way into articles I write, classes I teach and community engagement that marks my life. They also emerge in questions that fuel my research with young people in rural regions, ethical dilemmas that sometimes keep me awake at night and decisions I make in the light of day in collaboration with community people with whom I live, work, study and play.

In a moment of social and economic rearranging and heightened technological impact, rural regions are complex and dynamic spaces where local, global and cyber communities merge. There are commonalities in how researchers and participants respond to the broader conditions at work in their communities. Still, no two experiences are alike and our unique sociocultural standpoints frame how we conceive of 'the community'. How then, do researchers root their work in the rural communities where they learn and serve? A first step is to reflexively examine the conceptions they hold of the rural communities that are home to their research. In addition, they can create research spaces where their participants, too, can think about and articulate what community, specifically in the context of their own rural communities, means to them. Finally, researchers can contemplate how they share their research in ways that honour their participants, respect the broader community and still critically address the issues they set out to study. A key intention of such a reflexive exercise is to reveal threads that hold the research process in place and consider whether, as intended, the research is best rooted in the rural communities where researchers engage in their practice. In this chapter I draw from my own research to illustrate examples of what such a reflexive journey can uncover. I discuss factors that shape my own interpretation of the community where I conduct my research. I then describe, with examples, ways that I attempt to create opportunities for research participants to reflect on how they experience and perceive their community. Finally, I reflect on considerations that influence how I share my research with participants, the community and beyond. First, however, I outline how reflexivity is conceived in this chapter.

A framework of reflexive inquiry

Reflexivity has been taken up and applied in a variety of theoretical and method-ological ways (see, for example, Alvesson & Sköldberg, 2000; Bourdieu & Wacqant, 1992). Hence, researchers do well to articulate their own reflexive pro-cess. The approach I adopt in this chapter is relational, epistemological and socio-cultural.

By relational, I mean that focus is given to relationships among the people in the research process. As Stuart Hall (1996) reminds us, meaning is created among people. The relational dimension of reflexivity consists of researchers' acknowl-edgement that their relationships with participants and communities influence what emerges from their research. From an epistemological perspective, attention is paid to researchers' academic fields and the theories that frame their work. Bourdieu (Bourdieu & Wacquant, 1992) contends that theories that inform our study and assumptions upon which they are built figure in how we approach our research, how we engage with our participants and how we analyse and present our findings. The sociocultural piece of reflexivity is recognition of ways our social and cultural positions are central to how we engage in and make sense of the world. Hannah Arendt (1998) teaches that when we communicate with others we bring to the interaction all that we have in common and that which makes us unique. To ignore our commonalities is to miss opportunities for deeper mutual understandings. Temptations to dismiss the differences deny human plu-rality. As reflexive researchers, we can explore some of the sociocultural overlaps and distinctions in our work with research participants and their greater commu-nity. The sections that follow illustrate what attention to relational, epistemo-logical and sociocultural circumstances can reveal when reflexivity is used to understand 'the community' in rural community research.

Understanding community: a researcher's perspective

I am an ethnographic researcher whose work focuses on the lived practice of young people growing up in small post-industrial communities. I want to better understand ways in which they navigate their transitions to adulthood in spaces and times that are in flux. My agenda is to critically inform and promote civic engagement research, education and practice that facilitate with youth their engagement in ways that are meaningful for them and their communities. My research crosses the social sciences and humanities, as my learning is informed by education, sociology, cultural studies, and communication and media studies.

Much of my research is conducted in a semi-rural region of Atlantic Canada. A small municipality about 500 kilometres (300 miles) from the closest large urban centre, the region is rural, although there are some semi-urban character-istics. The local coal and steel industries have seen their demise, and the fishing, farming and forestry industries have declined and restructured in such ways that they are not what they used to be. As the region figures out its future I am particularly interested in the role the community plays in the experiences of local youth. I also engage with researchers, community youth organisations and young people in other small post-industrial regions, and we compare and learn from one another's experiences.

While this place informs my ideas about what constitutes *community*, my research is also framed by the teachings of others who have theorised the construct. Through this chapter I note, as I have elsewhere (see Brann-Barrett, 2011) the ideas of theorists such as Raymond Williams (1985) and Iris Marion Young (1990). As my research has evolved to focus more intently on globalisation, another theorist's work has become particularly meaningful to me – Doreen Massey. Massey (1994, 2005) has written extensively of place, and her insights are useful when considering place-based research. Massey contends that, while places are geographically situated, they are dynamic and evolving. She explains that places exist in relation to one another. In some post-industrial small communities, such as where I work, globalisation helps make those relationships visible. From international players' involvement in restructuring and remodelling industries to outmigration of citizens seeking social and economic security, signs of rural regions' connections to other places are present. Other markers of global relationships are evident in people's daily practices. Thanks to global media, many (not all) rural citizens can bear witness through television, film, radio and social media to ways ideologies and social constructs play out all over the world. Such access is commercialised and can influence consumption practices in rural communities. Meanwhile, through media and technology we can form global affiliations and feel expectations as world citizens. As globalisation works through rural communities, it is experienced differently by different citizens, and responses to global influences vary among people. Some influences are accepted as others are resisted.

Another significant factor influences my notion of community and how I reflect on my capacity to serve the places where I conduct research. I am an insider-outsider (Dwyer & Buckle, 2009). As someone who has spent much of my life in this community, it is my home. I am invested in the community on individual, familial and professional levels. I have an interpretation of the local history. I have witnessed the shift from an industrial to post-industrial place. I have my own perspectives of how the region's past and present influence our future. I am aware that despite global connections many citizens still feel a historically entrenched sense of isolation from prosperous regions of the province and country and a wariness of outside interest in the regional economy and landscape (Brann-Barrett, 2010). At the same time, I conduct research primarily with young people and I am not a twenty-first-century youth. My personal transition to adulthood was different in many ways in comparison to pathways available to youth today. Hence, while there may be similarities in how participants and I perceive the community, there are very likely differences as well.

From this multi-faceted viewpoint, I conceive of rural communities as evolving spaces including but not limited to geographic placement (Brann-Barrett,

2011). These spaces are made up of relationships among people and other places on a global scale. Hence, rural communities are local and global. A multitude of social, cultural and political structures of power relations help shape how rural communities are experienced and whose needs are best met. Accordingly, rural community experiences vary among people, including researchers and participants. As one of the most technologically connected generations, young people are on the cutting edge of the local–global citizenry. As such their perspectives are of particular interest to me.

Shaped by my conception of community, I engage in research that asks particular kinds of questions. How do local histories and practices and globalisation and technological advancement bear on young people's civic identities in rural places? How do race, class and gender play out in their sense of being and belonging in their communities? What are the implications of local and global expectations, limitations and opportunities, on the life chances of youth and rural post-industrial communities?

Understanding community: exploring participants' perspectives

As useful as it is for me to articulate how I understand the notion of community and the one where I work in particular, an intention of my research is to increase my understanding of how youth experience and perceive the rural communities to which they belong. I have spent years contemplating notions of community. I cannot expect that my participants have done the same. Subsequently, I am charged with creating research processes through which youth can think reflexively about and convey their conceptions of their rural communities in a globalised society. In addition, I want to avoid overwhelming them with my own perspectives and assumptions.

In small community research, broader relationships between researchers and participants warrant consideration when constructing research practices – particularly when both are from the same place. As is often the case with ethnographic research, it is commonplace to come to know your participants. In rural communities it is also possible to know your participants before the research begins. The circles through which I travel in my personal and professional life mean that I engage with young people daily through teaching, research, community work, family and social circles. I often know many of my participants in some capacity outside of the research. Even when I do not know participants beforehand, it only takes a few conversations to figure out some connection – such is the nature of research in many small communities.

These relationships can strengthen research. In some cases our previous insights about one another help us appreciate and make sense of one another's perspectives. Yet I am mindful of the temptation to assume I understand their ideas, thoughts, experiences and perceptions when deeper probing and inquiry are still needed. Similarly, I realise participants may assume I know what they mean and stop short of elaborating their point. For example, while conducting a study about youth civic engagement, a young woman described herself as uninvolved. However, through ongoing discussions I discovered the extensive degree to which she was informally engaged in her community. She assumed I knew of her activities and that I would not consider them as important as formal types of engagement. Hence, she had not mentioned them.

My work is informed by the contention that we can never completely understand another's experiences (Young, 1997). Therefore, we should never stop trying. Researchers must be vigilant when trying to make sense of others' perspectives. My approach is to spend as much time as I can with participants, minimise my voice and find multiple ways to watch and listen to them share their ideas. For this reason I adopt multi-method research designs.

Coupled with interviews, focus groups and participant observation, arts and media can enrich ethnographies. Visual research methods provide avenues in conjunction with interviews to facilitate reflexivity among participants (Bagnoli, 2009). Music can trigger discussion and reflexive thought among youth (Brann-Barrett, 2009). Art can be a meaningful method of communicating experiences (McNiff, 2008). Adopting research methods that include visuals, music and self-produced art gives participants myriad ways to contemplate and express their experiences and perceptions of their region and the world beyond. This is of particular benefit when participants and researchers are from the same small community. As noted, the temptation to assume we know exactly what our participants mean to convey based on our shared local experiences is ever-present. Multiple methods offer participants several avenues to express the subtleties and nuances of their experiences and numerous opportunities for researchers to clarify, question and discuss with them their thoughts and ideas.

Photo elicitation is a visual method in which photographs are used in interviews to generate in-depth responses from participants. Photographs do not just elicit more information. They can extract a variety of types of information, including memories and feelings (Harper, 2002). I have used photos in two ways in research. First participants create photo narratives. They take photographs that represent their ideas, experiences and perceptions about their community. They also prepare short written or verbal narratives to explain their photographs. Prior to engaging in the activity, I meet with participants and review the process and answer any questions. A few weeks later we meet and they share their photos and discuss the messages they want to convey. This technique works particularly well in focus groups. It opens doors for discussions among participants as they look at and listen to one another's visual narratives. Many of the photographs shared by participants capture the complex nature of their relationship with their post-industrial region. Images of forests, lakes and the ocean illustrate participants' connections with their physical environment. They value their proximity to the rural character of their community and they take offence when it is not respected by others. For example, they are angered by illegal dumping and littering. They also reference industries' disregard for the environment in the past

(Brann-Barrett, 2011). Some participants express their affection for community practices and rituals that are long held and, in their view, meaningful. Photos that represent sporting tournaments and community festivals that have run for generations seem important to them.

Participants also use photos to raise issues that trigger feelings of anger, frustration and sadness. A photo of a bag used to hold marijuana lying in a school playground highlighted extensive illegal drug use in some parts of the region. A picture of a school filled with empty classrooms brought attention to outmigration. Such photos served as points of critical discussions regarding implications of socioeconomic disadvantage and what many perceive as regional inequality. Without the photos it may have been more difficult to stimulate such conversations.

Along with taking photos, I sometimes ask participants to select lyrical music – from any genre – that captures their ideas about their community and issues important to them. In focus groups they explain why they selected a particular song. Their selections often focus on social issues. For example, they have chosen songs about world peace, global environments, slave labour and urban gang violence. Their choices evoke discussions regarding ways they see these issues as their concerns and emphasise the challenges of navigating local and global civic expectations. Interestingly, I conduct research in a disadvantaged region and some participants I work with experience serious social and economic barriers. Still, they minimise their own disadvantage in relation to how they perceive it is experienced in other places. They often base their comparisons on media and popular cultural representations of poverty, such as that described in their song selections. For example, one of the songs selected was 'We Are the World', written by Michael Jackson and Lionel Richie as a call for support for those living in famine-stricken regions of Africa and years later for those affected by the earthquake in Haiti in 2010.

One area of perceptual difference among participants is in relation to what they refer to as the 'drug problem'. Some participants live in pockets of the community where illegal drug use is visible and witnessed daily. They see similarities between themselves and those living in urban neighbourhoods where drug-related problems are prevalent. Those who do not see drug use disagree. They do not believe the problem is as serious in their region as it is in cities. These discussions have led to questions regarding the ways poverty and drug-related concerns manifest in rural regions and how it can look different than it does in urban centres. For example, economically disadvantaged participants note that, although we may not see people sleeping on streets and highways, homelessness is a problem. In small and rural communities it often appears as what some call *couch-surfing*, in that people go to friends' or family members' homes looking for places to sleep for short periods of time. Other participants were less aware of this reality. It becomes increasingly evident that, even in small communities, social issues are experienced differently among variations of youth (Brann-Barrett, 2011). This highlights what Young (1990) contends is a limitation in 'community' models premised on the ideal of sameness. There are important differences in ways participants with whom I work experience and perceive their community. Such distinctions highlight social arrangements that privilege some more than others. Again, these conversations would have been difficult to unearth with just questions. Participants' photos and songs led me to what was important to them instead of my questions leading them to what I thought was significant. I still had influence over the direction of the discussions but hopefully it was somewhat minimised.

I also use photos so youth can reflexively consider their relationships with the local past (Brann-Barrett, 2014). In historical photo/art-making focus groups, participants are invited to look at photos of their community from the early and middle part of the twentieth century. They discuss things about the photos that stand out and surprise them or seem to be missing. Photos are printed and displayed on computers. Then participants are provided with supplies including canvasses and paint to create artwork that illustrates their sense of connection and disconnection with the past. They discuss the meaning of their creations with the group. The historical photo activity appears to have particular meaning in a small post-industrial region. Many key fixtures and landmarks that were prominent when the region was more populated and prosperous no longer exist. Hence, participants note they have little visual evidence or memory of their local history unlike, from their perspective, youth in big cities (Brann-Barrett, 2014).

Many participants express sadness and frustration that the past in the photos seems better off than their community today. Their responses fuel critical discussions regarding changes in the social and economic health of the region. They considered ways gender, family and daily practices evolved and stayed the same. They discussed ways globalisation has changed the face of their small region (Brann-Barrett, 2014).

I was surprised by participants' emotional response to the past. I, too, feel regret over the downturn in our economy. However, I did not anticipate the degree of emotion that some of the youth expressed and I could not assume I understood why they felt the way they did. Given our unique sociocultural standpoints, the kinds of emotions we experience and the factors that influence those responses are unique. Their responses to the photos showed evidence of that and opened the door for more discussion.

Participants' paintings were equally insightful. For example, 'change' was a prevalent theme in their art. Interestingly, their interpretation of change involved a future that incorporated elements of the past. One participant painted a canvass and wrote the slogan 'Be the Change'. She included a historical photo of a people-filled street as an image to strive for in the future. Responding to the artwork, participants discussed the need for community change steeped in a deeper understanding and embracement of some historical practices that have eroded.

Even when photos and self-produced art capture participants' insights, possible misinterpretation remains as I read participants' work through my own sociocultural lens. It is incumbent upon me to continue to ask questions, clarify and leave room for further discussion. Because we all live in the same region, it is relatively easy to keep in touch with some participants. However, I try not to take advantage by intruding more than is needed. Still, the opportunity to follow up has enriched my understanding of their conceptions of the community.

The multi-media methods I use have limitations. For example, to comply with research ethics and diminish the possibility of harm, there are parameters that influence what participants can and cannot photograph. To protect participants and other citizens they are asked not to include photos of people. This seems particularly important in rural communities where people may be recognised by researchers, other participants and local citizens, who see the photos when the research is disseminated. On one occasion, participants said that they could take pictures of houses in their neighbourhoods where drugs were sold. For their own safety, and to protect the people who lived in the dwellings, I asked that they not include such photos. These homes would be easily identifiable by many people who live in the very small communities. If participants do submit pictures of people, I listen to their reasons and the messages they were trying to convey. I do not use the photos in focus groups or visual dissemination. I invite them to submit new photos. Accordingly, however, these boundaries limit the perspectives participants can visibly convey and may influence what emerges in discussions.

Other limitations require consideration when photographs are used in research. The historical images I shared with participants represented particular elements of the past. Accordingly, other perspectives of local history were inadvertently 'left out'. Photos can privilege certain standpoints and exclude others (Pink, 2011). Researchers can inform participants that photos are not an exhaustive historical record and encourage discussion regarding what is not in the photos and whose views are represented.

Another influencing factor that cannot be ignored, regardless of methods used, is the power relations between researchers and participants (Brann-Barrett, 2009). In my case, I live and conduct research in a small community. Many youth participants know me in hierarchical roles – as a professor, a parent, a coach/ trainer and simply an adult. For example, they sometimes adopt the role of a student when they work with me. They make statements such as 'I'm not sure if I did this right' and raise their hand to ask to go to the bathroom. Consequently, I wonder if they are sharing what they think I want or what truly reflects their ideas about the community. To address these concerns, I clarify throughout the entire process that I am not there to 'grade' what they share. I use descriptive feedback such as describing what I see in their artwork and giving them time to elaborate on its meaning. During interviews and focus groups, I paraphrase their comments and avoid evaluative statements such as 'Good answer'. I explain beforehand that notes I take during sessions are to jog my memory later so they do not think I am writing judgements about them. Moreover, I assure them in the consent form and verbally that, should I teach them in the future, their participation in the study will not influence how they are treated or assessed. Still, that may be hard for youth to accept, because hierarchies are difficult to ascend.

Issues surrounding confidentiality may also influence participants' disclosures. Hence, I spend significant amounts of time discussing this subject during information sessions, before they sign the consent form and before every encounter throughout the research process. Depending on the research I explain what I can and cannot guarantee in terms of confidentiality. For example, I will not repeat what they tell me to people in the community. However, there are certain pieces of information I am ethically obliged to share with authorities – namely, disclosures of child abuse. I inform participants that when we work in focus groups I request they respect one another's privacy. At the same time, I cannot guarantee that other participants will not disclose information shared by fellow group members. In the case of participants' art, they have the right to have their names attached to their work and to be included in photos that show them creating their art. Yet I explain that this means they will be identifiable as a study participant, particularly in a small community. When submitting the ethics applications for my research, I often include references to relevant articles and Canada's research agencies' policy statement on ethical conduct for research with human participants. Such references can clarify my approach particularly when incorporating arts-based methods in research with participants in small communities. The specifics of confidentiality can be complicated. Still, I hope that by explaining how I use their information, and how I can and cannot protect their privacy, participants can make informed decisions regarding what they share. While these steps may create a greater sense of trust and minimise the power scale between my participants and me, I accept there will still be limits to what they share and how they share it – regardless of methods.

Understanding community: sharing rural research with the community and beyond

My status as a member of the community and the rural nature of the region figure in ways I think reflexively about research dissemination. *Community* is a 'warmly persuasive word' (Williams, 1985, p. 76) that often avoids rigorous critique. This explains tensions I feel as a rural community researcher. I am committed to my community and how it is perceived by those within and outside its boundaries – I want my homeplace to be valued. I am also committed to my role as a critical researcher who investigates ways communities challenge and reproduce mechanisms of power that facilitate social inequalities – I want inequities in my region acknowledged and addressed. How I share my work can contribute to and/or challenge both the perceived value of the community and the community-based inequities. My job is to present my work in a way that respects my participants, the community and the analysis I have undertaken.

I give considerable thought to how I share my participants' perspectives. Something I struggle with is how they may interpret my analysis. While this is often a concern that researchers experience, I suggest there is an additional weight attached when participants and researchers live in the same small community. For example, much of my work is about challenging notions of community, civic engagement, schooling, and social and economic health that are narrowly conceived and reproduce social inequalities. Even when our intention is to do otherwise, humans are (often unwittingly) complicit in the reproduction of practices and beliefs that sustain the status quo, even when it hurts us (Bourdieu, 1990). I often see examples of this in the perceptions and experiences my participants share. For example, I refer to my research with young adults who experience serious barriers to social and economic health. Some of the men said that they believed it was more difficult to be a man in economic need than a woman. They felt that the social welfare system supported single mothers and not men. Some of the mothers in the study who received social assistance differentiated themselves from other mothers, who they felt were irresponsible with the money they received. I considered their responses in the context of the theoretical framework of the research and suggested that their positions inadvertently reinforced negative stereotypes often attached to single mothers living in poverty that blame the women for their situation (Brann-Barrett, 2010). By sharing this analysis, I did not want the study participants to interpret my reading of their comments as a negative judgement of them and a dismissal of the meaning and value in their perspectives. My intention was to challenge a perception of poverty as a character flaw, leaving people to justify their need for support.

For another example, early analysis of young people's ideas about their community and civic engagement suggested that they ascribed to notions of engagement that privilege particular practices such as formal volunteering, involvement in well-known events, and voting. Often, the activities were facilitated through schools or formal community institutions. While these are valuable contributions, there are other ways youth are involved that are important, yet do not receive the same kind of recognition. Moreover, some of the more prominent modes of participation are not accessible and desirable to all youth for a variety of social, cultural and economic reasons. It was important to figure out ways to honour participants' involvement as well as the local organisations and institutions that are valued by the community, while still challenging the prevalence of a model that can be exclusionary.

One way I address these ethical dilemmas is to be upfront with participants. From the beginning I state that my job is to analyse what they share in relation to the academic fields that inform my work. This is particularly important if participants know me in other capacities, because they may not be aware of my researcher responsibilities. When I do present participants' perspectives I make sure that their own words are prominent and kept in the context in which they were delivered. I also make it clear that some of the views and ideas presented by participants are widely held by many of us. I use it as an opportunity to critically discuss ways power functions at the level of our daily practices and attitudes. I know there are no guarantees participants will agree with my analysis. However, it is my job to balance my responsibility to them and my responsibility as a researcher to present an interpretation of findings grounded in a theoretical framework.

I also consider the broader community when I share my findings. If my purpose is to serve the community, I need to make my research accessible to those who may find it useful. Like most academics, I present my work at academic conferences and in peer-reviewed publications. However, many local citizens have limited access to such work. As such, I accept opportunities to speak about my research with local groups and media and as a public lecturer. I also volunteer to share my work – often through art-making sessions with groups and individuals who may be interested in or benefit from what I have learned.

As well as face-to-face engagements, web-based media has become an important way for researchers to disseminate information. This is particularly helpful in spread-out rural regions with limited public transit where everyone does not have opportunities to attend in-person events. It is also a method of communication typically meaningful to young people. My most recent research is housed on a research website. The project is multi-media and arts-based, so the website is set up to display participants' work like an online exhibition to appeal to viewers. I produced musical slideshows with music written and performed by local youth musicians that illustrate the art-making process and artistic messages conveyed by participants. There is also a place on the site where the public can access media coverage and documents produced as part of this research. Attached to the website is a blog that enables youth from the community and other regions to submit photo narratives through which they share their ideas, experiences and perceptions of their communities. A long-term intention of the blog is to link youth locally, nationally and internationally and to encourage discussion and debate about their communities and issues that are important to them.

In addition to 'official' research dissemination, I am often called upon to explain, debate and discuss my research in 'unofficial' ways. I have been questioned about my work in grocery stores, on beaches, at social gatherings, in a doctor's office and once at a funeral home during a wake. I have learned that it is important to be able to answer the questions 'What are you doing, anyway?' and 'What have you found out?' I sometimes feel caught off-guard or not in the mental space to have the discussions. Still, there are benefits. I seldom lose sight of my accountability to the community. I learn how to express my work in many ways and how to debate my analyses with people invested in the community. I have also learned that when people question me about my work they often have something to share, and the best thing I can do is listen. Informal dialogue serves as a source of continued motivation and it ultimately strengthens my work. I contend that research is never complete. Many of these discussions help me formulate new questions, lead me to contacts and resources and affirm if I am heading in the right direction. Ultimately such encounters encourage my own ongoing reflexive practice.

Conclusion

Researchers and participants bring to the research process the social and cultural positions that tie them together and distinguish them from one another. In rural research, where all parties call that place home, the tie may be the community. But how it is experienced and perceived can look vastly different from each person's perspective. Researchers must find ways to make those various perspectives explicit. Moreover, they must consider ways they convey such viewpoints and the implications for the greater community and society at large. Rural regions are as dynamic and diverse as their urban counterparts. To ignore that plurality is to privilege one notion of community over others. By acknowledging relational and sociocultural positions of researchers, participants and the wider community, and the epistemologies that inform their work, rural researchers can potentially contribute to the construction of more accurate and inclusive conceptions of rural communities. From this research juncture, rural researchers may be better positioned to do as Bourdieu suggested – serve the communities where their work is grounded.

References

Alvesson, M. & Sköldberg, K. (2000). *Reflexive Methodology: New vistas for qualitative research*. London: Sage.

Arendt, H. (1998). *The Human Condition*. Chicago: University of Chicago Press.

Bagnoli, A. (2009). 'Beyond the standard interview: The use of graphic elicitation and arts-based methods'. *Qualitative Research*, 9(5): 547–570.

Bourdieu, P. (1990). *The Logic of Practice*, trans. R. Nice. Cambridge, UK: Polity Press.

Bourdieu, P. & Wacquant, L. J. D. (1992). *An Invitation to Reflexive Sociology*. Chicago: University of Chicago Press.

Brann-Barrett, M. T. (2009). 'We're here, you just don't know how to reach us: A reflexive examination of research with citizens on the socio-economic margins'. *Canadian Journal for the Study of Adult Education*, 21(2): 53–66.

Brann-Barrett, M. T. (2010). 'Renegotiating family gender identities in a disadvantaged Atlantic Canadian working-class community: Young adults' perspectives'. *Community, Work & Family*, 13(2): 167–187.

Brann-Barrett, M. T. (2011). 'Same landscape, different lens: Variations in young people's socio-economic experiences and perceptions in their disadvantaged working-class community'. *Journal of Youth Studies*, 14(3): 261–278.

Brann-Barrett, M.T. (2014). 'How did we get here in the first place? The learning significance of perceived local histories in ways young people experience civic engagement in their post-industrial communities'. *Canadian Journal for the study of Adult Education*, 26(1): 1–18.

Dwyer, S. & Buckle, J. L. (2009). 'The space between: On being an insider-outsider in qualitative research'. *International Journal of Qualitative Methods*, 8(1): 54–63.

Hall, S. (1996). 'Introduction: Who needs identity?' in S. Hall and P. duGay (eds), *Questions of Cultural Identity*. London: Sage.

Harper, D. (2002). 'Talking about pictures: A case for photo elicitation'. *Visual Studies*, 17(1): 13–26.

McNiff, S. (2008). 'Arts-based research'. In J. G. Knowles and A. L. Cole (eds), *Handbook of the Art in Qualitative Research* (pp. 29–40). Los Angeles: Sage.

Massey, D. (1994). *Space, Place, and Gender*. Minneapolis: University of Minnesota Press.

Massey, D. (2005). *For Space*. Thousand Oaks, CA: Sage.

Pink, S. (2011). 'Sensory digital photography: Re-thinking "moving" and the image'. *Visual Studies*, 26(1): 4–13.

Williams, R. (1985). *Keywords: A vocabulary of culture and society*. New York: Oxford University Press.

Young, I. M. (1990). 'The ideal of community and the politics of difference', in L. Nicholson (ed.), *Feminism and postmodernism*. New York: Routledge.

Young, I. (1997). 'Asymmetrical reciprocity: On moral respect, wonder, and enlarged thought'. *Constellations: An International Journal of Critical & Democratic Theory*, 3(3): 340–363.

Chapter 6

Rural community research *process* as *outcome*

Approaching the community

Zane Hamm

Introduction

In this chapter, I explore the process of working with community members on a rural community research project, and draw on my lived experiences as I set a foundation for community-based dialogue between youth and adults. I focus on understanding and making sense of the initial research findings as an essential part of the methodology. A growing body of literature calls for rural research and policy development that involves participation and partnerships, specifically engaging youth and rural community members to build sustainable rural communities (Azano, 2011; Sherman & Sage, 2011; Vanclief & Mitchell, 2000). However, I struggled to reconcile this theory with the challenges I faced in the field. The purpose of sharing my experience is to demonstrate how the process of working with community members is part of the methodology, and requires time and commitment to understand the unique and idiosyncratic nature of a specific community. In this case, identifying participants and constructing dialogues was part of the research process that I undertook. This commitment to *process* and *engagement* is part of the discourse on community development that is attentive to different rural contexts.

This chapter is divided into three sections. First, I describe my research methods and provide an overview of the literature, then I share some of the challenges I faced early in the research process, specifically relating to recruitment and selection of rural participants for the research dialogues. Next I discuss some of the gaps between my initial ideas or 'ideal' proposal stage and the 'real' experience of gaining access to a rural community in which members did not have a point of reference that attests to my integrity as a researcher. Finally, I position this experience in the literature and explore how this learning contributes new ways of thinking about how we grapple with the challenges of this process of building and maintaining relationships. I argue that this process of connecting with rural community members is a vital part of the research findings.

The study

The purpose of my study was to gain a deeper understanding of the issues and possible responses to youth out-migration. I explored the reasons youth choose to stay or return to a rural community, and why they leave, and extended this exploration by connecting generations to explore the context, drivers, and playing fields that can shape a rural community. Scholars stress the importance of rural community history and context (Epp, 2008; Epp & Whitson, 2001) and sustaining rural communities (Longo, 2007; Meyer Lueck, 2012). For my study, I reviewed literature on conducting rural research, rural community development and examined issues such as youth out-migration, transitions and potential for return (Corbett, 2007; Dupuy, Mayer, & Morisette, 2000; Looker, 2001; Cicchinelli & Dean, 2005; Raffo & Reeves, 2000). I was interested in methods to engage with youth (Dagnino, 2009; Heartland, 2008) and across generations through dialogue (Vella & associates, 2004). Designing and facilitating two focus group dialogues served to unpack and explore rural community members' experiences, and gain a richer, more complex understanding of why rural people and places matter and how youth and adults might be engaged in making decisions that impact their future.

The starting point for this exploration was the question 'Can an intergenerational dialogue lead to a better understanding of these issues, and a better understanding of possible solutions?' My objective was to explore the issue together with rural community members, and develop a framework for dialogue between youth and adults. The framework for intergenerational dialogue could then be applied to strengthen and support other rural communities that are interested in communicating across generations to share local knowledge and engage with local issues. In my study, I explored the potential for dialogue by testing the process with one specific community, and then considered how dialogue may be applied to other communities facing similar challenges (see Vella & associates, 2004). The 'big picture' application of my work, and my contribution, was to demonstrate the process of dialogue and how it might be used to engage youth and adults as it is applied to explore and deepen our understanding of issues like youth migration. My position as an emerging scholar with roots in a rural community solidified my commitment to explore alternatives to out-migration from rural communities.

Data collection and handling

For this study, I chose methods that were consistent with a community-based approach to research and used both qualitative methods and a survey to collect my data. For methodological work on mixed methods research approaches, see Creswell (2007) and Seale (2005). The study included a survey of 158 participants, semi-structured interviews with 27 participants, and two community focus groups with a total of 10 participants, in the form of dialogues that I called 'intergenerational dialogues' with youth (18 to early 30s) and adults. Interview respondents were identified through the initial survey, key stakeholders who work with youth, dialogue with participants, and 'snowballing' of networks and referrals (Seale, 2005, p. 177). This study involved a sample of current and former members of rural communities, and included youth and an older generation of community leaders and mentors. Interviews and dialogues were fully transcribed and coded. Policy analysis of provincial rural community development and national and provincial youth migration was also included in my research design to strengthen the depth of understanding of the issue and context, as well as the current and possible responses.

I applied a form of grounded theory to my data analysis where theory is developed from data that are generated from real experiences. The aim of a grounded theory approach is to develop new theory that is 'grounded' in lived experiences (Glaser & Strauss, 1967). Previous assumptions about the research questions were examined through a process of reviewing the data and examining the lived experiences and stories from participants (Clandinin & Connelly, 2000; van Manen, 1990) and relationships between the concepts (Piantanida, Tananis & Grubs, 2004). Thus, through a rigorous process of conceptual coding and constant comparative analysis, new knowledge was generated from qualitative data, based on the validity of knowledge shared by rural participants. I explain this research methodology and process here because it illustrates the connections between planning and engaging with rural community members. I turn now to the process of gaining trust and rapport with community members to learn from their experiences.

Selecting a rural community

From document analyses, survey responses, initial interviews and careful attention to secondary data, I selected Kitscoty, in east-central Alberta, as the community in which I would conduct the intergenerational dialogues. I considered criteria such as age and migration of rural youth in specific communities over time, and gender, region and community, and subgroups that exist in the rural community such as children of farm families and Aboriginal youth (Looker, 2001; Tremblay, 2001).

The population of Kitscoty is 892 (Statistics Canada, 2006). It has a rich history of farming, some oil-related development, a strong volunteer sector and recreational spirit, and it celebrates local community achievements in sport and the building of recreational walking trails. The Chamber of Commerce has invested in community mapping and reports a large youth population on their town website. The rural location, at the juncture of two highways that lead to larger centres, impacts education and work opportunities for youth. In this study, I was interested in how these factors impact out-migration, and where the respondents feel most at home: their sense of place, rural identity and belonging.

Learning from the research process

When I began this study I did not intend to write about the experience of being immersed as an outsider in a rural community. I consider myself an insider in a rural context, but not in the specific community where my dialogues were conducted, and I did not have a formal connection to this particular group of participants. Although I had insights into rural community life, I was not a true insider. However, while I now live in an urban setting, during the most challenging times in the research process I found myself drawing on my rural experiences and background to connect with community members. Perhaps not surprisingly, these familiar patterns helped build trust and rapport by communicating with rural community members in an authentic and credible way (Marquart-Pyatt & Petrzelka, 2008). I kept coming back to two simple statements: 'Rural is important'; 'I care about this work.' However, questions from the literature caught my attention and I reconsidered two essential ideas. Do qualitative researchers examining rural community issues need to be a part of the rural population they are studying? Do they need to be presently living there, or have a rural background? What I learned through the process of facilitating the rural dialogues is an *outcome* of my research. Now I explore some of the questions about membership posed by scholars and talk about insider/outsider dynamics as they relate to the process of research in rural communities.

Duality of research

There is a duality to the role of qualitative researcher. While closely examining the lives of others and learning about their experiences, I simultaneously weigh and account for my own assumptions. Maykut and Morehouse (1994) speak about the perspective of the qualitative researcher as 'paradoxical, as we try to be aware of how our own biases and preconceived ideas impact our work' (p. 123). In this process I considered my own understanding of the phenomenon, holding it up against the literature about the role of the qualitative researcher, and dug into my research questions and data to explore the broader questions of membership and belonging in a rural community. While my experience and perspective add value to the research process, participants' own words about being part of the community are critical for a broader understanding of my research questions.

An exploration of the researcher's role and membership in rural communities is critical, because researchers are in a position of power and play an intimate role in observation, data collection and analysis. In other words, there is immense power in what is seen, and what remains unseen; what is included, and what is left out. It is crucial to gather data with an awareness of our own assumptions while maintaining openness about the research questions. Asselin (2003) asserts that, while the researcher might be part of the culture under study, they might not be part of the subculture. The subtleties and differences are important to understand the phenomena and the researcher's power. To what extent, then, is it vital to identify the researcher's position in relation to the phenomena in the research study? Some scholars suggest that researchers are increasingly aware of their membership identity (Dwyer & Buckle, 2009) and there is now greater attention to the researcher's 'context,' or gender, class, and ethnicity (Angrosino, 2005). In this study, my farm background and experience living, volunteering, and working in rural communities in Canada as well as other countries, informed my general understanding of the rural phenomena being studied. However, it was necessary to attend to my biases and challenge my own assumptions.

A sense of my own identity and history motivated me and shaped the type of project I designed, but my assumptions, values and bias required adequate analysis. For this reason I examined my position as a researcher with insight into rural community life. We are shaped by our history and landscapes, including the 'way people talk, argue, and hold their values as residents of a particular regional culture and particular geographical locality' and, further, the 'particular spaces and places in which we do our thinking contribute to the knowledge we create' (Preston, 2003, p. 74). In the next section, I discuss the role of the rural researcher, and how this status impacted my process of setting up the dialogues.

Insider/outsider

The concept of a researcher as insider, outsider or somewhere in between has been discussed across disciplines. Breen (2007) provides insight and a comprehensive review of how researchers from fields as diverse as anthropology, education, nursing and psychology approach qualitative methodologies. When a researcher studies a group, community or culture to which they belong, they often begin the research process as an insider (see also Bonner & Tolhurst, 2002; Harklau & Norwood, 2005; Hewitt-Taylor, 2002; Kanuha, 2000). Current scholarship stresses that a researcher can be in between the roles. They can identify and reflect on bias, and gain insight through observation and experience (Breen, 2007; Dwyer & Buckle, 2009). For example, Breen (2007) argues that 'the insider/outsider dichotomy is simplistic, and the distinction is unlikely to adequately capture the role of all researchers. Instead, the role of the researcher is better conceptualized on a continuum, rather than as an either/or dichotomy' (p. 163). A role as neither an insider-researcher nor outsider-researcher then allows the researcher to benefit from the advantages and minimise the potential barriers of one status or another.

The place in between, or along a continuum, as Breen (2007) suggests, is the place where I ultimately feel I belong. For example, through initial challenges I considered the strengths and limitations of conducting qualitative research as an outsider in this particular community, and weighed it against the relative merit of conducting the same research study in my home community with a status closer to an insider. It would have been a very different research study in the hometown in which I grew up. On one hand I have networks and contacts gained from years of volunteer work, sports, music, family connections and Mennonite roots. On the other hand, being known in the community may create some resistance to participate in a study with someone 'known' – an insider, with a familiar family name. Though I often visit the family farm, ultimately I chose to leave the community. Issues of trust, confidentiality, and perhaps a perceived pressure to volunteer for my research, may have impacted participation, either increasing or decreasing the numbers of participants. Further, participants may perceive similarities or differences that cause them to leave out parts of their experience, with an assumption of common ground.

The nuanced position between these dichotomous points of insider/outsider that Dwyer and Buckle (2009) call the 'space between' perhaps best describes my status as a researcher. I grew up on a farm and was raised in a rural community, but I am now at home in an urban center. My commitment to rural community development and ties to rural communities are demonstrated through membership in community supported agriculture (CSA), as well as land ownership, and more nuanced notions of family history and rural identity. How, then, does this affect my role as a researcher and the research process? In the next section I discuss my experiences in the rural community, why and how I revised my timeline for my study and what variables I considered as I made those decisions.

Initial contact in a rural community

The selection of Kitscoty, Alberta as a rural research site was an important step because my experiences within this community frame my discussion about membership roles, insider and outsider status, and how I conducted the qualitative research. My first contact was with the Chamber of Commerce, where I was advised to speak with the local youth worker for the region. Through a process of internet research and telephone conversations, I prepared a list of key contacts who worked with youth and who were embarking on a partnership with youth and adults/seniors. Through the key contact people, I aimed to identify three or four youth, and three or four adults, who were willing to be interviewed and be paired for the intergenerational dialogue. I hoped to conduct an initial interview with each of the youth and adults, based on my interview protocol and informed by responses from the survey data. The next step was to meet with the participants and explain the framework for the dialogue. I would provide a set of introductory questions and a tape recorder. In my initial design, these youth and adults would then be given the parameters of the dialogue and asked to interview *each other* two to three times during a set period of time. During this time I would check in and monitor their interactions. Finally, the pairs (six to eight people) would come together for a collective dialogue and process of a guided reflection on key themes that emerged from the dialogues.

My research plan was my 'ideal' scenario. I will now describe the 'real' process and some of the challenges along the way. Throughout this process I asked the question, 'What would change if I was an insider in this community?' I also considered, 'How does this research compare or contrast with a study I might conduct in my home rural community, in which I am on the cusp of the insider/outsider polemic?' These are critical questions concerning membership, validity and specifically whether a qualitative researcher should be a member of their study population (Dwyer & Buckle, 2009). This literature will provide a lens through which I will discuss the 'lived experience' of research involving a population with which I share similarities and differences.

Learning and action in context – ideal meets real

I was relieved to read (alas, in hindsight) the experiences of other researchers who faced challenges. Longden (2005) asks, 'Was the research process as smooth, logical and as organized' as the final text might imply, and does it account for the research process; 'all the failed starts, compromises in research design because of external and internal factors, and serendipitous occurrences that in retrospect saved the research design from certain failure' (p. 107). I ponder these questions as I reflect on how the research process unfolded. Initially I visited the community of Kitscoty after writing a letter to the mayor to express interest in research with the community, and after calling contacts I found on the community website.

My initial attempts to set up an in-person meeting with community leaders did not come to fruition, but I was connected through the county office with a youth resiliency worker. However this contact person changed during the course of my project. The importance of family connections and networks in rural communities became increasingly evident when one of my aunts from a rural Alberta community in the same school district suggested that I contact the school principals and guidance counsellor, noting their excellent reputations for supporting students. The high school guidance counsellor connected me with the Safe and Caring Communities group. I went to a meeting to talk with members about my study and encourage them to to participate in the dialogue that I would facilitate with youth and adults. This was an important step in developing networks.

Reflections on the selection and engagement process

Through my past experiences living and working in rural communities, I have learned the importance of having allies and key contacts or informants to connect with local youth and adults. In several rural communities in Alberta I had contacts through local teachers or youth workers. I anticipated that building relationships with these initial contact people would be an asset to help me build trust as I entered the community and as I set up interviews and prepared for the dialogues. These initial contacts are vital; the research process takes time and the participants are volunteers (Seale, 2005). This is an important process and, although it can be very discouraging, these are important steps (with ethical considerations) to ensure that potential research participants have a clear understanding of the research and know that their participation is voluntary.

What I had not anticipated, and a detail that proved challenging, was the gap between the ideal initial contacts and feedback I received and the ongoing steps it took to complete the study. Seale (2005) refers to having realistic expectations of timelines and volunteer participation and working through setbacks at least three times before considering an alternate plan. While I had some very fruitful conversations by telephone, there were changes in staff (the first youth resilience worker left for a position in a larger centre twenty minutes away). This change in staff, though challenging in the beginning stages of my research, also reflected the very issue I was investigating. In this case the new youth worker was from the community and knew the dynamics very well. These changes in roles can add extra months to the study as a researcher gains new ground and establishes trust with a new member.

Learning from field notes

My initial research plan was to host two research dialogues with ten participants. With a change in key contacts, I revised my plan and requested the support of the new youth worker to help me to identify young people in the community, aged 18 to 30, who might be willing to participate in the dialogues and an in-depth interview. It became clear to me that this was going to be a more challenging process than I had anticipated. The setback prompted me to revise my initial plan and seek input from potential respondents about timing and potential barriers to participation. I took the new youth worker and a youth worker from a neighbouring community for lunch and they agreed to help me connect with rural youth over age 18 for my sample. We discussed a plan to facilitate a dialogue between five youth and five adults, and proposed a timeline. I was advised to advertise in the local newsletters that were 'read by everyone' and place posters on local bulletin boards. The next set of challenges provided a pathway into the community as I searched for a place to copy my posters with revised dates. It became clearer why residents drive twenty minutes to the nearest city for office supplies. I could not find coloured paper in town, and the internet connection was not working at the local library. However, the school receptionist copied my posters and provided more contact names.

Through this initial process of advertising and recruiting I learned that my vehicle was visible as a 'newcomer' in the community, and there was a curiosity about what I was doing there. A local antique store owner noticed that I had left my car lights on and said he would have switched them off for me if I had not returned. My sense was that my visibility in the community was increasing and that prominent members of the 'Main Street' or community life might mention their interactions with me to others. Seale (2005) describes this as a snowball effect, where local community members connect the researcher with other potential participants. I hoped that this 'effect' might increase the understanding of my study, attest to my credibility and encourage participation from a wider sector of the community. It became clearer to me that there was not a lack of interest in the research issue, but rather that community members needed more time to get to know me and my interest in the community. I gained confidence and felt braver asking more questions and speaking about my research project, and local community members seemed more at ease. These insights into rural dynamics proved to be valuable. At the local coffee shop, I sat with the local newsletter editor, and mentioned to those who stopped to chat that my grandfather's farm was an hour away. Those details alone seemed to help me to gain some trust and smoothed the way for further conversation about the rural area.

Emerging challenges from constructing the dialogues

With my posters at the local Seniors Centre, town boards and cafés, I telephoned service clubs, teachers, community groups and churches to explain the project and recruit potential participants. However, ten days before my proposed first dialogue evening, only two participants had confirmed and, at the last moment, the youth resiliency worker cancelled. I had requested an RSVP – with a promise of food and drinks – but I wondered if folks might just 'show up'. Despite planning *with* several local youth, and calls to local organisations, this first attempt at hosting the dialogues was not a success. These urgent telephone calls proved beneficial, however, as I talked with key stakeholders about the research questions. I gambled, and drove out to the community on the scheduled evening. By this point I did not want to lose credibility, even if one person came, but it was evident that farming schedules and holidays might impact participation. I hoped I could overcome discouragement and analyse 'why' it was not successful, as part of the research process.

I drove the two and a half hours to the rural community for the first dialogue date, prepared the meeting hall, and waited. And I waited. After half an hour it was clear that no one was coming. This was a setback for my research methodology and timeline, but I hoped these were lessons I would write about later – the energy, time and commitment required for community organising. A longer-term vision and time to build relationships with community members was needed to build trust with participants who did not know my background, as an individual or as a researcher. Although no participants came that evening, I set up the equipment, prepared my resources for the dialogue, and brought coffee and snacks. The lack of research participants in my first efforts illustrates the need for the researcher to know in advance if there will be not be participants attending, by formally or informally checking in with community members. From these conversations, the researcher can begin to ask 'why'. Although the experience of uncertainty about numbers of participants was disheartening, I decided to think of it as a 'rehearsal' and, like a drama production, go through the steps of preparing for the dialogues to be clear about how I would facilitate them when (not *if*) I had the participants.

This experience of the empty hall, coffee brewing and no participants twenty minutes after official starting time was the low point of the research journey. I questioned my outsider position as researcher in this rural community and wondered how a different rural community might have responded to my study. This research would have been a different project if I had conducted it in my own rural community, where I may always be received as an insider, even though I have left. At this stage I considered a 'Plan B' – choosing other rural communities in which

I had some initial contacts and the positive reputation of my previous work to draw on if needed. Clearly, this would change the study. Further, I selected this rural community based on my research questions and responses to initial data collection. Beginning from the assumption that there was interest, based on conversations with helpful community members who seemed supportive, I forged ahead. The phase of building trust and rapport with potential participants was going to take longer than I had planned. It took courage and what I call 'emotional fortitude' to stay confident in the process, to ask more questions and to continue to explain my interest in the rural community.

My doubts about *how* to engage rural community members in my study lingered. At this critical point I was still 'cold-calling', but one kind, helpful contact agreed to an interview, and these contacts began to snowball. I built a network through referrals of people who shared similar characteristics, and through personal recommendations. As Seale (2005) explains, this snowball approach to building a network is especially useful when local community members can speak to others about the legitimacy of the researcher, and connect with people who may not otherwise participate. As I gained ground in recruiting and retaining participants for my study, I took field notes about the experience. I slipped back into what I began to think of as 'rural language', relating to local events I had seen posted. I felt more comfortable in the town, and the 'local' culture. I wrote notes on a napkin in a truck stop on my way back into the city late one night, and thought about ways in which I would like to be approached if a researcher wanted me to participate in a dialogue or interview. I needed to talk more with potential participants about how they were involved in the community and find ways to connect through these conversations.

I rescheduled the dialogues, participated in a community meeting to talk about my research, and I asked more questions about local activities. These efforts provided critical insight into community life, civic participation, and decision-making. After a Safe and Caring Communities meeting, several people came up to me to volunteer for my study. With those first expressions of interest, I had the momentum – and courage – to move forward.

At this point I wondered how many research projects are adversely affected by their perceived 'outsider' status and how many projects are abandoned or reconsidered when researchers are faced with barriers such as limited participation or challenges when approaching community members or local organisations. Since writing this chapter, I have learned that the answer to that question may be 'Lots, maybe most'. As Seale (2005) concedes, gaining access and building trust is a time-consuming process. I took advice from a community member and registered for the local volunteer sign-up night. At this stage I was building trust, but I was still not an insider. In a sense I was moving to acceptance as a participant in some important events in rural community life. Drawing on my rural background in a community where it was important to demonstrate investment, I participated in an event to confirm my understanding of membership and worthiness of belonging. Though there was still tension inherent in my position as a researcher who was not a true insider but had insight into rural community life, I was gaining trust.

Learning through language, observation and participation

I arrived early at the volunteer night to help set up for the event. Swarms of young people grabbed free hotdogs and quickly signed up for minor hockey league. There were also seniors, educators, youth workers, and young families with school-aged children and infants. The booths ranged from Minor Hockey League (wildly popular) to 4-H, the local library, civic projects and a bereavement society. Many people stopping at my booth seemed interested, but declined to participate, which took the wind out of my proverbial sails. I tried to ask why, but ultimately the choice not to participate was voluntary. Some possible barriers might include busy schedules, lack of transportation or a hesitation to be involved in a research process. Other community members pointed out young people who had stayed in the area or returned. By the end of this evening I had a list of contacts and sufficient initial face-to-face contact with potential participants to feel confident that, with a lot of work to build these relationships, the dialogues would be completed. Ultimately, I had three generations participating in the dialogues, ranging in age from early 20s to 60s. In the end, the youth participants in the dialogues ranged in age from early 20s to 30s, rather than 18 to 30. All of the participants contributed phenomenal perspectives and ideas about their lives and their rural community in the process. My gratitude is deep.

Over the next weeks, the dialogues finally came to fruition. During the data collection phase when I was setting up the community dialogues I visited a sheep farm and dairy about five minutes from town. This impromptu field trip added not only local cheese and chorizo sausage to my itinerary, but also a vital glimpse into the way that the local economy is diversifying, and the 'lived experience' of one of the participants. At a local hockey rink for dinner, I observed grandparents, parents and siblings prepare the players for practice. There were forty-three vehicles in the parking lot and side streets. That was where the community members were focused that evening.

As I prepared for the second intergenerational dialogue a senior farmer, aged 76, saw the lights on in the Seniors Centre and came in to visit me and lock the door. It was the last harvest day for him on a farm that had been in the family for a hundred years. Though he did not participate in the dialogues, he invited me for coffee. His insight and the time he invested in me attests to the importance of one-to-one connections and building relationships within the community.

These examples, along with the challenges and the successes in setting up the dialogues in Kitscoty, demonstrate that our roles as researchers permeate all aspects of the research process. It was fundamental to the completion of my research. Dwyer and Buckle (2009) articulate that, as qualitative researchers, 'we are not separate from the study'. As they emphasise, researchers are an essential part of the process as they listen to the stories of research participants:

> We carry these individuals with us as we work with the transcripts. The words, representing experiences, are clear and lasting. We cannot retreat to a distant 'researcher' role. Just as our personhood affects the analysis, so too, the analysis affects our personhood.
>
> (2009, p. 61)

This process brings 'real' individual voices to the forefront, and '[w]ith this circle of impact is the space between' (Dwyer & Buckle, 2009, p. 61).

Finding my place in rural community research: the space between

The 'space between' is where I fit. The push and pull reflected in the previous quotation illustrates how inhabiting this place between is not always comfortable, but a place of discomfort may be the best possible ground for challenging assumptions and learning with participants. Straddling insider/outsider status while building rapport took time and patience, but I maintain that it would not have happened, or would have been a much longer process, without a reference point to gain access into the rural community's life. The hockey rink, antique store, schools, community events and the local coffee shop are a few examples of spaces and places where connections were made, step by step. This insider/outsider status, though unsettling and uncomfortable at times, provides a foundation for understanding local dynamics or what makes a community a welcoming place, a grounding for interactions between generations, and a reason why young people might stay or return. As a young person growing up in a rural area, I witnessed the efforts that newcomers made to 'fit in' to the local community, and the assumption that if you were not born there you were always on the fringes. It is my goal to work in partnerships with rural community members and educators to understand these dynamics and ask questions about what makes a rural community a welcoming place. The initial discomfort as a researcher in an unknown community may also spark questions about why young people may or may not feel welcome to stay or return.

In Kitscoty, the walking and biking paths, built by local residents, are pathways that serve as an analogy for my experience as a rural researcher. The importance of the connections between community members and their natural surroundings was suddenly visceral for me as I walked the trails, breathed in the cool fall air and reveled in the beauty of a lake full of snow geese in early autumn. Although I did not realise it at the time, residents who talked with me about the trails connected with me as someone with a shared experience – one who appreciates the natural beauty of this rural community and values the importance of community efforts to address a broad scope of rural community issues.

As I have shared in this chapter, connections with rural community members happen in local spaces like the coffee shop or hockey rink, and at local events such as the volunteer sign-up night. These early connections can impact on the data because before, during and after the dialogues I asked questions about the places and activities in the community that were important to participants. My experiences also guided the questions I asked. For example, I asked for participants' reflections on what makes an outsider feel like they belonged in a rural community. Not surprisingly, they all mentioned participation as a key to being part of community life. It is significant to me that they shared these responses despite of, or because of, my insider/outsider role as a researcher. I can relate these examples back to my home community and think of similarities and differences, but my next challenge was to analyse them with open eyes in response to my research questions. The voices of the participants were dynamic, and listening to the interview transcripts continues to remind me that these are stories of real people living in a real rural place. The long, nail-biting process described in this chapter was worth every moment. It shaped the study. Though I struggled to stay attentive to the process, the challenges required me to reflect upon and challenge my own bias and assumptions.

Concluding perspective

In this chapter I shared some of the challenges I faced early in the research process, specifically with participant recruitment for my research dialogues. Through these experiences I learned that the formal and informal ways in which I engaged with community members throughout the process of setting up the dialogues were outcomes of my research. Ultimately I am both an insider and outsider as a researcher working within a rural community that is not my home, and yet I carry with me a rural history and identity. From this perspective, researchers working with rural community members are uniquely positioned to advance new research in the field. Their experiences contribute a broader range of understanding the experience, and emphasise the complexity and ambiguity of human experiences with attention to both similarities and differences.

I have shared some of the gaps between the real and the ideal I had imagined in the research proposal and relayed some key challenges I faced gaining momentum in the community and confirming participants for my research dialogues. The overview I provided of community selection, recruitment efforts and how I gathered my initial contacts has been intended to challenge others to think about these aspects of the research project as part of the process, and to consider observations and learning during this phase of the research as a key component of the research findings.

By exploring the supports and barriers during the research process, researchers in rural communities may add a nuanced perspective to the question, 'Should qualitative researchers examining rural community issues be part of the population they are studying?' In my study, the research questions were ultimately suited to a rural population that was receptive to my insider status as a researcher with rural roots, while my outsider status provided a perspective that allow for a depth of analysis in a rural community different from my own. My experience has taught me the importance of reflecting on how researchers engage with communities and make sense of their insider/outsider status. I will continue to explore how this learning might contribute to the field of rural research methodology and community development, and examine the insider/outsider status of the researcher in more detail. Invariably, insider/outsider status has limits, risks and possibilities.

Although there is not a prescriptive methodology to follow when working with rural communities, my experience conducting qualitative research in rural communities suggests that there are some considerations that might be helpful to explore. I learned that a flexible research design creates space to connect with community members and allows one to be more 'human' as a researcher. These entry points for both planned and serendipitous conversations may provide opportunities for personal sharing and points of connection to surface. Finally, key questions developed by Rutley (2013) focus on learning from the rural community members and may be useful for other rural researchers:

1)   Are you working *with, on* or *for* rural community participants?
2)   Who else should be included in the conversation?
3)   Listen, and ask questions first to understand the context.
4)   Identify needs and priorities with community members.
5)   Stay engaged with community members through the process.

By asking members of a community to participate in research, and validate or expand on their own interpretations, you are inviting them to engage in a process that is complex and messy. This 'process as outcome' approach to research reflects what it means to be part of a dynamic rural community.

References

Angrosino, M.V. (2001). Recontextualizing observation: Ethnography, pedagogy, and the prospects for a progressive political agenda. In N. K. Denzin and Y. S. Lincoln (eds), *The Sage handbook of qualitative research* (pp. 377–392). Thousand Oaks, CA: Sage.

Asselin, M.E. (2003). Insider research: Issues to consider when doing qualitative research in your own setting. *Journal of Nurses in Staff Development, 19*(2): 99–103.

Azano, A. (2011). The possibility of place: One teacher's use of place-based instruction for English students in a rural high school. *Journal of Research in Rural Education, 26*(10). Retrieved from http://jrre.psu.edu/articles/26-10.pdf

Bonner, A., & Tolhurst, G. (2002). Insider outsider perspectives of participant observation. *Nurse Researcher, 9*(4): 7–19.

Breen, L. (2007). The researcher 'in the middle': Negotiating the insider/outsider dichotomy. *Australian Community Psychologist, 19*(1): 163–174.

Cicchinelli, L., & Dean, C. (2005). It's all about the quality of advice, guidance, and research for rural educators: A rejoinder to Howley, Theobald, and Howley. *Journal of Research in Rural Education, 20*(19).

Clandinin, D. J., & Connelly, F. M. (2000). *Narrative inquiry: Experience and story in qualitative research*. San Francisco, CA : Jossey-Bass.

Corbett, M. (2007). *Learning to leave: The irony of schooling in a coastal community*. Halifax: Fernwood Publishing.

Corbett, M. (2009). Rural schooling in mobile modernity: Returning to the places I've been. *Journal of Research in Rural Education, 24*(7). Retrieved from http://jrre.psu.edu/articles/24-7.pdf

Creswell, J. W. (2007). *Qualitative inquiry and research design: Choosing among five traditions*. Thousand Oaks, CA: Sage.

Dagnino, M. (2009). *An exploration of youth engagement: Inspiring tomorrow's leaders*. Retrieved from http://www.ophea.net/Ophea/PARC/upload/An-exploration-of-Youth-Engagement.pdf

Dupuy, R., Mayer, F., & Morisette, R. (2000). *Rural youth: Stayers, leavers and return migrants: Report submitted to Rural Secretariat of Agriculture and Agri-food Canada*. Ottawa, Ontario: Minister of Public Works and Government Services Canada.

Dwyer, S. C., & Buckle, J. L. (2009). The space between: On being an insider-outsider in qualitative research. *International Journal of Qualitative Methods*, pp. 54–63. Online.

Epp, R. (2008). *We are all treaty people: Prairie essays*. Edmonton, Alberta: University of Alberta Press.

Epp, R., & Whitson, D. (eds). (2001). *Writing off the rural west: Globalization, government, and transformation of rural communities*. Saskatoon, Saskatchewan: Houghton Boston.

Glaser, B., & Strauss, A. (1967). *The discovery of grounded theory*. London: Weidenfeld & Nicolson.

Harklau, L., & Norwood, R. (2005). Negotiating researcher roles in ethnographic program evaluation: A postmodern lens. *Anthropology and Education Quarterly, 36*: 278–288.

Heartland (2008). *A come-back/give-back approach to rural community building, HomeTown YouthForce: Engaging the entrepreneurial generation*. Retrieved from http://www.heartlandcenter.info/documents/YouthForcebrochure2.pdf

Hewitt-Taylor, J. (2002). Insider knowledge: Issues in insider research. *Nursing Standard, 16*(46): 33–35.

Kanuha, V. K. (2000). 'Being' native versus 'going native': Conducting social work research as an insider. *Social Work, 45*: 439–447.

Longden, B. (2005). Cameo: Methodology and methods. In J. Wellington, A. C. Bathmaker, G. Hunt & P. Sikes (pp. 106–110). *Succeeding with your doctorate. London*: Sage Publications.

Longo, N. (2007). *Why community matters: Connecting education with civic life*. New York: State University of New York Press.

Looker, D. (2001). *Policy research issues for Canadian youth: An overview of human capital in rural and urban areas*. Human Resources and Social Development Canada. Retrieved from http://www.hrsdc.gc.ca/en/cs/sp/hrsd/prc/publications/research/2001-000179/page08.shtml

Marquart-Pyatt, S., & Petrzelka, P. (2008). Trust, the democratic process, and involvement in rural community. *Rural Sociology, 73*(2): 250–275.

Maykut, P. & Morehouse, R. (1994). *Beginning qualitative researchers: A philosophical and practical guide*. Washington, DC: Falmer.

Meyer Lueck, M. (2012). *Remaking the Heartland: Middle America since the 1950s* – by Robert Wuthnow. *Rural Sociology, 77*(1): 138–141.

Piantanida, M., Tananis, C. A., & Grubs, R. E. (2004). Generating grounded theory of/ for educational practice: The journey of three epistemorphs. *International Journal of Qualitative Studies in Education, 17*(3): 325–345.

Preston, C. J. (2003). *Grounding Knowledge: Environmental philosophy, epistemology, and place.* Athens: University of Georgia Press.

Raffo, C., & Reeves, M. (2000). Youth transitions and social exclusion: Developments in social capital theory. *Journal of Youth Studies, 3*(2): 147–166.

Rutley, B. (2013). Process to develop a research project. Presented by Bruce Rutely, Grande Prairie Regional College, at Alberta Rural Development Network [ARDN] Reseach Boot Camp, Edmonton, Alberta.

Seale, Clive. (2005). *Researching society and culture.* London: Sage.

Sherman, J., & Sage, R. (2011). Sending off all your good treasures: Rural schools, brain drain, and community survival in the wake of economic collapse. *Journal of Research in Rural Education, 26*(11). Retrieved from http://jrre.psu.edu/articles/26-11.pdf

Statistics Canada (2006). Community profiles. Retrieved from http://www12.statcan.ca/english/census06/data/profiles/community/Index.cfm?Lang=E

Tremblay, J. (2001). Rural youth migration between 1971 and 1996. *Rural and Small Town Analysis Bulletin, 2*(3) Catalogue no. 21-006 XIE.

van Manen, M. (1990). *Researching lived experience: Human science for an action sensitive pedagogy.* New York: State University of New York Press.

Vanclief, L., & Mitchell, A. (2000). *Working together in rural Canada: Annual Report to Parliament.* Ottawa, Ontario: Minister of Public Works and Government Services Canada and Rural Secretariat, Agriculture and Agri-food Canada.

Vella, J., & associates. (2004). *Dialogue education at work: A casebook.* San Francisco: Jossey-Bass.

Chapter 7

Researching within and for a rural community

Research journey

Cath Gristy

Introduction

Whilst working as a community based teacher in a rural area of Southwest England, I became aware of a group of young people from one particular isolated local community who appeared to be disconnecting from their secondary school. It was clear that once separated from school, the young people became disconnected from more than just the institution, with its collected resources and services; they also became disconnected from their wider community of peers. I recognised an insatiable desire (Deleuze, 1997) for a greater understanding of the situation I had been observing which appeared to be leading to exclusion from school and injustice for a group of young people I cared about. As a result of these experiences, I began my doctoral study research, which was driven by a desire to develop an understanding of the way young people in rural areas like this make connections (or not) with school and begin to develop understandings of how schools can be better serve their students. The research was a critical engagement with social justice and set out to investigate how injustices and inequalities are produced, reproduced and sustained in schools, particularly in rural contexts. This chapter records my journey through the research, engaging with the complexities of living, working, researching and reporting research in a rural place.

The geographical context

The research took place in a small, isolated village community known as Morton (a pseudonym), which I visited regularly as a teacher. Morton is in a harsh geographical locality and isolated in UK terms; it's 'such a remote out place' (Jo, student from Morton) and 'people are never meant to have lived here' (John Seccombe, Morton resident). It is clearly a 'community of place' (Delanty, 2003), being a large compact village, centred on a crossroads with a few outlying farms, 9 miles away from the nearest town, Riversville. There is a small primary school (64 children on roll in 2012). Many of its inhabitants experience poor housing and socio-economic disadvantage, and access to services is a particular problem.

Morton is no rural idyll (Bunce, 1994; Cloke, 2003). The young people of Morton go to secondary school (with students aged 11–18) in the market town of Riversville. The secondary school is identified as a community college serving an extensive rural area, with an almost entirely white, English speaking population. It is much larger than the average secondary school in the UK, with a student population (in 2012) of nearly 1,800. The community was undergoing 'Neighbourhood Renewal' at the time of the research, an organised programme of community regeneration in deprived areas coordinated by a Local Strategic Partnership (LSP) group convened by the local government authority.

The rural, social and geographical context of this research, the secondary school, the market town of Riversville and the rural isolation and associated deprivation of Morton are not unique to this region. These contexts are recorded across rural areas of the UK (Shucksmith, 2000) but rarely acknowledged in contemporary UK education policy.

The researcher

Coffey (1999) asks that researchers are positively present throughout their research and must identify themselves as part of the world they know (Ballard, 1995). Ballard requires researchers to write their stories into their reports so they are available for public scrutiny and this seems particularly pertinent to researchers working in and around rural places where their presence as a researcher in the locality is probably very obvious (Anderson and White, 2012). I work and research in the rural localities in which I live. I have a multitude of roles (Castells, 1997), professional and other, which include that of a teacher working with young people who do not go to school. During this project I added the role of researcher. I found the work of Henry Giroux useful to help conceptualise my life, work and research, and saw myself working in the 'borderlands' as a 'border crosser' (Giroux, 2005: 25). Like many people in rural places, I work 'on the edge' of a number of professional jobs, existing at the boundaries of schools, families and communities. Here in the borderlands, there is a sense of being 'in-between' (Griffiths, 1998; Mirza, 1995), which offers spaces in which to work and think. These spaces between different groups of people, ideologies and practices are useful places to conceptualise my work. I can be both 'in' and 'out', both or neither, avoiding binary positions like this and embracing a multitude of roles whilst living, working and researching in my rural place.

The research project

The case study set out to investigate the role school plays in the lives of young people in this isolated rural community by exploring the motivations that the young people have to overcome exclusionary barriers and attend school. The study was based in Morton and the secondary school, and I was a regular visitor at both places. I used the connections I had in these places to facilitate the project.

My reflections on these and other methodological decisions appear later in this chapter.

The 'pilot phase' of the project began at the Morton Youth Club, where I was known to many of the young people as a local teacher. As part of the 'youth empowerment programme' being run there, I was invited to a session where young people talked about their experiences at school. Some young people agreed to talk to me in more detail. These initial self-selected volunteers included Jo and Ivor (aged 16) and Marty (aged 17). They recommended that some younger Morton young people also take part to give their different perspectives. They suggested Lenny (aged 13) and Ali (aged 15), who both agreed to be involved, and Lenny brought his friend Mike (aged 13). Some young people chose not to take part, including Robert and JR, whose silences were acknowledged. This 'snowball sampling' worked well in this rural place where there were strong connections between the young people and led to a group of six young people being involved in the project over a two-year period. The small size of this group (which, although small, represented a significant proportion of regular school attendees from this community aged 13–18) clearly limited the breadth of the information collected but offered the opportunity for sustained, deep engagement. All the young people were regular school attendees, which was important, as the research set out to find out the connections individuals had with school and why they went. A great deal was already known locally about why other young people from Morton did not go to school. The research approach was informed by grounded theory interpreted from a social justice perspective (Charmaz and Mitchell, 2001). The methodology is based on empirical evidence (interviews with young people) in order to 'turn up the volume' (Clough, 2002: 67) on quiet voices and hopeful that these voices would not be overwhelmed by the 'grand narrative' of research.

Reflection 1 – voice, participation and a space to listen

Recognising the call for social research to be participatory, particularly research in vulnerable communities, this research work began with an aim for it to be 'participatory', acknowledging that this is complex and problematic territory. The aim was for the young people to be involved in every element; a way to foreground the perspectives of the 'marginalised youth' and to identify and challenge the exclusion they were facing (Alderson, 2000; Cahill, 2004). It has been argued that participatory methods are more ethically acceptable and offer epistemological advantages (Pain, 2004) and, operating in a rural place, this was a particularly important consideration.

There has been a rapid popularisation of the idea of 'voice' and 'participation' in many aspects of society – financial, social and public financial policy in spaces such as communities and schools. It is rarely acknowledged that this is complex territory. For example, the Neighbourhood Renewal programme Morton was undergoing promoted the participation of community 'stakeholders', so their

voices were heard in the planning of community development. There were problems with this and the chairperson of the LSP declared the 'stakeholders' had
been 'consulted to death' and the process seemed to have alienated many local
residents, who were now refusing to be involved in what one resident referred to
as the 'social engineering project' (John Seccombe, Morton resident). Ruddock
and Fielding (2006) have tracked the development of the idea of 'student voice'
in schools and are suspicious of recent growth in government support. They see
'perils in the popularity', 'despite rhetoric of agency the reality is that students
remain objects of elite adult plans' (Gunter and Thompson, 2007: 181).

Some writers argue that participatory techniques can reinforce rather than
challenge hierarchical power relations (e.g. Cooke and Kothari, 2001). There are
also some inherent risks with the consultation of young people in their schools.
For example, school systems advantage students who have the recognised forms
of cultural and linguistic capital (Bernstein, 1970; Bourdieu and Passeron, 1990)
and there is a very real danger that 'uncritical adoption of student voice initiatives
may reinforce existing hierarchies' (Noyes, 2005: 537). It could be argued in this
study, for example, that the attempt to include young people in the study further
alienated them and reinforced their position as 'different'.

As the research project entered its main phase, it was clear to me that a truly
participatory project was unachievable. Although the young people helped plan
the project and I consulted them in various ways throughout, I accepted that they
had little scope for what I would consider real participation. It was clear that in
reality I would be controlling the data collection, analysis and reporting. I really
struggled with this, but could not reconcile, in a way I considered ethical, the
theory and the practice I had hoped for with the realities of carrying out and
reporting the research. So the methods I used were not participatory but they
were about 'voice' in the sense that those involved were 'subjects' actively
involved in development of the project (Gunter and Thompson, 2007). It became
a work of listening (Mazzei, 2007), which offered a space to really listen and take
seriously (Giroux, 2005) what the young people had to say. It was also a space
where attempts were made to minimise the indignity of speaking for others and
the imposition of meaning on their words (Lather, 1991), whilst acknowledging
that it is ultimately my interpretation that is recorded.

Reflection 2 – reconceptualising the research

Another starting point for this project was a serendipitous event (a meeting of the
Morton LSP) to which I was invited as a teacher. The young people of Morton,
their poor school attendance and problematic behaviour in the community were
discussed. I wanted to understand how this separation from schooling and poor
behaviour had developed and how this understanding might illuminate structures
and systems in the school that excluded young people from this isolated community. The initial stages of the development of the methodology were informed
by Foucault's ideas of 'archaeology' and 'genealogy', with the aim of looking

back into an 'archive' of data gathered from as many of the elements of 'the case' as possible. A Foucauldian genealogy begins with the premise that the problem is complex, which seemed very appropriate to the project. In his work on 'archaeology' as method, Foucault asks that 'one ought to read everything, study everything, one must have at one's disposal the general archive of a period at a given moment' (Blacker, 1998: 263). This 'archive' should include statements from as wide a range of sources as possible – with no difference being made between official and private. It 'requires patience and knowledge of details and depends on a vast accumulation of source material' (Foucault, 1984: 76). As a natural collector and hoarder of information of all kinds, this approach resonated with my own perspectives on life and it became a central tenet in the conceptual underpinning of the methodology leading to an intense period of data collection from a very diverse range of public sources through my local community and school connections. I interviewed a significant number of Morton residents and people working for the community, the primary school headteacher and members of the LSP. At the secondary school, I interviewed teachers, support staff and the senior managers. I also collected published material from the village (council publications, local papers and newsletters, etc.) and the school. ·

As the research progressed, it became clear that it was being dominated by the researcher. The huge 'archive' of material and the 'grand narrative' of the Foucauldian methodology was turning up the volume of the researcher and the research project and overwhelming the voices the study had set out to listen to. The research was becoming a project about research and the researcher rather than about young people and their experiences of school. The project's role in consciousness raising was being lost, as it became something too complex to share with colleagues, friends and others met during the research. It eventually became clear to the researcher that the political purpose of the research – the village of Morton, its young people and the issues they were dealing with – was being usurped by the research and the researcher. The awareness developed as a result of an event (attending a meeting with other doctoral students) that resulted in my 'stepping away' from the study community and reporting on progress of the project with 'interested others'. It took this moment of being 'out of the thick of it' to see what was happening. There are a number of similar 'stepping away' events recorded in my research diaries that show the importance of these opportunities on later reflection.

This period of reflection raised questions about the framework underpinning the research. First, even with a lifetime's worth of collecting, there cannot be a complete 'archive' required for Foucault's archaeological approaches. The researcher cannot avoid making what is in the end, 'an arbitrary selection of historical materials' (Castel, 1994: 242), although 'consistency and rigour' in data collection may go some way to overcoming these difficulties (1994: 242). It can also be argued that in this kind of study all discourses 'appear equally truthful' (Henriques et al., 1998: 109), which is also problematic. Second, it also became clear that there are obvious dangers in producing writing that confirms the view of the world by powerful groups such as the ones the researcher is associated with by default, providing yet more material for classification by the dominant culture in its own academic terms (Mirza, 1997). Mirza argues that explaining the research to others becomes an act of confirming the domination of the researcher. Sitting in meetings with the Morton LSP was teaching me a great deal about the domination of the people in Morton through the practices of those given power by their role in the LSP.

I became acutely aware of the myriad risks associated with my role as researcher and made a decision to reposition my methodological approach. A simpler approach was needed to reduce the volume of the grand narrative. A repositioning was also required which allow the researcher to examine her own role in the construction of what was going on whilst ensuring quiet voices could be heard. This less complex approach was also important for effective communication of the important and challenging findings that were emerging from the data. I made the decision to use the conceptual framework of Foucault's 'ethical project' to underpin the methodological approach, and this ensured I was constantly aware of the effects my practice and presence in the research had on any outcomes.

Foucault's framework of ethics focuses on 'the forms of relations with the self, on the methods and techniques by which he works them out, on the exercises by which he makes himself an object to be known, and on the practices that enable him to have his own mode of being' (Foucault, 1987: 30). Ethical work as practice has a 'readiness to find what surrounds us strange and odd; a certain determination to throw off familiar ways of thought ... a lack of respect for the traditional hierarchies of what is important and fundamental' (Foucault, 1988: 132) and offers individual researchers the chance to experience 'the self as agent' (Warren, 1988: 138).

Julie Allan (2005) translates the four elements to Foucault's ethical practice into a form we can use as 'method'. These four elements are:

1. Determination of the ethical substance: identification in one's self of the things that need to be worked on which encourages acknowledgement of the individual's role in creating exclusionary pressures.
2. The mode of subjection: the ways in which an individual lives within the 'rules'. The exclusionary nature of 'rules', structures and systems in and around a community and a school are scrutinised in this research.
3. Self-practice or ethical work: the way in which an individual can change the way they live. Key activities in ethical work are deconstruction, criticism and reflexivity. Deconstruction helps to subvert the 'ideology of expertism' (Troyna and Vincent, 1996: 142) so offers 'ways to throw off familiar ways of thought'. Criticism should produce writing 'that creates openings rather than closures through certainty' (Allan, 2005: 290). The researcher here is reflexive, having an alternative perspective, to 'make strange' the familiar, to explore new ways of seeing and being.

4. The ultimate goal of ethical work, Foucault calls the telos. In this context, the telos is social justice, for those subject to the exclusionary forces in and around Morton and their secondary school.

With a simpler approach informed by ethics, it soon became clear that data derived from listening to the young people from Morton would be of primary importance. It was here, through 'a readiness to find what surrounds us strange and odd' (Foucault, 1988: 132), that lay the key insights into the exclusionary school structures and systems and the way young people were making connections (or not) with school. The research strategy of this 'ethical project' from this moment then set out to 'turn up the volume' of the voices of the young people and focused on listening.

Reflection 3 – ethical considerations

In order to minimise the risks to people and places, very careful attention was paid to research ethics throughout the project. The planning and implementing of the research was informed by the British Education Research Association (BERA) 'Ethical Guidelines for Educational Research' (2011). The principles underpinning the BERA guidelines, as with other international education research ethical procedures, are based on an ethic of respect for persons, knowledge, democratic values, quality of educational research and academic freedom. There are often conflicts between these and various positions are taken as to what is of most importance (Christians, 2005). Researchers involving young people must comply with Articles 3 and 12 of the UN Convention on the Rights of the Child, which require that the best interests of children (and young people) must be the primary consideration and that children who are capable of forming their own views should be able to express their views freely. This principle is at the core of this piece of research and is applied throughout.

Researchers must recognise the right to privacy for participants in research and this is problematic for case study work (Mahbub, 2008), particularly in small communities and places where it is difficult to guarantee anonymity for the case location and inhabitants. The reporting of data from this study had to be sensitively handled to minimise risk to the young people, the community and the school, as some of the findings were very challenging. Dialogue with the school principal was maintained throughout the project, although there was a series of events at the school during the period of the research which led to a great deal of change in the school management. Pseudonyms were used throughout, for places and individuals (Delamont, 2002), and care was taken in placing the school and study community within the reporting. In his well-known case study of an English secondary school, Ball (1981) paid very particular attention to removing all identifying geographical references for the study school and advocates the active misleading of the reader if necessary. As it was the relative rather than the particular geographical location of the school and study community that was important in my research, all details of the geographical locations were carefully removed from the report.

My research was driven by two key motivations: my desire to further understand the apparent injustice being experienced by the young people of Morton and my need to complete my doctoral study. I was clearly to be a beneficiary of the research, and Oliver (1992) asks researchers to consider whether it is ethical that researchers should benefit from the experience of the research, leaving the researched subjects just as they were before. I struggled with this dilemma throughout this project. Len Barton, in the context of disability research, argues that able-bodied researchers should accept the power they have and exploit them whilst asking:

> What responsibilities arise from the privileges I have as a result of my social position? How can I use my knowledge and skills to challenge, for example, the forms of oppression disabled people experience? Does my writing and speaking reproduce a system of domination or challenge that system?
>
> (in Barton and Clough, 1995: 144)

A similar argument is used in research on poverty, where the question is whether or not researchers who do not share the social and economic context of those they are researching, have a right to be there. Here there are demands for those in poverty to be heard directly, but acknowledgement that due to the 'collective weakness' of people in poverty as a political constituency there is a continued need for researchers and activists to continue to work as a 'poverty lobby' (Lister, 2002: 43). In this research project, I accepted my position of 'privilege' as a researcher, used Foucault's framework of ethics as a guide and firmly positioned the research as an engagement with the systems of domination.

Reflection 4 – marginalisation and risk

The young people central to this project were considered marginalised, coming from a community isolated geographically, socially and economically. I was aware that there are advantages, disadvantages and risks associated with research of such marginalised groups. The margin 'offers to one the possibility of radical perspective from which to see and create, to imagine alternatives, new worlds' (hooks, 2000: 207) and provides critical feedback to policy makers (Glenny and Roaf, 2008). Apple (1990) argues that seeing things from the standpoint of those with the least power can be beneficial to researchers looking to raise consciousness, offering a way to subvert traditional hierarchies (Foucault, 1988). However, there are also risks, and particular risks for research studies taking place in isolated, rural places; risks that the research can lead to further marginalisation through 'otherising' or do damage in other ways (Bines, 1995) and that the researcher's actions can confirm or even promote separation. There are also risks that 'the demand for narrative can become part of a renewal of colonising power'

(Allan, 1999: 113) and research becomes little more than voyeurism (Spivak, 1988) by dominant groups and intellectual tourists.

Risk, however, also gives the chance to break out of the cycle of certainty (Lather, 1994), in this case the certainty that these young people in this community will continue to face disadvantage. Skrtic (1991) encourages brave thinking and action in order to emancipate one's self from the 'machine bureaucracy', and Fulcher (1995) asserts that research must be political if it is to counter dominant readings. Research which is designed to struggle with an injustice and bring about some kind of change is going to be political (Clough and Nutbrown, 2007). I managed (and continue to manage) the risks of this research through my engagement with the ethical framework at every stage of the project, including its reporting and dissemination.

What the study heard

An implicit purpose of the research reported here was 'consciousness raising', so it is important to report some findings of the project and listen to what the young people had to say. Although their talk was 'full of oscillations, uncertainties and ambivalences' (Allan, 2008: 1), which disturbed clear conclusions, the young people revealed a deep sense of injustice as to what was happening to them in school and their community, but also their own exclusionary, labelled views of others.

To hear from one of the young people and illustrate the interview process, here is part of the transcript of the first interview with Lenny. Lenny began by talking about what people in Morton say about their secondary school.

Lenny: yeah I mean normally when I come back from the bus around the bus stop there's a whole load of people and I say why weren't you in school today and they say I just don't want to go and I ask them why and they say because they just don't like it there. I don't know why but maybe they are nervous or rather like-they – some people say they get treated unfairly by teachers

Cath: right, so what do you think?

Lenny: One or two teachers maybe – but I mean most people don't like it because they are like – you miss one day and you'll be behind for the rest of the term that's why they don't come

Cath: so once you've missed one …

Lenny: you've got behind with your work and get found out

Cath: so they tend to be around the bus stop when you get home?

Lenny: yeah I mean it's a small village so if you do get a bit off you'll be alright that's why they wait at the bus stop – I was trying to get on the bus the other day and this guy came up to me don't go to school today and I said what do you mean? – come and have a day off with me and I said I can't because of my education and I want a good life but he went don't mind I'll get someone else and I saw him at the bus stop where he gets on and I asked him what did you do and he said nothing so I said why didn't you go to school because it's just normal.

Cath: do you think there are a lot of people doing that?

Lenny: well I think people – what they want to do, they walk to the bus and get in Morton or they go on the bus walk into school and then walk straight out.

Cath: really?

Lenny: and then go around the town, that's what happens.

(Lenny, 16 May 2006)

The issues that arise in this excerpt – truanting from school, poor relationships with teachers and the school bus – are recurrent throughout the data. It also illustrates the flow of conversation begun by the young person and developed with responses, questions and contributions by the researcher. During these interviews I sensed that the quest for data had a powerful effect on me and there was a need to consciously remind myself of the need to listen, really listen.

The overwhelming sense gained from listening to the students is that school is seen as primarily a social place, a place where they make friends and enemies, meet with friends and deal with disagreements. For the small group of young people from the rural community of Morton, social opportunities in their home community are limited by, amongst other things, small numbers of young people and lack of provision of suitable 'meeting spaces'. Similar situations are recorded across rural areas of the UK (Fabes et al., 1983; Howard League for Penal Reform, 2005; Shucksmith, 2000). In all the interviews with young people, the social aspect of their school experience dominates the conversation. School was seen as a place for connections and relationships with peers. It was clear that these connections were not always beneficial. Lenny, Mike, Ali and Jo were all in trouble at school for their behaviour. Nowhere in data collected from interviews with school managers and from the reading of school policy documents is there any acknowledgement of the central significance of the school as a social place. There the discourse is soaked in the language of the 'standards agenda' and concerns about attendance and behaviour. There were also very limited spaces in the school buildings and timetables for student social activity.

The transition to secondary school is a time of great change for young people and is well documented by researchers (e.g. Weller, 2007). For young people from rural communities, moving to secondary school offers opportunities for many new encounters and connections, but is also a time for disconnection from primary school teachers and friends, and of course a journey to school by bus, a key part of the day for rural students. It emerged that one of the 'barriers' to attending school for some Morton young people was the journey to school and the poor behaviour and trouble on the school bus. This important finding emerges as a key issue for the young people of Morton and may well have been missed without a research approach that was focused on listening. For some, the school bus is seen as a facilitator to 'getting out of Morton'; for others, the bus is a barrier. Data collected from the community showed a link was made with young people not going to school on the bus and the young people causing criminal damage and general rowdiness in Morton.

There is acknowledgement by the Morton students both explicitly and implicitly that they see school as a place for learning and getting qualifications, and some express anger and frustrations about what they perceive to be teachers' lack of control, fairness and poor classroom management. There was a clear overlap in the aspirations of the Morton students and the teachers. The school's vision statement identifies academic achievement as a priority and the teachers and students share the desire for school as a place for learning. What seemed to be missing for the students interviewed in this study was communication with their teachers about this shared aspiration.

Reflection 5 – sharing the findings

Disseminating the reporting of consciousness-raising research activity raises certain ethical dilemmas and these are heightened in places such as small rural communities where anonymity may be impossible. Ethical research promotes the individual researcher as agent but also demands attention to the effects of the actions of individuals on others. In a search for justice for some, injustices should not be meted out to others. I was acutely aware of the risks of presenting some elements of the data collected from individuals, aware that respect for all persons must be maintained at all times. I argue that it is the relationship and interaction between what is said by individuals, the contingency, that is important. For example, the setting of the students' words against those of the senior managers at the school illustrates the separation between their two perspectives. Exactly who these individuals are is of less importance. Great care was taken throughout the study to use pseudonyms for geographical and professional labels, so that the study could be located in a secondary school in a rural area of the UK. Precisely where is not important.

Reporting the findings locally brought with it great challenge. This was helped in my case by a number of significant events, some serendipitous and some that I managed consciously. The main data collection period required extensive amounts of time being spent in Morton and the school. Once the majority of the data were collected, I consciously withdrew from the school and community, assisted by changes in my teaching commitments. The following period away from the locality allowed time for reflection and analysis of the data and time for those involved in the research to 'move on'. During this time a great deal of change happened, particularly at the school, including the departure of the four senior staff interviewed and two cohorts of students. A further cohort, including the youngest students interviewed in this study, departed before the report of the case study was disseminated. There were changes in Morton, too. The funding for the Neighbourhood Renewal programme came to an end and sadly both youth workers left as their funding also ceased. With all these local changes in personnel, the data could be seen to document the past and the findings to inform the future.

This space between the past and the future was envisioned as offering 'spaces in between' (Stronach, 1996) for mutual engagement in change.

Final reflections

It is argued that inclusion and research about inclusion such as this project should be undertaken as a political project, 'a disturbing and challenging activity essential of the struggle for change' (Barton, 2003: 13). Slee (2001) argues that if inclusion is seen in terms of 'cultural politics' rather than as a technical problem, it can then be seen to be about rights of citizenship for all rather than the solution for a few. Barton argues that 'hope is central to the struggle for inclusion' and 'involves an informed recognition of the offensive nature of current conditions and relations and the belief that the possibilities for change are not foreclosed' (2005: 23). Certainly, 'no advantage is derived through a calculus of emiseration' (Slee, 2001: 174) but a sustained examination of what was clearly a miserable situation for the students who contributed to this study, needed the maintenance of hope.

As a place to begin, Slee invites us to 'explore our own knowledge … and to examine the implications of the kinds of beliefs we hold' (2001: 169). If everyone were to engage in ethical work on themselves, with the resulting increased awareness of how our beliefs, actions and language have the potential to oppress others, 'oppression would be reduced' (Allan, 2008: 116). Seeing research in this way, as an examination of oneself, gives agency to individual researchers working in rural places and offers the opportunity to see possibilities for change at the individual level. It also offers the possibility of this personal (and then shared) consciousness-raising activity spreading across groups of individuals and organisations. The 'ethical project' framework seems particularly pertinent for research in rural communities where risks associated with marginalisation need to be minimised.

All the young people were surprised at the interest of the researcher in what they had to say, and seemed to welcome the opportunity to talk about their experiences in school, and it could be argued that this was a way in which the young people benefited from being involved in the research. It was the young people who provided new insights into the dividing practices in and around a school, including their school transport, and confirmed the importance of listening to and turning up the volume of voices from rural places. The young people showed a growing awareness of 'self as agent', which resonated with the researcher's own experiences during the research. This work drew to a close, hopeful that it had demonstrated that this kind of ethical project is possible for any individual researcher and that if we all embarked on this kind of work on ourselves, oppression in all its forms would be reduced.

References

Alderson, P. (2000). Children as researchers: the effects of participation rights on research methodology, in P. Christensen and A. James (eds), *Research with children: perspectives and practice*. London: Routledge Falmer.

Allan, J. (1999). *Actively seeking inclusion*. London: Falmer Press.

Allan, J. (2005). Inclusion as an ethical project, in S. Tremain (ed.), *Foucault and the government of disability*. Ann Arbor: University of Michigan Press.

Allan, J. (2008). *Rethinking inclusive education*. Dordrecht: Springer.

Anderson, M. & White, S. (2012). *The rural researcher and rural research: examining the footprint*. European Conference for Education Research, Cadiz. September 2012.

Apple, M. (1990). *Ideology and curriculum*. London: Routledge and Kegan Paul.

Ball, S. (1981). *Beachside comprehensive: a case study of secondary schooling*. Cambridge: Cambridge University Press.

Ballard, K. (1995). Inclusion, paradigms, power and participation, in C. Clark, A. Dyson and A. Millward (eds), *Towards inclusive schools?* London: David Fulton.

Barton, L. (2003). *Inclusive education and teacher education: a basis for hope or a discourse of delusion*. London: Institute of Education.

Barton, L. (2005). *Special educational needs: an alternative look. A response to Warnock (2005)* Special educational needs: a new look. London: Institute of Education.

Barton, L. and Clough, P. (1995). Conclusion: many urgent voices, in P. Clough and L. Barton (eds), *Making difficulties: research and the construction of SEN*. London: Paul Chapman.

Bernstein, B. (1970) Education cannot compensate for society. *New Society*, 26: 344–347.

Bines, H. (1995). Risk, routine and reward: confronting personal and social constructs in research on special educational needs, in P. Clough and L. Barton (eds), *Making difficulties: research and construction of SEN*. London: Paul Chapman Publishing.

Blacker, D. (1998). Intellectuals at work and in power: towards a Foucaultian research ethic, in T. Popekewitz and M. Brennan (eds), *Foucault's challenge: discourse, knowledge and power in education*. New York: Teacher's College Press.

Bourdieu, P. and Passeron, J. (1990) *Reproduction in education, society and culture*. London: Sage.

British Education Research Association (BERA). (2011). *Ethical guidelines for educational research*. London: British Education Research Association.

Bunce, M. (1994). *The countryside ideal*. London: Routledge.

Cahill, C. (2004). Defying gravity? Raising consciousness through collective research. *Children's Geographies*, 2: 273–286.

Castel, R. (1994). Problematization as a mode of reading history, in J. Goldstein (ed.), *Foucault and the writing of history*. Oxford: Blackwell.

Castells, M. (1997) *The power of identity*. Oxford: Blackwell.

Charmaz, K. and Mitchell, R. (2001). Grounded theory in ethnography, in P. Atkinson, A. Coffey, S. Delamont, J. Lofland and L. Lofland (eds), *Handbook of ethnography*. London: Sage.

Christians, C. (2005). Ethics and politics, in N. Denzin and Y. Lincoln (eds), *The Sage handbook of qualitative research*, 3rd edition. Thousand Oaks, California: Sage.

Cloke, P. (ed.) (2003). *Country visions*. Upper Saddle River, NJ: Prentice Hall.

Clough, P. (2002). *Narratives and fictions in educational research*. Buckingham: Open University Press.

Clough, P. and Nutbrown, C. (2007). *A student's guide to methodology*, 2nd edition. London: Sage.

Coffey, A. (1999) *The ethnographic self: fieldwork and the representation of identity*. London: Sage.

Cooke, B. and Kothari, U. (eds) (2001). *Participation: the new tyranny?* London: Zed Books.

Delamont, S. (2002). *Fieldwork in Educational Settings*. London: Routledge Falmer.

Delanty, G. (2003). *Community*. London: Routledge.

Deleuze, G. (1997). *Essays Critical and Clinical*, trans. D. W. Smith and M. A. Greco. Minneapolis: University of Minnesota Press.

Fabes, R., Worsley, E. and Howard, M. (1983). *The myth of the rural idyll*. Leicester: Child Poverty Action Group.

Foucault, M. (1984). On the genealogy of ethics: an overview of work in progress, in P. Rabinow (ed.), *The Foucault Reader*. New York: Pantheon.

Foucault, M. (1987). The ethic of care for the self as practice of freedom. *Philosophy and Social Criticism*, 12: 112–131.

Foucault, M. (1988). Practising criticisms, in L. Kritzman (ed.), *Michel Foucault: politics, philosophy, culture*. New York: Routledge.

Fulcher, G. (1995). Excommunicating the severely disabled: struggles, policy and researching, in P. Clough and L. Barton (eds), *Making difficulties: research and the construction of SEN*. London: Paul Chapman Publishing.

Giroux, H. (2005). *Border crossings: cultural workers and the politics of education*. London: Routledge.

Glenny, G. and Roaf, C. (2008). *Multiprofessional communication: making systems work for children*. Maidenhead: McGraw Hill/Open University.

Griffiths, M. (1998). *Educational research for social justice: getting off the fence*. Buckingham: Open University Press.

Gunter, H. and Thompson, P. (2007). Learning about student voice. *Support for Learning*, 22(4): 181–188.

Henriques, J., Holloway, W., Urwin, C., Venn, G. and Walkerdine, V. (1998). *Changing the subject: psychology, social regulation and subjectivity*. London: Routledge.

hooks, b. (2000). Choosing the margin as a space of radical openness., in J. Rendell, B. Penner and I. Borden (eds), *Gender space architecture: an interdisciplinary introduction*. London: Routledge.

Howard League for Penal Reform (2005). *Once upon a time in the west: social deprivation and rural youth crime*. London: Howard League for Penal Reform.

Jones, A. (1998). Pedagogical desires at the border: absolution and difference in the university classroom. Winds of change: women and the culture of the universities. International conference, Sydney, July 1998.

Lather, P. (1991). *Getting smart: feminist research and pedagogy within the post modern*. New York: Routledge.

Lather, P. (1994). Textuality as praxis. *Annual Meeting of American Educational Research Association*. April 1991, New Orleans.

Lister, R. (2002). A politics of recognition and respect: involving people with experience of poverty in decision making that affects their lives. *Social Policy and Society*, 1(1): 37–46.

Mahbub, T. (2008). Inclusive education at a BRAC school: perspectives from the children. *British Journal of Special Education*, 35(1): 33–41.

Mazzei, L. (2007) *Inhabited silence in qualitative research: putting poststructural theory to work*. New York: Peter Lang.

Mirza, M. (1995). Some ethical dilemmas in field work: feminist and antiracist methodologies, in M. Griffiths and B. Troyna (eds), *Antiracism, culture and social justice in education*. Stoke on Trent: Trentham.

Mirza, H. (ed.) (1997). *British black feminism: a reader*. London: Routledge.

Noyes, A. (2005). Thematic review. *British Educational Research Journal*, 31(4): 533–540.

Oliver, M. (1992). Changing the social relations of research production. *Disability, Handicap and Society*, 7(2): 101–114.

Pain, R. (2004). Social geography: participatory research. *Progress in Human Geography*, 28: 652–663.

Ruddock, J. and Fielding, M. (2006). Student voice and the perils of popularity. *Educational Review*, 58(2): 219–231.

Shucksmith, M. (2000). *Exclusive countryside? Social inclusion and regeneration in rural areas*. York: Joseph Rowntree Foundation.

Skrtic, T. (1991). The special education paradox: equity as the way to excellence. *Harvard Educational Review*, 61(2): 148–206.

Slee, R. (2001). Social justice and the changing directions in educational research: the case of inclusive education. *International Journal of Inclusive Education*, 5(2/3): 167–177.

Spivak, Gayatri Chakravorty (1988) 'Can the subaltern speak?', in C. Nelson and L. Grossberg (eds), *Marxism and the interpretation of culture*. Urbana: University of Illinois Press.

Stronach, I. (1996). Fashioning post-modernism, finishing modernism: tales from the fitting room. *British Educational Research Journal*, 22(3): 359–375.

Troyna, B. and Vincent, C. (1996). The ideology of expertism: the framing of special education and racial equality policies in the local state, in C. Christensen and F. Rizvi (eds), *Disability and the dilemmas of education and justice*. Buckingham: Open University Press.

Warren, M. (1988). *Nietzsche and political thought*. Cambridge, MA: MIT Press.

Weller, S. (2007). Managing the move to secondary school: the significance of children's social capital, in H. Helve and J. Bynner (eds), *Youth and social capital*. London: Tufnell Press.

Chapter 8

A conversation about research as risky business

Making visible the invisible in rural research locations

Robyn Henderson and Sherilyn Lennon

Introduction

Doing research in rural locations can present researchers with exciting possibilities, but also with challenges. In this chapter, we discuss some of our own experiences and reflect on the implications for researchers when preparing themselves for conducting research in rural communities. Specifically, this chapter foregrounds ethical and methodological issues faced by researchers working in these diverse locations and suggests tools that rural researchers may find useful. We present a conversation where we talk together (Sherilyn as a recently graduated doctoral student; Robyn as her doctoral supervisor) about some of our considerations when undertaking research in rural communities. Both of our projects investigated educational issues in our respective communities, and in many discussions during Sherilyn's candidature it became apparent that there were similarities, not only in the nature of our research in and about rural areas but also in the challenges that we experienced.

Through exploring some of the synergies between our doctoral studies – Sherilyn's completed at the end of 2012 (Lennon 2013) and Robyn's completed in 2005 (Henderson 2005) – our conversation highlights the sometimes risky business of trying to trouble the taken-for-granted social practices that can exist in a given community. In our research projects, we attempted to make visible particular inequities that seemed to be operating in the rural communities in which we lived or had lived for some time. These related to gender in Sherilyn's study and to the educational disadvantage, particularly literacy underachievement, that seemed to be experienced by itinerant farm workers' children in Robyn's study. In both studies, we set out to make visible the invisible.

In this chapter, we aim to make explicit or visible some of the considerations that would seem important for those wanting to conduct research in rural contexts. From our perspectives as insider researchers, we consider some of the methodological issues that we experienced as we conducted our research. We also extend our discussion to include possible implications for researchers who do not reside in rural communities. Before presenting our conversation, we describe briefly the approach taken in this chapter and our doctoral research projects that were conducted in rural areas.

Using a reflective conversation to frame the chapter

In our preparation for this chapter and in the tradition of Shor and Freire (1987), we recorded a conversation where we reflected critically on our experiences of conducting educational research in a rural context. Following transcription, we reordered and edited elements of the conversation to eliminate pauses, false starts and irrelevant or extraneous information. If necessary, we added details that would ensure that readers – most of whom we realised would not have specific contextual knowledge of relevance to our discussion – could make sense of what we had discussed. This *said it and edit* process has resulted in a more coherent conversation that illustrates the points that we wish to make about doing educational research in rural settings.

In a sense, we present a text that draws together elements of autobiography and academic research (Lather and Smithies, 1997). We used the process of critical reflection suggested by Macfarlane, Noble, Kilderry and Nolan (2005), thus framing our conversation with the four steps of deconstructing, confronting, theorising and thinking otherwise. In the final version of our conversation, however, we downplay the theorising aspect by keeping references to the literature to a minimum. We think this has achieved our purpose of maintaining readability.

Where necessary, we refer to relevant literature in the commentary that links sections of the conversation together. Our commentary serves a purpose similar to the production technique that is often called a 'voiceover'. It allows us to use a shared research voice, thus ensuring that particular points are noted by readers. In effect, this technique has activated the theorising step of Macfarlane et al.'s (2005) model of critical reflection, allowing us to maintain the informal style of our conversation while still providing an academic perspective.

Sherilyn's study

Sherilyn's research (Lennon 2013) stemmed from her concern over the disproportionately high number of boys performing poorly at her local high school. Unlike the situation reported in other locations, where schooling is set up 'to usher young people out of the community and into opportunities' elsewhere (see Corbett, 2007: 1), this community provided many skilled and unskilled employment options for its boys, regardless of their schooling performances. Indeed, as one 15-year-old boy explained to Sherilyn, 'I've already got three jobs lined up … I don't need to pass anything for any of them!'

Sherilyn's research was conducted in a traditional Australian bush town complete with wide tree-lined streets and a skyline dominated by hotels. The township is a service centre for the surrounding industries of dry land cropping, grazing, cotton and irrigation. With a town and shire combined population of more than 8,000, the diversity of agricultural industries in the community means that it has managed to thrive despite prolonged droughts and recent record-breaking floods.

Sherilyn has been a teacher at the local high school and a member of this community for more than a quarter of a century. She understands her hometown as a place where most people know each other and one another's family histories, where lives are dependent on and interconnected by the seasons, and where individuals are governed by a strict but unwritten code of cultural beliefs and practices. She recognises dominant discourses that circulate in the community and support practices whereby farming land is passed down from fathers to sons and men are encouraged to take chief financial and civic responsibility for their families and the wider community. Other dominant discourses she has identified construct women as the community's homemakers, caregivers and cultural gatekeepers. They also naturalise and normalise the construction of girls as outperforming boys at school. The photograph in Figure 8.1 shows part of a rural landscape that is typical in the context where Sherilyn's research was conducted.

By adopting sociocultural understandings of gender, Sherilyn used her study to focus on the gender messages local boys were receiving from home, school, sporting clubs and community texts. Initially she sought to deepen her understandings of what it was boys were valuing if it was not their schoolwork. However, as the study progressed and Sherilyn's understandings of the links between heteropatriarchal constructions of gender and boys' schooling performances deepened, she felt compelled to act. This led her to publish a letter in the local newspaper, challenging a well-known local logo that she interpreted as perpetuating discourses of white male entitlement and violence against women. Sherilyn's letter to the editor opened up a space for community members to engage in extensive public and private discussions relating to local gender beliefs and practices. Considerable data were generated as these discussions spread across, and occasionally beyond, the community.

Figure 8.1 A typical rural landscape in the location where Sherilyn's study was conducted.

Sherilyn drew on case study traditions (e.g. Merriam, 1998), critical discourse analysis (e.g. Fairclough, 2001), reflexive dyadic interviewing techniques (e.g. Kincheloe & Berry, 2004), critical ethnography (e.g. Foley & Valenzuela, 2005), autoethnography (e.g. Ellis, 2004), and aspects of radical (e.g. Giroux, 2001) and public pedagogy (e.g. O'Malley & Roseboro, 2010). Her approach built links between community constructions of gender, schooling performances and local power inequities. It also enabled Sherilyn to add to knowledge in the emerging fields of transformative and activist pedagogies.

Robyn's study

Robyn's research (Henderson, 2005) was conducted in a coastal town in North Queensland, where she had lived and worked for almost 25 years before beginning doctoral studies. During the winter harvesting season each year, the town's population was swelled by up to 3,000 itinerant farm workers, many of whom returned to the town on an annual basis. Figure 8.2 shows some of the farms that provided seasonal work. With the influx of farm workers, approximately 100 school-aged children also arrived in the town and enrolled in the local schools, with 60 of them enrolling in the primary school where Robyn conducted her research. Depending on the factors that influenced the harvest, including the weather and market prices, children sometimes stayed for as long as six months, although they often stayed for a much shorter time.

Using ethnographic techniques for data collection, including semi-structured interviews, informal conversations, classroom observations and an artefact collection, Robyn conducted six family case studies. Drawing on Fairclough's (2001) text–interaction–context model, she used critical discourse analysis to do both textual and

Figure 8.2 Farms in the location where Robyn's study was conducted.

social analysis. This yielded insights into the social and discursive construction of itinerant children and their families within the school and the wider community, as well as the literacy learning of this particular group of itinerant children.

The study found that teachers' narratives about itinerant farm workers' children were predominantly negative. They constructed the children and their families in deficit and stereotypical terms and identified the families' itinerant lifestyles as impacting negatively on the children's literacy learning. These narratives contrasted with those told by the families as they provided insights into what it meant to live an itinerant lifestyle. The families' practices were often very different from the commonsense assumptions of teachers. Robyn concluded that there was a desperate need for teachers to shift the focus away from deficit stories towards the literacy strengths that itinerant children bring to school. She sees this as a first step towards ensuring more productive and responsive pedagogies that will assist the children with being successful at school literacy learning.

Beginning the conversation: being an insider researcher in a rural community

In the next two sections, we present the conversation that resulted from the *said it and edit* process that we implemented. We begin by talking with our shared researcher voice, which reappears in places throughout the conversation.

Research has acknowledged that there is a 'lack of research on diverse rural populations' (Donehower et al., 2012: xiv). This absence of research has enabled mainstream perceptions of rurality to shape and inform how particular communities are conceptualised. As a result, those who live in the Australian 'bush' are often described in stereotypical ways. These include romantic notions that celebrate and mythologise people's 'rural past and character' and deficit stories that depict 'rural places and people as lacking educational, economic, and cultural resources' (Donehower et al., 2012: xiv).

Although educational research is often confined to schools and events inside the school gate, Giroux's 'correspondence principle' (2001: 56) highlights the way that the microcosm of a school often reflects what is happening in the wider community. In both of our research projects, we applied this principle to the research we conducted. In attempting to understand particular dynamics in schools – gender in Sherilyn's study and literacy underachievement in Robyn's – we collected data from school and community sources.

Sherilyn: Apart from the extended period of time that we both spent in our communities prior to our research, where I also see us overlapping is in our decision to go beyond the school and into the wider community to collect data. Did you make a conscious decision to do this?

Robyn: Yes, I did. From living in the community, I was aware that the stories I had heard in the school about itinerant farm workers were similar to stories I had heard in the community; plus I was using Fairclough's context–interaction–text model, from his book *Language and Power*. In using that model, I had already decided that I was interested in the context. I wanted to investigate the broader community context and the stories that were in circulation there. How did you come to the conclusion that collecting community data was important?

Sherilyn: I had been working with other teachers and across schools on projects to re-engage boys in their schooling for many years and, while I certainly had some successes, I noticed that when the boys finished the class or the project or the year and moved on to another teacher they would, more often than not, just revert to their previous patterns of behaviour. I started to realize that what I was doing was just band-aiding an issue. If I really wanted to make a difference, then I had to start thinking about the boys' schooling performances, or lack thereof, differently. The problem couldn't just be explained away as a faulty school curriculum or inadequate teaching. I had to start thinking about the issue of underperformance as a cultural issue. I needed to understand what boys were really valuing if it wasn't their schoolwork, how gender roles were being acted out within and across the community, and what the hidden curriculum might be teaching our boys about schooling and its place in their lives.

Robyn: It seems that our inclusion of the wider community in our research had advantages and disadvantages. On the one hand, it offered insights into how and why particular practices within the school came to be. Yet, on the other hand, the involvement of the wider community had particular implications for us as researchers. And these are worthy of discussion.

Sherilyn: Yes. While we overlapped on some things we operated in really different ways on others, didn't we? We were both insider researchers, but you worked at making school discourses and practices visible, to show how they worked against the itinerant farm workers' children. In contrast, I set out to deliberately and publicly confront some of the inequitable gender practices and discourses that were operating in my community.

Robyn: You were definite in your plans to change the community. My research was aimed at understanding why the itinerant farm workers' children were not achieving at school, despite appearing to be bright and capable in so many ways.

Sherilyn: Your research didn't set out to confront members of the community as mine did. You were seeking to understand the issue more deeply in a non-confrontational way, but I set out to provoke a reaction from community members, as a way of challenging the status quo.

Although our research projects were quite different in their intent, we were both positioned as insider researchers, with knowledge about and experiences of

the communities in which we were conducting our research. Both research projects were investigating aspects of the social world and, as Austin (2012: 221)
highlighted, this type of research 'is always a troubling and frequently a morally
tortuous process'. Social research uses 'other people's lives as data' (Lather 2007:
52) and, in small communities where almost everyone knows one another, this
can provide challenges for researchers. In the conversation that follows, we begin
to identify some of those challenges and some of the benefits that we experienced
as insider researchers.

Robyn: I know one day you talked about how the 'bush telegraph' operated in
           your community.
Sherilyn: Yes, it was amazing how quickly news of my research was transmitted
           within, across, and even beyond the community. Whilst many admitted
           to never having read my original letter to the editor, it seemed as
           though everyone was talking about it and had an opinion on it. When
           you've challenged something that hasn't been challenged before
           or questioned something that has become so familiar that it is invisible
           in the cultural landscape, you can create enormous unrest in a com-
           munity. And news about that can travel through the community really
           quickly.
Robyn: Can you give me an example?
Sherilyn: As you know, I wrote a number of letters to the editor of the local
           newspaper, questioning the use of what I thought was an inappropriate
           logo. The editor told me that in his 25 years in the community there
           had only ever been one other issue that had created such unrest. In
           some ways it was validating that my voice could have such an impact in
           my community, but in other ways it was quite unsettling. My actions
           and the reactions I got from others made me reconsider who I was,
           where I was, how I was positioned in my community, and how I was
           positioning others.
Robyn: Being an insider researcher seems to have been an important part of
           your study.
Sherilyn: Yes. Yes. Most definitely. Having been on the inside for more than a
           quarter of a century before conducting my doctoral research meant
           that I had the time to build a very deep knowledge of the community
           and its cultural beliefs and practices. Once I started looking at my com-
           munity through critical lenses, I knew almost immediately where I
           should start collecting data. Yet in some ways that *already there knowl-
           edge* had the capacity to limit my thinking and blind me, blind me in
           two ways. Firstly, because I already knew whose stories would be useful
           to my study, there was a temptation to ignore other sources of data or
           not to go looking for alternative stories. Secondly, researching from the
           inside meant that the ideologies, discourses, practices, traditions,
           behaviours, customs and gender performances I was exposed to daily

had become so normal and natural to me that I sometimes found it hard to look at them differently.

Robyn: So how did you get around that?

Sherilyn: One of the methods I used for overcoming these dilemmas was to deliberately wear lenses that distorted my readings of local media articles. I would mentally change around the gender roles or the cultural representations of the people appearing in the images and stories in the local newspaper. If I did that and it transformed the story into one that I considered would be confronting for most community members – you know, one that I knew would never appear in the local newspaper – then I knew that I had something that was worth examining further. I adopted this process from McLaren's 2003 work. He calls this process, which makes the familiar strange and vice versa, 'pedagogical surrealism'. In my research, it helped me to move beyond the view that it's normal for girls to outperform boys at school, that it's normal for women to drive their men home from parties after the men have had too much to drink, that it's normal for men to control the finances, and that it's normal for women to serve and for men to be served.

Robyn: Ah, so you used a role swapping technique to see if the data were useful for confronting and challenging community practices. Interestingly, if you were a researcher from outside the community, then you would probably not have been privy to that information at all.

Sherilyn: True. Being an insider gave me insider knowledge of school and community discourses, beliefs and practices and ready access to these.

Robyn: So how do you think outsiders might deal with access issues?

Sherilyn: It's really important to know who to contact and where to go to collect useful data. As insider researchers we already had extensive knowledge of our communities. Perhaps one strategy for outsider researchers would be to find ways of accessing local knowledge. What do you think?

Robyn: I think you're right. When I go back to the town where I collected my data, there are always two places I go – the pie shop and the supermarket. It probably seems strange to those who don't know the community, but those are places where it pays to be seen. I always spend time there, because I know that word gets around really fast that I'm in town. People are always interested to know how my life is going in the outside world and they want to talk and fill me in on happenings in the community since my last visit.

Sherilyn: That obviously helps to maintain your insider status.

Robyn: Yes, it does, even though I haven't been a resident in the community for quite some years now. When I began my doctoral research, many years ago, I was told that a group of researchers from another university had tried to conduct research relating to farm workers. However, because they weren't living and working in the particular community they had chosen, they had trouble finding research participants. When you have a relationship with a community, you know who to ask, where to go, and the types of protocols that you need to follow.

Sherilyn: I feel guilty – and I hate to admit it – of having been selected for research surveys on email or on the phone and, because I'm so busy and because I don't know the researcher, I sometimes say, 'No, I'm sorry I can't help you out at the moment.' So being an insider gives you an advantage because of those personal relationships that you've built.

Robyn: There are clear messages for outsider researchers, aren't there? They need to build a relationship with the community and that can take time.

Our conversation highlighted important relational considerations that we had used as insider researchers. We acknowledge that our long-term relationships with our respective communities were helpful, particularly in terms of knowing who to contact and what community protocols to follow. Yet we also recognise that closeness to a community can make it difficult to critique the community's hegemonic beliefs and practices and its social and cultural traditions. As Sherilyn highlighted, she used a particular process (see Lennon, 2013), based on McLaren's (2003: 189) concept of 'pedagogical surrealism', to make the familiar strange.

Positioning self and others; repositioning self and others

It was important for us to acknowledge that we had probably been acculturated by our communities into accepting certain beliefs and practices as normal and natural. Our considerations about these issues involved making ethical decisions and consciously repositioning or decentring ourselves (Berry, 2006), in order to see with 'new eyes' our cultural landscapes and the issues being investigated. This was not always an easy task.

Our conversation now continues and we further explore some of the complexities associated with being positioned as insider researchers in small, somewhat isolated, rural communities.

Sherilyn: One of the things I noticed during my study was the gap between how I was trying to position my research and how others expected me to position it – and how they expected me to position them in it. There seemed to be an assumption that I would present the dominant social order in a favourable way. When I started to question commonsense practices and beliefs, it was as if I was threatening established power bases. That wasn't always comfortable.

Robyn: I know what you mean. I had worked in the school where I conducted my research. The principal seemed to think that my study was going to solve 'the problem' of farm worker students. It was as if I'd be able to produce a magic bullet.

Sherilyn: And that didn't happen?

Robyn: As we know, research often helps us understand the problem in more detail rather than solving it.

Sherilyn: Yes.

Robyn: I found that the more data I collected, the more complicated it became. For example, when I started to collect the families' stories and began to compare the families' stories with the teachers' stories, I realised that I had two completely different perspectives. One particular teacher story was about a Tongan family. The teachers regarded the parents' absences away from the town as evidence of poor parenting. However, my interviews with the parents suggested that there was much more to the story than teachers knew about. I began to understand that the family worked hard to make sure that their children's schooling wasn't too disrupted by their itinerant lifestyle. They tried really hard to keep their children in the same school.

Sherilyn: So did this impact on your research?

Robyn: Yes, it impacted on my thinking about how I would represent the stories. I didn't want to set up a binary of teachers' stories against parents' stories. It wasn't as if one set of stories was right and the other was wrong.

Sherilyn: So what did you do?

Robyn: I thought about how I could theorise the different stories that were evident in the data. I was investigating discourses, so that helped to shift the focus away from the individuals who told the stories. There were times, though, when I chose to not record conversations with research participants. Some of the issues were sensitive and recording the conversations seemed too intrusive. Instead I wrote my recollections of those conversations in my researcher journal.

Sherilyn: I can so identify with your stories of turning off the audio recorder and the principal making an assumption that you were going to present his perspective and his school favourably. Another issue that I am starting to identify as problematic for rural researchers is the potential for our work to reposition us in our communities. There can be that perception that we are 'digging for dirt' or somehow trespassing on hallowed ground because we are documenting or challenging deeply ingrained assumptions.

Robyn: Challenging taken-for-granted assumptions, practices or beliefs isn't easy.

Sherilyn: I think one of the biggest challenges is finding ways of making sure the research is meaningful, yet also maintaining good relationships with the community. If you want your research to be productive, then you probably need to shift people's thinking. But how do you do that without breaking trust or distancing yourself too far from the very people who need to be a part of the change-making process?

Robyn: And that comes back to the position of the researcher and how, regardless of the perspective you take, you need to maintain a positive relationship with the community you're researching. Part of doing that involves trust.

Sherilyn: You have to be trusted to be able to do that in a professional and ethical way.

Robyn: The community needs to trust that you are going to represent them in a way that they see as okay.

Sherilyn: And, on that, my experience has been that particular groups within a community can be somewhat suspicious or mistrusting of outsiders. If you're an academic or researcher from a university, then you're probably operating from an unknown for a lot of people – and I certainly don't mean that in a disrespectful way.

Robyn: No.

Sherilyn: What I am saying is that it is rare to have universities or tertiary institutions located in isolated rural communities. It's not likely that the residents of these communities will have had much exposure to researchers or academics. If you're a long-term member of the community then I guess you have some advantages over an outsider researcher, but it really keeps coming back to the importance of taking the time to form those relationships, doesn't it?

Robyn: I know with my study that some of the information that came from families was information they had tried to hide from the community. On the one hand, I knew I was at the point where they trusted me completely and were willing to reveal such information, but I also knew that my use of that information would have been doing exactly what the families had tried to avoid. That meant that there were ethical issues involved.

Sherilyn: In some situations there could even have been legal issues involved. Even though you do everything you can to protect identities, if people recognise themselves, or recognise their partners, or recognise other members of the community, then the reality is that you can destroy lives.

Robyn: That goes back to it being a small community, doesn't it? Even though we say we will maintain confidentiality and we will use pseudonyms to offer anonymity, sometimes there is a risk that people will be identified by others in the community, especially when the community is small and most people know one another.

Sherilyn: Yes. Exactly. You need to weigh up that risk and make a decision about whether to use the data or not. I knew that including some of the data

I had collected could have been harmful to certain people, their reputations and their relationships. For example, there were a number of sexual assaults that I was told about and some of them involved minors. These had either been dealt with by the authorities or happened a long time ago and the victim didn't want to press charges. I needed to be very, very careful when dealing with this information.

Robyn: How did you handle that?

Sherilyn: I had to make decisions about what to put in my study and what to leave out. Research can be a risky business. Whilst someone might argue that leaving certain data out watered down my study, I think I could argue that leaving them out increased the study's integrity and ethical standing.

Robyn: What about in terms of having to live in that community? As part of your research you've done quite a bit of disrupting and unsettling, but you want to stay in the community.

Sherilyn: Yes. That's right. What I said and did throughout my research broke a lot of cultural boundaries and certainly unsettled particular groups within the community. There is no doubting that. There are some individuals who will probably never be comfortable speaking to me again. I've been publically branded a 'nihilist' and an 'alarmist' by some and I don't think I will ever be able to change those perceptions. But I'm not sure that I want to either. I'm comfortable with my stance. I believe in what I am doing. I've been accused of being a man-hater and I get irritated when I hear that because I know I'm not. But I have to balance that with 'Well, what have I done to make you feel that way? How much must I have challenged your thinking and practices for you to say that or react like that?' I set out to irritate the taken-for-granted and I certainly did that but, in the process, I also unsettled myself. This reciprocal unsettling incorporated some steep and deep learnings about the power of the insider researcher but also about the potential for impact on the insider researcher.

Robyn: But interestingly, if you were a researcher from outside the community, then you would probably not have collected that rich data or had such an impact. Yet, an outsider researcher who did so much disrupting and unsettling might close the doors to all future research in that community.

Sherilyn: So true. And that leads me to another dilemma that I had with my study. Because I was using a critical framework, I needed to represent and critique the views of others, but somehow I had to avoid setting myself up as some sort of judge and jury who alone knew 'the real truth'. Such an approach would not have endeared me to anyone.

Robyn: Of course.

Sherilyn: I think that's why polyvocality became so important to my study. Whilst my voice was obviously the dominant one, because I decided what to do, what to include, what to exclude and how to analyse it, it became really important for me to include a whole plethora of voices and different belief systems in the study. Some of these aligned with my thinking, but some didn't.

Robyn: Yes.

Sherilyn: I felt it was important to include substantial extracts presenting others' points of view, without censoring or editing them to death first. After I'd typed up the transcripts of interviews, I gave the interviewees two weeks to do any editing they wanted and make changes before adding the transcripts to my data bank. In my study there was a whole chapter where community members told their stories, you know, talked about how they were thinking or feeling about the gender issue. I wanted to let the community speak for itself. I think as researchers we need to keep reminding ourselves that we are working with real people who can offer different but equally valid insights into community issues. They are not just pieces of data for us to manipulate, use and analyse.

Our conversation has highlighted some of the important decisions that we had to make as researchers. These related to our own positioning in the research, the ways that we could present and represent data and data analysis (see Henderson, 2005, 2009; Lennon, 2013), and the ethics of our decisions (see Henderson, 2008). In particular, we recognise how vital it was to think through such issues, especially when challenging seemingly accepted sociocultural practices, either in the school or in the wider community (Lingard et al,. 2000).

Concluding comments

Rural communities present varied opportunities for research. Each community has its own issues, stories and life rhythms. Schools servicing such communities cannot help but be influenced by the ideologies, discourses and practices of these diverse, but often distinctive, cultural contexts. Whilst schools like to see themselves as social sites which teach 'democratic values while demanding social control' (Giroux, 2001: 54), educators and researchers working in rural communities sometimes fail to notice and make explicit the links between the wider community's dominant ideologies, discourses and practices and students' schooling performances – or lack thereof. As a result, schools and their teachers can end up perpetuating social inequities inherited from the hidden curriculum operating within and beyond the school gates.

Our doctoral research projects set out to 'open up and disrupt taken-for-granted ways of interpreting the world' (Somerville, 2012: 71). While such research practice can be a potentially risky business, we posit that if long-lasting and far-reaching cultural change is to be achieved for some of our most marginalised schools and their students, then it is necessary for educational researchers to move beyond the school site and into the wider community that supports it.

Keddie and Mills (2007: 204) hinted at the value of doing this when they stated that 'schools do undergo change ... school structures and procedures are not fixed by their histories and are always open to transformation ... such transformations require a knowledge of and engagement with the local community'.

In our conversation about our own doctoral research projects, we identified some of the challenges and issues that researchers can face when doing research in rural places. Because we lived, or had lived, in the rural communities where we conducted our research, we became aware of some of the difficulties of wanting to make visible the invisible. However, both of us were insiders and that meant that we brought long-term knowledges, experiences and insights of our communities to our research.

Using our insider perspectives, this chapter has explored some of the risks and rewards of conducting research in rural locations. In particular, we highlighted some of the methodological issues that challenged us. We noted Sherilyn's use of McLaren's (2003: 189) process of 'pedagogical surrealism', ways of accessing local knowledge, the importance of building relationships with community members, the need to engage with and reflect on ethical dilemmas, and the effects on the researcher of being an insider.

The chapter has presented a case for moving beyond the school setting and into the wider community in order to deepen understandings of students' performances and address issues associated with discourses and practices that can work to limit students' lives. It has also argued for the importance of building relationships of trust with those whose lives the research touches, including those who are participants in the research as well as the broader community. Additionally, the chapter suggested some considerations and strategies for those who wish to research in communities where they would be regarded as outsiders.

We recognise that our conversation focuses on only two rural communities. Although they were more than 1,000 kilometres (600 miles) apart, both were located in Queensland, Australia, and each was within three hours' drive from a regional city. While we do not intend to stereotype rural communities or generalise from our experiences in these particular communities, our critically reflective conversation (Macfarlane et al., 2005) has highlighted aspects of our research that were potentially risky and therefore warranted our consideration. In exploring our actions and thinking about these issues, we have presented practical strategies that may help others deal with some of the dilemmas of conducting educational research in communities where everybody knows one another. Our own position 'should always be held in a critical light' (Leistyna 2012: 216) and our research responses should, of course, demonstrate an ethical and responsible approach.

References

Austin, J. (2012). 'Enlightening the stranger within: (re)viewing critical research from/ on/in the centre'. In S. R. Steinberg and G. S. Cannella (eds), *Critical Qualitative Research: reader*. New York: Peter Lang.

Berry, K. (2006). 'Research as bricolage: embracing relationality, multiplicity and complexity'. In K. Tobin and J. Kincheloe (eds), *Doing educational research: a handbook*. Rotterdam, The Netherlands: Sense Publishers.

Corbett, M. (2007). *Learning to leave: the irony of schooling in a coastal community*. Halifax, Canada: Fernwood Publishing.

Donehower, K., Hogg, C. & Schell, E. E. (2012). 'Preface'. In K. Donehower, C. Hogg & E. E. Schell (eds), *Reclaiming the rural: essays on literacy, rhetoric, and pedagogy*. Carbondale: Southern Illinois University Press.

Ellis, C. (2004). *The ethnographic I: a methodological novel about autoethnography*. Walnut Creek, CA: Altamira Press.

Fairclough, N. (2001). *Language and power*, 2nd edition. London: Longman.

Foley, D. & Valenzuela, A. (2005). 'Critical ethnography: the politics of collaboration'. In N. Denzin & Y. Lincoln (eds), *The Sage handbook of qualitative research*, 3rd edition. London: Sage.

Giroux, H. (2001). *Theory and resistance in education: towards a pedagogy for the opposition*. London: Bergin & Garvey.

Henderson, R. (2005). 'The social and discursive construction of itinerant farm workers' children as literacy learners'. Unpublished thesis, James Cook University, Queensland.

Henderson, R. (2008). 'Dangerous terrains: negotiating ethical dilemmas'. In R. Henderson and P. A. Danaher (eds), *Troubling terrains: tactics for traversing and transforming contemporary educational research*. Teneriffe, Queensland: Post Pressed.

Henderson, R. (2009). 'Itinerant farm workers' children in Australia: learning from the experiences of one family'. In P. A. Danaher, M. Kenny & J. Remy Leder (eds), *Traveller, nomadic and migrant education*. New York: Routledge.

Keddie, A. & Mills, M. (2007). *Teaching boys: developing classroom practices that work*. Crows Nest, NSW: Allen & Unwin.

Kincheloe, J. & Berry, K. (2004). *Rigour and complexity in educational research: conceptualizing the bricolage*. Berkshire, England: Open University Press.

Lather, P. (2007). *Getting lost: feminist efforts towards a double(d) science*. Albany: State University of New York Press.

Lather, P. & Smithies, C. (1997). *Troubling the angels: women living with HIV/AIDS*. Boulder, CO: Westview Press.

Leistyna, P. (2012). 'Maintaining a vibrant synergy among theory, qualitative research, and social activism in this ever-changing age of globalization'. In S. R. Steinberg & G. S. Cannella (eds), *Critical qualitative research: reader*. New York: Peter Lang.

Lennon, S. (2013). 'Reconceptualising research using an insider activist approach to seek social transformations around issues of gender'. Unpublished thesis, University of Southern Queensland, Queensland.

Lingard, B., Mills, M. & Hayes, D. (2000). 'Teachers, school reform and social justice: challenging research and practice'. *Australian Educational Researcher*, 27(3): 101–115.

Macfarlane, K., Noble, K., Kilderry, A. & Nolan, A. (2005). 'Developing skills of thinking otherwise and critical reflection'. In K. Noble, K. Macfarlane & J. Cartmel (eds), *Circles of change: challenging orthodoxy in practitioner supervision*. Frenchs Forest, NSW: Pearson.

McLaren, P. (2003). *Life in schools: an introduction to critical pedagogy in the foundations of education*, 4th edition. Boston, MA: Allyn and Bacon.

Merriam, S. (1998). *Qualitative research and case study applications in education*, 2nd edition. San Francisco, CA: Jossey-Bass.

O'Malley, P. & Roseboro, D. (2010). 'Public pedagogy as critical educational and community leadership: implications from East St Louis School District governance'. In J. Sandlin, B. Schultz & J. Burdick (eds), *Handbook of public pedagogy*. New York: Routledge.

Shor, I. & Freire, P. (1987). *A pedagogy for liberation: dialogues on transforming education*. New York: Bergin & Garvey.

Somerville, M. (2012). 'The critical power of place'. In S. R. Steinberg & G. S. Cannella (eds), *Critical qualitative research: reader*. New York: Peter Lang.

Chapter 9

Researching from the standpoint of the rural

Philip Roberts

Introduction

In this chapter I aim to outline a perspective on what a rural standpoint in research may be, and to encourage you, the reader, to consider your own 'rural' standpoint. My perspective on this is informed by the view that, while rural meanings are clearly important and need to be valued in research, methodological orthodoxy and the need to produce clear numbers for policy impact often erase the particularities of these meanings. Central to my argument is a perspective that the rural needs to be more than a setting for research or a point of difference justifying publication. Instead, it should be generative for, or pertinent to, the purpose of the research, and more than a category of description. In advancing this perspective, I suggest that some of what purports to be rural research tends to use the rural more or less as the setting or as a convenient example, and consequently does little to add to an understanding of the rural or how issues uniquely play out in the rural. As such, they tacitly assume a metropolitan norm, where the point of difference is the context of rural, without understanding the conditions of the rural and how the category influences the interpretation or advances knowledge. If the research is not advancing an understanding *of* the rural, *for* the rural, it may be just enacting symbolic violence (Bourdieu & Wacquant, 1992) against the places it purports to represent by inadvertently treating them as a curiosity or constructing them as deviant. Thus, I will argue that an important component of rural research is its focus upon the particularities and subjectivities of places, and the opportunity this affords to illuminate the modern condition in what is arguably an increasingly placeless metropolitan 'first' world (Roberts & Green, 2013).

What is a rural standpoint, as I understand it? Briefly, by using the concept standpoint I am drawing on the work of feminist theorists (Harding, 2004) to suggest a philosophical position from which one examines an issue or understands the world. I suggest that it is the basis of the ontological and epistemological position from which an issue is researched. However, the labeling and identification of a standpoint indicates that it is a position associated with an identity that is marginalised in some way. It is through this identification of a standpoint that we come to see that what is regarded as the normal state of affairs is in fact imbued with powerful social and cultural knowledge, and that this 'normal' position actively marginalises other forms of knowledge. A standpoint therefore comes from a position of the least advantaged. In this chapter, indeed in my research, the least advantaged I aim to associate with is the rural. Thus, for me, in the terms used by Sher and Sher (1994), a rural standpoint refers to approaching my research from a position that rural people and communities *really* matter. That said, I will now firstly introduce my own background as relevant to the development of my understanding of a rural standpoint. I will then return to the concept of rural standpoint itself, to elaborate on it in more depth and detail.

Positioning myself in the research

As a number of authors in this book have suggested, many researchers of the rural live in urban contexts and are in a way revisiting a rural childhood in their work. This implied biographical authority to conduct rural research is problematic, as it assumes that the person comes before the issue being researched and is open to potential criticisms of romanticising the rural. I don't neatly fit this biography, and I am not convinced that such biography leads to effective rural research; indeed, I have a suspicion that by itself this standpoint may be an impediment to seeing the bad, along with the good. What really matters is our position vis-à-vis the research and how we account for that position. That said, as there is an inherently ethnographic component of coming to appreciate rural meanings, some time spent with rural communities is an important factor in developing a researcher's understanding.

I grew up near Bondi, the iconic beachside suburb of Sydney, in Australia. This is about as urban as it gets. However, I guess it is also far removed from the urban expanses of suburban Sydney to the west and southwest. Ironically, perhaps, I am now based in a university in what is essentially the city-state of the nation's capital, albeit commonly regarded as a 'bush capital'. However, I am writing this in a small town in a regional area nearly two hours away, where I live. But how did I get here?

I cannot quite explain why things transpired the way they did. All I know is that my initial position in a private school didn't fit the sociopolitical ethos I had developed. Trained as a history teacher, it may have been my specialisation in Russian revolutionary history and Marxist history that influenced my social attitudes. As it transpired, I resigned my initial private school position to take up temporary positions in schools generally regarded as remote and hard to staff, and eventually was appointed into a permanent position in the semi-arid marginal farm lands of northwestern New South Wales (NSW), Australia. The school where I spent the next four and half years is generally regarded as remote and isolated, with the nearest town an hour away, and the nearest regional centre about four hours away. I subsequently took up an appointment as headteacher in another small rural school, though not quite as remote, before my final position as a headteacher in a large regional high school. This is not as dramatic a shift as it may initially seem. My mother's side of the family had a rural settler heritage that was central to their identity, while my father was a Sydney-born-and-raised agricultural scientist. Thus, the rural loomed large within the family mythology as an imagined other (Soja, 1996).

It was the initial position in that remote western NSW school that was formative for my subsequent work in rural education and my current academic work. The school was one of many regarded as hard to staff, with high staff turnover rates, yet for some reason I immediately felt at home there. As it transpired, many teachers came and went, while a few of us stayed on, *dwelling* within this community, while others merely *inhabited* it during the school term. Watching this passage of transience, physically and mentally, attuned me to the qualitatively different engagement with the community of a number of my peers. There was the usual difficulty in attracting and retaining staff (Roberts, 2005) but, also, the quality of the engagement of those who did remain was often deeply concerning, especially when one considered what this meant for the students. I came to see that staffing these schools was a constituent factor in the quality of teaching the students received. It seemed that the disproportionate effort of the students to get to school was not always matched by what they received when they got there. Staffing shortages, mostly teachers in their first appointment (or first leadership appointment), limited access to professional development for staff, and some staff who would clearly rather not be there, seemed like a fundamental injustice (Roberts, 2005). To be fair, many of these teachers were learning to live and teach in a social environment vastly different from where they had lived their lives to that point (McConaghy, 2005). However, that students' futures were involved quickly removes any relativistic justification.

Stirring the anger of injustice within me further was the structural disadvantage the students in my community experienced – from the time they travelled to their nearest school each day (especially in the wet, when the short route was impassable, adding another 50 minutes to the journey), to being senior students studying for competitive exams by candlelight after helping on the farm and after the generator was turned off each night. These students were battling an unjust system. In a competitive system, they were like a football team competing against students on the same field, with the same rules, but without the same equipment or training.

Standing up to what I saw as inequality, and highlighting the associated issues and challenges, led me on a path of activism, punctuated by positions within the State's teachers' union. This afforded some amazing opportunities, like a grant for a research project (Roberts, 2005), which I will discuss further later in this chapter, and positions within the curriculum authority, equity funding schemes and the teacher registration authority. However, these experiences ultimately led me away from activism and into the standpoint from which I now write. While this work may have achieved some positive changes for students in rural schools, it always seemed that I was standing outside 'common sense', or having to compromise what was, in my opinion, genuinely needed. Upon reflection, I was developing a rural standpoint that was in conflict with the dominant discourse of the time.

My purpose in recounting this extended biography is to highlight two important points about standpoint: first, it doesn't necessarily imply a position germane to the self like the location of our childhood, gender or ethnicity; second, we cannot control who we have become or how we arrive at researching (in this instance, the rural) any more than we can separate ourselves from it. I've been grappling with what this means for my own work and wondering if somehow it undermines any aspiration towards quality research or potential policy impact. I don't think it does. More importantly, I think it is important to embrace my experience, as it has (hopefully) allowed me to speak about these issues in a knowledgeable and compassionate way that may be helpful for others in understanding the experiences and challenges of rural communities. Indeed, this chapter is as much about encouraging you, the reader, to reflect upon biography as part of uncovering and understanding your research motivations as it is about the position on a rural standpoint I have developed.

As I write elsewhere, the significance in researching the rural is in its attention to the particularity and subjectivity of places (Roberts & Green, 2013). In a globalised world, the rural allows us to see the impact of policies and ideologies that have become obscured by the familiarity of modern metropolitan life. Thus, our research speaks not only to the rural, but to the non-rural as well, in that it can shed light on what it takes for granted and what it has lost in the process of modernity. To be clear, I am not implying here only a qualitative approach to research. I am questioning the traps of chasing the chimera of objectivity implied in forms of methodological purism and suggesting that there is more to be gained from openly embracing the opportunities of experience in all forms of research.

Developing a standpoint through research

Part of the activism I referred to earlier included obtaining a study grant from the New South Wales Teachers' Federation to research the staffing of rural, remote and isolated schools in Australia. These grants are aimed at allowing the recipient to travel and research a topic of importance to the Union in order to assist in the development of union policy. Rather than travel overseas, where the issues seemed ubiquitous and equally intractable in sparsely populated areas, I chose to fill what I saw as a policy gap in our understanding here in Australia. There seemed to be a lot of hearsay and assumption in relation to these matters that were largely unhelpful in coming to clear, definite and evidence-based policy. For example, at the time, the recent Human Rights and Equal Opportunity Commission Report (HREOC, 2000) into rural and remote education was highlighting the staffing of these schools as a significant, and perhaps most important, factor in raising the educational achievement of rural and remote students. In doing so, it suggested the expansion of 'incentives' to attract and retain teachers, and better prepare them. Just what this might mean practically, however, was left as assumed.

The report, *Staffing an Empty Schoolhouse: Attracting and Retaining Teachers in Rural, Remote and Isolated Communities* (Roberts, 2005), set out to investigate the problem of the attraction and retention of staff in rural schools and propose new approaches to overcoming these intractable problems. Not having any formal research training, I decided to take an evaluative approach and look at the experiences and insights of people working in the various jurisdictional staffing directorates, and also the different approaches to staffing these schools around Australia and their effectiveness, as well as directly surveying teachers in these schools themselves about their experiences and perspectives on what would work. Consequently the report comprised tables and descriptive statistics from a survey, comments from survey participants, union officials and education department officials, a policy analysis and a limited review of the literature. Overall it proposed a model of staffing rural schools that involved four components: the *economic*, that is, making rural teaching economically attractive; the *social*, offsetting or compensating for social isolation; *professionalism*, that rural teaching is a distinctive professional-teaching activity; and *rural difference*, recognition that the rural is a distinct educational context (Roberts, 2005).

Notably both personal professional interests and those of the funder weighed into decisions of method and, equally importantly, presentation. A few assumptions come into relief here. The first is a view about 'evidence-based' policy. I had indeed come to a position that we needed evidence in order to make decisions about the Union's policy positions, as well as to mount a convincing case to the media and government. Thus, the objective of achieving change was at the forefront of my decisions. Second, I consciously intended throughout to position myself as 'expert' on these matters, and to carve out an important political niche. I like to hope that this position taking was motivated by a genuine concern and that I respected the values and experiences of rural teachers. However, a positioning as a political activist/researcher representing the struggles of marginalised groups raises particular ethical concerns (see Gristy, Chapter 8 this volume).

Clearly the standpoint from which the report was produced had more to do with traditional notions of class and marginalisation than with rurality. However, the inclusion of the two areas of professionalism and rural difference (that I downplayed at the time because they conflicted with my unionist orientation and industrial motivation) signals a subtle shift I was undertaking, largely influenced by my experience in rural schools and through the course of the research project. I came to understand, and have since developed the view further, that the issues impacting on rural students are at the intersection of the traditionally separate areas of policy and curriculum (Rizvi & Lingard, 2010). At issue was more than just a matter of getting a teacher into each classroom: these teachers needed to be appropriate. I do not mean here the recent obsession with a standardised form of quality. I mean someone who could relate to the students and, through that relationship, make what was being taught meaningful. That some teachers only lived in the community for as little time as possible, and didn't mix in the community, meant that they didn't understand the students' lives and the 'funds of knowledge'

(Moll, Amanti, Neff & Gonzalez, 1992) they brought to school. Instead, these teachers persisted with attempting to transmit a curriculum in terms meaningful to them based on their metropolitan mindsets, resulting all too often in student disengagement, their own diminishing professional satisfaction and, ultimately, staff turnover (see Roberts, 2013). There existed a blurring between the professional and industrial – with the professional here leaning more towards an accountability to students, rather than focusing on general work practices. Importantly, that again references the idea of standpoint. Looking at the issue from the position of the rural necessitated recognising and acknowledging the difficult reality, for a unionist, that there was more at issue than ensuring just working conditions.

At this point I would encourage you to consider both the influences and experiences that have led you to researching the rural, and how they may impact upon your subsequent work.

On standpoint

In using the label 'standpoint', I am building upon the tradition of *standpoint theory*, which assumes that a person's perspectives are shaped by their social locations. Rather than being a singular perspective, such as gender, a standpoint works at the intersection of a person's various positions, such as gender, class, ethnicity and (in this argument) rurality, to influence how they see the world. It recognises that, while everyone's experience is different, there are also broadly identifiable perspectives that either constitute the dominant culture or are marginalised by it (Williams, 1958). In this way, the dominant culture sets the tone of society and those outside it need to put their way of being aside and learn to pass in it (Griffin, 2012). The idea of a 'standpoint', arguably begun by Hegel and his discussion of master–slave relations, and also Marx on the positioning of labour, was brought into popular usage by Nancy Hartsock, looking at the relations between men and women, in what she would explicitly call a feminist standpoint (Griffin, 2012). Whilst initially remaining rooted in feminist theory, the development of a feminist epistemology has contributed a number of important concepts for social research, and potentially to the development of a rural standpoint. Notably, Haraway's notion of 'situated knowledges', that knowledge is socially situated and therefore only ever partial (Haraway, 1988), and Harding's (1993) notion of 'strong objectivity', suggest that the perspectives of the marginalised can help create more objective accounts of the world and should therefore be the starting point of research.

This approach of starting with those who have traditionally been outside the dominant mode of production of knowledge and the institutions in which it is generated has enabled standpoint to be applied more generally to facilitate the perspectives of other marginalised groups – for example, in Australia by Martin Nakata as an Indigenous Standpoint (Nakata, 2007). This general applicability may deem the appending of adjectives like 'feminist' or 'Indigenous' superfluous, as standpoint comes to represent working from the situated perspectives of all peoples and groups. However, initially at least, the appending of such adjectives is valuable, as it signals a group or perspective that has not previously been identified or able to speak on its own terms, and thus has remained outside knowledge production. While Nakata brings an Indigenous perspective, an equally important perspective he includes for the purpose here is the location of the learner as a site of interaction of competing perspectives (Nakata, 2007). He points out that standpoint is not simply another perspective on knowledge that exists simply by virtue of a person's biography or ethnicity. Rather, it is something that has to be *produced* to engage with the questions found in that perspective and, crucially, a distinct form of analysis to that which influences other people's understandings and is accountable beyond the inherent standpoint (Nakata, 2007). This is an extension of Harding's 'strong objectivity', emerging from Haraway's 'situated knowledge', which seeks to transform everyone's understandings of the world. In a research approach, it draws in various perspectives, while requiring them all to account for themselves and their production in order to expand everyone's understandings.

The notion of standpoint as produced is central to Reid and Green's (2009) use of standpoint in relation to professional practice theory. Illustrating standpoint as epistemology, the appended adjective of 'feminist', 'Indigenous' or even 'rural' is not used in this construction. This gets away from a potential limitation of other approaches, which imply that the researcher must in some way have a lived or organic affinity with the perspective. For this argument, such an approach would imply that a 'rural' standpoint could only be achieved by someone with extensive rural experience or heritage. Instead, Reid and Green suggest that professional practice research 'has different aims from conventional scientific research, in that the knowledge produced is "insider/outsider" knowledge *in, for* and *with* the profession, rather than external knowledge generated *about* the profession' (Reid & Green 2009: 174). This approach is highly relevant to rural educational research on at least three fronts: first, as rural educational research is about the production of knowledge and understandings in rural schooling, it is professional practice research; second, rural educational research is inevitably about insider/outsider knowledges (see Brann-Barrett and Hamm, Chapters 5 and 6 in this volume, respectively), and the place of the rural in a cosmopolitan world; and, finally, rural educational research needs to be about, as I have argued, rural meanings rather than endeavouring to impose non-rural values.

Valuing situated knowledges and building upon strong objectivity, Reid and Green implore researchers to do the 'intellectual and imaginative work that is required to "keep ourselves honest"' (2009: 180). Additionally, Green suggests that standpoint requires '*will, intellect*, and *imagination* to take up a standpoint that is not organically one's own' (personal communication, 2013). This construction suggests that a standpoint other than that occupied through biography can come to be appreciated if we, as researchers, are willing to do the hard work. We must have the *will* to understand other ways of seeing and experiencing the world to invest the effort to undertake the necessary ethnographic and intellectual work. *Intellectually* we must engage in the hard work of both coming to know our own predispositions and position in relation to the research, and doing the reading and research to come to know other accounts of the world. Finally we must put this will and intellect to work in *imagining* the world as another. We may not be able to know the world from another's perspective, but with *will*, *intellect* and *imagination* we are able to engage on the terms of another and represent this with honesty and integrity.

At this point the question for you, the reader, to consider is just how you would engage with, and account for, this issue in your research.

Using a rural standpoint

A standpoint in research is more than an intellectual position. It embodies an epistemological dimension and predisposes an approach to research. Here I examine just what a rural standpoint includes in my experience and how it influences the research task. I'll again develop this discussion in relation to the report mentioned earlier to suggest an approach to rural research that develops through a rural standpoint. I aim to raise issues that you may come across in your own research, and show the importance of reflecting critically on our work.

An initial re-examination of the evidence for that report, using more sophisticated statistical approaches and qualitative methods, and now more informed by research, indicates that understanding place is an important component in the professional lives of teachers in rural and remote schools (Roberts, 2010). The method used in the report matched the intent, and this intent structured the organisation of its arguments and conclusions. It was essentially what I would now call 'mixed method'. This is particularly the case in that it exhibits the failing of much of what is termed 'mixed method', as the components were conducted independently and brought together to illustrate the main arguments that arose. It was essentially the sequential use of quantitative (often a mix of surveys and statistics) and qualitative (often interviews or survey comments) methods to investigate the same issue (Johnson & Onwuegbuzie, 2004), or their simultaneous use without really influencing each component (Denzin, 2010). However, when deployed strategically, in an integrative fashion, a mixed method approach can assist the researcher obtain a fuller and more informed picture of the issue being investigated (Torrance, 2012). However, such approaches are still often limited by a predication to put method over subject (Denzin, 2010). Such an emphasis can result in the problem remaining obscured by concerns about the independent validity of each method used.

This is where a standpoint becomes important. I return to the work of the report I described earlier to illustrate this point. The report was primarily concerned with impact, and traditional notions of disadvantage influenced it. This emphasis in turn obscured the real problem and limited its effectiveness in representing and acting in the interests of rural students and communities. Instead,

I suggest now that *focusing on the problem to be investigated, rather than the method of investigation*, should be a central tenet of rural educational research (Roberts & Green, 2013). Such an approach forms part of the philosophical foundation that should inform a mixed method approach (Madsen and Adriansen, 2004), resulting in different paradigms informing and influencing each other, as well as the research problem. By not taking such an approach with the initial report, and by only applying the most basic frequency statistical calculations, I missed an opportunity to deeply interrogate the influences on teachers' motivations to work and stay in rural schools. (However, this new understanding opens up new opportunities to revisit and reread that report, as I have begun here.) This disposition to focus on the problem over method in rural research (Roberts & Green, 2013) is part of what can be called a rural standpoint, with this perspective having significant implications for the methods used and drawing to the forefront the intent of our research. This standpoint seeks to get away from the rural–urban, local–global binaries, and to position and recognise the inherent value in places and rural meanings. Following on from this is a concern for social justice and with representing the interests of those otherwise marginalised by the dominance of the urban as the accepted 'normal'.

Using a rural standpoint raises two problems: first, the difficulty in defining the rural and, second, the challenge not to treat all the rural as the same. As Cloke (2006) suggests, the primary problem in studying the rural is the difficulty in defining what the site of study is, because the rural is a socially constructed space with competing and layered conceptions of its meaning and value. Modernism has tended to position the rural on the negative defining side of the binary, with the future, sophistication and advancement associated with the cosmopolitan urban (Corbett, 2006; Cuervo & Wyn, 2012; Popkewitz, 2008), and therefore preferred, future. However, this is also rural research's greatest opportunity, as the value of studying rural places is in fact within the problem of method and the difficulty in defining the rural: that the multiplicity of rural places and perceptions of the rural remind us of the forces that have become otherwise invisible, and that, inevitably, place matters. Implicitly this is shown by the fact that much rural research uses the theoretical tools of place and situated practice (e.g. Green, 2008; Gruenewald, 2003). Similarly, much 'place-based' education research uses rural examples (e.g. Gruenewald & Smith, 2008; Sobel, 1994; Somerville, Power & de Carteret, 2009). In so doing, they recognise that it is through a connection with the physical and social environment, and increasingly the local economy, that we come to 'know' the rural. With such an approach, we can better understand the larger (global) social, political and economic forces that treat all places, including all rural places, as the same.

In recognising the multiplicity of rural places, and therefore making space to observe the particular way that broader social forces intersect and construct place, Reid et al. (2010) propose a model of rural social space that links demography, economy and geography. It is, they argue, the unique connection of each of these with the others that constructs each place and the way it is perceived and lived by those occupying the place in any particular instance. This attention to the construction of place reminds us that meaning is made in place from the intersection of our understandings, perceptions and expectations, and that educationally this in turn not only influences students' understandings of the world through their experiences of place, but also mediates their expectations and aspirations (Dalley-Trim & Alloway, 2010). The existence of binaries, however, brings with it implicit value-judgements about the relative importance, appropriateness and even 'normality' of aspects of geography, demography and economy that are equally powerful as any objective construction of place. In countering this, a rural standpoint inherently values the particularity and subjectivity of places, and reconstructs any binary as an opportunity.

This is certainly something I did not appreciate in my initial report. It was, after all, conceived in a deficit frame of rural 'disadvantage' and proposed incentives to help ameliorate what teachers not from these places would see as negative aspects, and therefore disincentives to staying. However, such a construction did not address the attitude to place and the subsequent nature of learning produced by those who merely *inhabited*, compared to those that *dwelt* in, these places. It was only after developing a rural standpoint that I have retrospectively been able to recognise and articulate this new understanding. Furthermore, this realisation has allowed me to move to an enlarged view of social justice (Cuervo, 2012) for rural communities that incorporates a form of spatial justice (Soja, 2010), built on recognising the subjectivity and specificity of rural places (Roberts & Green, 2013).

Returning to Green's construction of standpoint as comprising '*will, intellect, and imagination*' (personal communication, 2013), my reflections on the earlier report reminded me that those of us involved in rural research have perhaps a dual responsibility to recognise rural meanings, while guarding against limiting notions of rurality or romanticising the rural. Instead, research needs to be able to speak from and with the rural, but also speak back to the rural: it needs to be able to sensitively raise uncomfortable truths for both the rural and the non-rural. To do this, a rural heritage may indeed be problematic for bringing strong objectivity to research, or at least is not a necessity, in that a combination of 'will', 'intellect' and 'imagination' can allow us to empathise with the perspectives of others. Furthermore, 'will', 'intellect' and 'imagination' suggest that there are other 'objective' perspectives on the world, and that a rural standpoint is not merely just another viewpoint. While it is hard to be sure, I think for me the imagined rural of my family's mythology helped me understand that the rural – or, more broadly, how we understand other places – is as much imagined as real. Thus Soja's (1996) trialectic of space as 'perceived', 'conceived' and 'lived' resonates with me and gave me a theoretical entry point to thinking about the rural in the modern world.

Looking back, it is apparent that I brought many of the limitations I have highlighted to the original Schoolhouse Report I began this chapter revisiting. Subsequent reflection has exposed their influence and allowed me to reconsider that work and reinterpret many of its findings. In other ways, though, the report provides evidence that a rural standpoint can be developed. More importantly, though, the experience of reflecting on that report has changed my standpoint as a researcher investigating the rural, and shaped my approach to subsequent projects and reporting from them. The lessons as I see them are that, as researchers, we can choose to see things differently only if we are willing to take on the perspectives of others and, further, that our personal biographies are opportunities to engage with rather than limitations to exclude. A standpoint changes how we understand, and entails a particular approach to research, containing aspects of reconstructing understandings through enlarging the range of accounts of the world. It recognises that not all groups experience the world the same, nor are groups homogenous. In rural terms, a standpoint values the situatedness and subjectivity of rural places and rural meanings, though it must also contain a reflexivity to acknowledge that these meanings are entwined with their different rural contexts and communities and that they are produced differently on a variety of scales. In so doing, the rural works as a metaphor for the local, as we are able to observe how dominant global cosmopolitan knowledges and understandings are produced, and the processes through which they marginalise other ways of understanding the world and deny situated knowledges. But this is the position I have come to, and I would encourage you, the reader, to explicitly consider how you understand a rural standpoint and incorporate this understanding in your work.

References

Bourdieu, P. & Wacquant, L. (1992). *An Invitation to Reflexive Sociology*. University of Chicago: Chicago Press.

Cloke, P. (2006). Conceptualizing rurality. In P. J. Cloke, T. Marsden & P. H. Mooney (eds), *Handbook of Rural Studies*. London: Sage.

Corbett, M. (2006). Educating the country out of the child and educating the child out of the country: An excursion in spectrology. *Alberta Journal of Educational Research*, 52(4): 289–301.

Cuervo, H. & Wyn, J. (2012). *Young People Making it Work: Continuity and Change in Rural Places*. Carlton, Victoria: Melbourne University Publishing.

Cuervo, H. (2012). Enlarging the social justice agenda in education: An analysis of rural teachers' narratives beyond the distributive dimension. *Asia-Pacific Journal of Teacher Education*, 40(2): 83–95.

Dalley-Trim, L. and Alloway, N. (2010). Looking 'outward and onward' in the outback: Regional Australian students' aspirations and expectations for their future as framed by dominant discourses of further education and training. *Australian Educational Researcher*, 37(2): 107–125.

Denzin, N. (2010). Moments, mixed methods, and paradigm dialogs. *Qualitative Inquiry*, 16(6): 419–427.

Green, B. (ed.) (2008). *Spaces & Places: The NSW Rural (Teacher) Education Project*. Wagga Wagga: Centre for Information Studies, Charles Sturt University.

Griffin, E. (2012). Standpoint theory of Sandra Harding and Julia T. Wood. In E. Griffin, *A First Look at Communication Theory*. New York: McGraw Hill.

Gruenewald, D. (2003). The best of both worlds: A critical pedagogy of place. *Educational Researcher*, 32(4): 3–12.

Gruenewald, D., & Smith, G. (eds) (2008). *Place-Based Education in the Global Age*. New York: Lawrence Erlbaum Associates.

Haraway, D. (1988). Situated knowledges: The science question in feminism and the privilege of partial perspective. *Feminist Studies*, 14(3): 575–599.

Harding, S. (ed.) (2004). *The Feminist Standpoint Theory Reader: Intellectual & Political Controversies*. New York: Routledge.

—— (1993). Rethinking standpoint epistemology: What is 'strong objectivity'? In L. Alcoff and E. Potter (eds), *Feminist Epistemologies*. New York: Routledge.

HREOC (2000). *Emerging Themes: National Inquiry into Rural and Remote Education*. Canberra: Commonwealth of Australia.

Johnson, R. B. & Onwuegbuzie, A. J. (2004). Mixed methods research: A research paradigm whose time has come. *Educational Researcher*, 33(7): 14–26.

Madsen, L. M., & Adriansen, H. K. (2004). Understanding the use of rural space: The need for multi-methods. *Journal of Rural Studies*, 20(4): 485–497.

McConaghy, C. (2005). *Transience and Teaching: Place and the New Psychoanalytic Sociologies of Teaching*. Paper 4 of the Bush Tracks Symposium. Australian Association for Research In Education Annual Conference, Parramatta, University of Western Sydney, November 2005.

Moll, L. C., Amanti, C., Neff, D. & Gonzalez, N. (1992). Funds of knowledge for teaching: Using a qualitative approach to connect homes and classrooms. *Theory into Practice*, 31(2): 132–141.

Nakata, M. (2007). The cultural interface. *Australian Journal of Indigenous Education*, 36: 7–14.

Popkewitz, T. S. (2008). *Cosmopolitanism and the Age of School Reform: Science, Education, and Making Society by Making the Child*. New York: Routledge.

Reid, J. & Green, B. (2009). Researching (from) the standpoint of the Practitioner. In B. Green (ed.), *Understanding and Researching Professional Practice*. Rotterdam: Sense Publishers.

Reid, J., Green, B., Cooper, M., Hastings, W., Lock, G. & White, S. (2010). Regenerating rural social space? Teacher education for rural-regional sustainability. *Australian Journal of Education*, 54(3): 262–267.

Rizvi, F. & Lingard, B. (2010). *Globalizing Education Policy*. New York: Routledge.

Roberts, P. (2005). *Staffing an Empty Schoolhouse: Attracting and Retaining Teachers in Rural, Remote and Isolated Communities*. Sydney: New South Wales Teachers Federation.

—— (2010). Rebuilding the schoolhouse: From the 'empty schoolhouse' to a schoolhouse in each place. Australian Association for Research In Education Annual Conference, 29 November–2 December 2010, Melbourne, Australia.

—— (2013). The role of an authentic curriculum and pedagogy for rural schools and the professional satisfaction of rural teachers. *Australian and International Journal of Rural Education*, 23(2): 89–99.

Roberts, P. & Green, B. (2013). Researching rural place: On social justice and rural education. *Qualitative Inquiry*, prepublished. doi: 10.1177/1077800413503795.

Sher, J. P. & Sher, K. R. (1994). Beyond the conventional wisdom: Rural development as if Australia's rural people and communities really mattered. *Journal of Research in Rural Education* 10: 2–43.

Sobel, D. (1994). *Place-Based Education: Connecting Classrooms & Communities.* Great Barrington: The Orion Society.

Soja, E. W. (1996). *Thirdspace: Journeys to Los Angeles and Other Real-and-Imagined Places.* Cambridge, MA: Blackwell Publishing.

—— (2010). *Seeking Spatial Justice.* Minneapolis: University of Minnesota Press.

Somerville, M., Power, K. & de Carteret, P. (2009). *Landscapes and Learning: Place Studies for a Global World.* Netherlands: Sense Publishing.

Torrance, H. (2012). Triangulation, respondent validation, and democratic participation in mixed methods research. *Journal of Mixed Methods Research,* 6(2): 111–123.

Williams, R. (1958). *Culture and Society.* London: Chatto and Windus.

Part III

Ethics and reciprocity

Chapter 10

Research and remembrance in a rural community

A step toward ethical learning[1]

Linda Farr Darling

> Wouldn't everybody be happier knowing, knowing all this happened? And then let it go – let it go – now it's finished ... and go on with our lives in a better direction ... peacefully.
>
> (Karen Markin, interview 9 May 2012)[2]

The woman's voice, Karen's, is laced with a soft Russian accent. Between phrases she pauses as if to make certain each word is right. Karen looks to be in her late sixties with warm brown eyes, and calloused hands that lie quietly on her lap. She swallows once, then looks out at her interviewer, who sits holding a flip video camera. Her question hangs in the air. The interviewer shifts a little as if searching for a comfortable position. Karen signals with a wave that she has finished speaking and the camera is turned off. An electronic hum is now the only sound in the room.

The room is a multi-grade secondary classroom in a small school (kindergarten through Grade 12) in a rural community located in a mountainous region of south-eastern British Columbia, Canada. Although working independently this morning, Karen and her interviewer are participating with dozens of middle- and high-school students, teachers, professional filmmakers and community members in a semester-long research project to 'learn about and from' (Britzman, 1998, p. 18) members of a minority group who settled in this valley. Present-day Doukhobors are descended from a group of Russian Christians whose non-Orthodox religious beliefs forced their migration from Siberia to Canada around 1900. The students are studying archives, consulting historians online and exploring historic sites so they can bring to light Doukhobor values and practices that have left traces here. They will also produce short films for a public screening. At the heart of the exploration are interviews with Doukhobor elders who, like Karen, live in the valley and have stories to share about their childhoods, many of them troubling to hear.

My own role is that of a researcher at the side, where the project on Doukhobor history becomes a space in which I consider the ethical dimensions of remembrance that unfold within rural contexts. My enquiry reflects one facet of my work as a teacher educator responsible for preparing, recruiting and supporting teachers for rural communities in British Columbia, places where finding and keeping teachers can be challenging. Importantly, my responsibility includes learning about the complex relationships that exist between small schools and the communities in which they are nested, in part so I might be able to contribute to the flourishing of both. In collaboration with college and university colleagues, graduate students, rural educators and community participants, I engage in research that I hope will shed light on living, learning and teaching in these special places.

With this project, I want to better understand encounters with troubling knowledge in a community; to find out how students and other researchers ethically engage with participants through listening and questioning; and discover what it may mean to work though loss (including one's own) when dwelling in other people's memories, in what Levine (2000, p. 1) calls 'a vicarious past'. Examining a school project steeped in local history represents rich opportunities for me to come to a deeper appreciation of what rural teachers need to know when engaging students in place-conscious learning. In turn, I hope this knowledge can help me and other teacher educators more effectively prepare rural teacher candidates, and more thoughtfully pursue our own studies within rural contexts.

At times in the project, those involved will be confronted by what Britzman and others have called 'difficult knowledge' (Britzman, 1998, 2000; Simon et al., 2000) – difficult with regard to its traumatic content, and difficult because of the ethical and psychic demand it makes on the listener. Within each telling is a call to bear witness to the suffering of another, suffering caused by deliberate human action. It's an unsettling demand to attend to another, and be implicated in knowledge that often comes too late for the listener to intervene or respond directly. Difficult knowledge holds potential to shake prior beliefs we have about people or historical events, and it can disrupt understandings we have of ourselves as ethical subjects experiencing our own contemporary 'crises of witnessing' (Britzman, 1998, p. 120). Difficult knowledge can be felt as 'a critique of the self's coherence or view of itself in the world' (Britzman, 1998, p. 118). Our first impulse may be to resist or refuse it.

With her question 'Wouldn't everybody be happier knowing all this happened?', and her subsequent entreaty to '*then* let it go – now it's finished', Karen has reminded listeners of the troubled history of Doukhobors in the valley, including her own childhood experiences. In interviews, she and others have described painful events that students have also discovered in their studies: from 1953 to 1959, their own village was the site of a residential school for Doukhobor children taken forcibly from their families, and Karen was one of these. She has asked students to hear her out, to bear witness to her memories. Karen has also, though unwittingly, reminded teachers of several risks entailed. First, important as it may be for students to hear, historical knowledge may cause more unhappiness than ignorance. Second, the story itself is not over, the past is not 'finished'. It needs to be recognised as a concern of the present. Remembering the Doukhobor past is, in this sense, an ethical obligation to examine what might be learned from it. Karen's question also contains a glimmer of hope. By facing difficult knowledge instead of turning away, listeners might begin working through the rupture it presents to their own historical thinking in and about this place. They might grasp more fully what happened in the community sixty years ago and how it has affected the world-views and self-understandings of the people here (including themselves), whether or not they claim Doukhobor ancestry.

As an educational researcher looking in, I am asking questions about difficult knowledge that are pedagogical in the broadest sense, important for learning to engage with others as well as understanding the past. I believe the questions matter to anyone who feels the force of Arendt's appeal to approach history 'as an incomplete project of becoming an ethical subject in relation to other ethical subjects' (Britzman, 2000, p. 37). Within particular communities, where place is never a fixed site but 'an articulation of social relations and cultural and political practices' (Schafft, 2010, p. 11) continually in flux, these questions play out in different ways. In small rural communities, they may, in fact, be magnified. The intensity of rurality (Balfour, Mitchell & Molestane, 2008) – that is, the ways in which life is experienced in a geographically and socially isolated place – likely affects how community members see themselves, and how others see them: as neighbors, as ethical subjects in relation.

For researchers attending to rural places, the questions we ask take on the distinctive hues of identities, histories and cultures that intersect, both harmoniously and divisively, within a small community. These are places where, in some capacity, everyone knows everyone else. Anonymity is impossible, or nearly so. In rural places researchers' questions risk upsetting a delicate balancing act between community members or groups. In these close settings, the ethics that animate questions and inform data gathering and analysis are coloured by a place where multiple generations interact on a daily basis and where one need not disturb the soil much to find the layered, the variegated past underneath. Our 'research footprint' (White et al., 2012) or the effects of our work on the wellbeing and the self-understandings of a community is always a question (Gruenewald, 2006); encounters with difficult knowledge bring it to the foreground.

There are additional questions. This chapter tells one story of a school's attempt to re-examine historical episodes through the voices of some of its elders and the listening ears of its youth. These local events reflect universal concerns such as freedom of expression, self-determination and pacifism, alongside world-wide phenomena of diaspora, religious persecution and exile. As a place-conscious project attempting to address global issues through local lenses (Corbett, 2009; Gruenewald, 2003; Gruenewald & Smith, 2008) it inevitably raises ethical questions about how to live with others (Putnam, 1987) as well as how to live well in a particular place (Orr, 1991; Gruenewald, 2003). 'Can there be a more hopeful way to live historically?' asks Simon (2000, p. 18). How should teachers and students approach history so close at hand and how should they engage with those who lived through the traumas they are recounting? What are the obligations of researchers, including students, teachers and academics, when revisiting issues that may still carry potential to divide a community? And, finally, how should these stories be interpreted, presented and shared?

The Doukhobors

Toil and a peaceful life.

(Doukhobor maxim)

In 1885 in Russia, a small Christian sect whose members were called Doukhobors (literally, 'spirit-wrestlers') set fire to their weapons in a dramatic refusal to swear allegiance to the Tsar and register for the military. In response, the Tsar banished Doukhobors to Siberia and Georgia for their pacifist beliefs. In 1899, 7,500 exiles migrated to the prairie provinces of Canada. The immigrants were told they would be free to follow their spiritual calling to 'toil and a peaceful life' within traditional communes. However, by 1908, new legislation required registration of births, marriages and deaths, and men needed to become naturalised citizens in order to own property. Guided by their leader, Peter Verigin, over 5,000 Doukhobors refused to comply and headed west to the province of British Columbia to start over again on land held in Verigin's name (Plotnikoff, 2013).

Doukhobors were farmers and the rich, temperate valleys of the Kootenay region of British Columbia provided what they needed to build communal villages, create vegetable gardens and pastures and plant fruit trees (Hayward & Watson, 1919). The families grew what they ate and shared labours and harvests equally. During the first half of the century, they thrived in tight-knit communities, where they educated their children, built sawmills, grain elevators and jam factories, and dressed as they had in Russia, in home-spun blouses and headscarves. Leading separate lives from people nearby, Doukhobors were nonetheless known for their willingness to help those in need, particularly Japanese-Canadians interned in the area through World War II. However, their tenacious commitments to pacifism, shared ownership and homeschooling sparked repeated conflicts with provincial and federal governments. Especially troublesome were the actions of 'Freedomites', the most radical and controversial of Doukhobor sects (even controversial among Doukhobors) that became nationally infamous for nude protests and acts of arson.

Clashes culminated in 1953, when two empty schoolhouses were burned to protest government interference in homeschooling (Tarasoff, 1995). One hundred and fifty-three children, most from Freedomite families, were rounded up and forced into residential school to rid them of Doukhobor heritage and assimilate them into Canadian life. The children, many under the age of 10, lived in the New Denver dormitory for up to six years. Family interactions were limited to moments at the chain-link fence on alternate Sundays. Other Doukhobor children spent these years in hiding. Although the British Columbia government later expressed regret, there has never been an official apology to those who endured life in an institution they remember as violent and harsh. The niece of one of these survivors expressed a common sentiment: 'The children want an apology – they deserve an apology … when I look at some of them now, I see sadness in their eyes' (Netta Zeberoff, interview 5 October 2011, from 'Behind the Chain-Link Fence', retrieved February 5, 2013, http://www.ruralteachers.com).

The Doukhobor legacy has marked this place: stately square houses of pink brick nestle into hillsides, cherry and apple orchards line highways, and local place names and mailboxes reveal Russian roots. The vegetable soup, borscht, is served at most roadside restaurants. One cultivated delta is called Ootishenia, Russian for 'Place of Consolation'. Several museums are located on former communes, preserving Doukhobor traditions by showcasing handwork like embroidered scarves, woven sashes and wooden furniture. The effects of 'toil and a peaceful life' are honoured at these sites; the effects of so much conflict and dissonance through history are not as apparent, if there at all.

Despite its presence on the landscape, and despite many children with Doukhobor backgrounds, Doukhobor history is little known to students here. Russian is an optional second language in several schools, but Russian without its local context. The topics of Doukhobor diaspora, imprisonment of war resisters, labour camps, the residential school and decades of conflict with the government rarely appear in textbooks or provincial Ministry of Education documents. So, as in many rural places, the history curriculum in schools in the Kootenay region of British Columbia is mostly about somewhere else (Corbett, 2007).

The lack of Doukhobor history in schools is exacerbated by the fact that many with Doukhobor ancestry have disassociated themselves from their heritage since the conflicts between the government and Freedomite extremists. Although 40,000 Canadians claim to be descended from the original immigrants who fled Russia, most have assimilated into mainstream life and intermarried. Some have Anglicised their surnames. Parents and grandparents have told children not to stir things up; a museum guide noted that, in her family, the past 'was a topic you didn't talk about because it brought out really hurtful feelings' (Netta, quoted in student film 'Behind the Chain Link Fence' retrieved 3 February 2013 from http://www.ruralteachers.com).

Within this shadow, a partial eclipse of Doukhobor history, several teachers at Lucerne School in New Denver decided to develop the interdisciplinary, multimedia project for Grades 6–12 called 'Doukhobor Values: Then and now'. Though the project was infused with ethical themes and questions of social justice that could be examined in myriad ways, teachers believed students should decide the focus of their own enquiries and films, and that each conversation with a Doukhobor elder offered opportunity for a meaningful encounter in which powerful content would emerge. My own research focus remained on how these encounters, as possibilities for ethical learning, would unfold.

A place-conscious exploration

> When I first heard the word 'Doukhobor' I remember being filled with a sentiment of mixed terror, curiosity and admiration that I find hard to admit.
>
> (Gabrielle Roy, 1942)

The aims of the project thoughtfully aligned with rationales for place-conscious learning found in the literature where 'place' is viewed as both a resource for curricular exploration and a site for meaningful inquiry into broader human concerns (Gruenewald, 2003; Schafft, 2010; Sobel, 2003). Project leaders, including middle and secondary level Social Studies and English teachers, wanted to make visible the effects of Doukhobor culture on the valley. They were keenly aware that formal schooling has little to say about local experience (Schafft, 2010) and what it does say is permeated with negative stereotypes. Doukhobor values, in fact, represent the rural values of 'community, hard work, stewardship and frugality' increasingly viewed throughout North America as 'unsavory – backward, conservative and irrelevant – a native anathema to be eradicated' (Howley & Howley, 2010, p. 47).

As antidote to pervasive accounts about the irrelevance, if not unsavouriness, of rural values, teachers wanted to provide students with opportunities to make positive connections between their own lives and the values and practices of Doukhobors as exemplified by their commitments to pacifism, sustainable agriculture, craftsmanship and self-sufficiency. Many Lucerne students come from families whose occupations and preoccupations are defined by close relationships to the land, so teachers believed personal links would be easy to forge. If relevance to students' own lives was established, perhaps the Doukhobor way of life would be seen to have contemporary significance.

Following their trip to the Doukhobor Heritage Center at the valley's southern end, students generated a list of commitments they believed were foundational to practices in Doukhobor communes. They toured the nearby memorial to Verigin, the charismatic leader who brought the immigrants here. Students wrote that Doukhobors 'stood up for their beliefs' and 'helped whoever needed it', no matter their 'race or religion'. A number were impressed by Doukhobor practices of 'gathering, recycling and reusing everything', seeing connections to their own environmental concerns. Several noted that over time the region and their village have become home to other pacifists, including draft resisters from the United States during the Vietnam War.

The teachers were interested in pursuing these connections more deeply through archival studies and, most importantly, interviews, in almost all cases with seniors who live in the valley and are identified as Independents, members of the faith living within mainstream society. Because the history and landscape of the region has been significantly shaped by Doukhobors, their narrative is woven into the story New Denver tells about itself. Every community 'has an appreciation of its own historicity premised on the promise of its own continuity, its own futurity, that which is yet to come' (Simon, 2000, p. 20). New Denver is no exception. It regards itself as a village strongly committed to stewardship, ecological preservation and sustainable living, ideals with particular meanings and applications in practice that are hotly debated by residents. This lived reality comes as no surprise to rural researchers who 'suggest that place is generally an arena of both meaning and conflict' (Hayes-Conroy, 2008, p. 2). Through investigating how Doukhobor interpretations of these ideals were negotiated with others in the region, it was hoped students would come to see that 'place is itself an ideological-discursive concept; with positive and negative dimensions, and that placemaking is always a political act, with inherent problems and possibilities' (Cormack, Green & Reid, 2008, p. 74).

Interviews with elders were important parts of students' enquiries into the processes of 'placemaking' that characterised the Doukhobor community's relationships with the land and other valley inhabitants, even as they lived apart from them. As children of these communal homesteaders and strict religious devotees, those interviewed said they were pleased to share stories about growing up Doukhobor. Most welcomed the chance to engage with students, regarding focus groups and interviews as liberating exercises, and chances to interact with another generation. One elder explained on camera, 'It opens it up when you watch each other, when you communicate. You're asking questions, you're answering questions' (Peter Malloff, interview 9 May 2012). Several student-led meetings on Skype brought together Doukhobor descendants from communities isolated from each other on either end of the valley. The interactions prompted one participant to remark, 'Seeing the communities come together … it was like wildfire … in a good way! I've seen that through the technologies, through the children' (Leonard Markin, interview 9 May 2012).

Initially, interviews focused on activities and qualities of life in Doukhobor villages. Filmed conversations emphasised agrarian practices, religious principles and domestic responsibilities that struck resonant chords with young rural listeners who may have felt them as 'points of connection' (Simon, 2000, p. 12) to the Doukhobor settlers. These memories, ones that might easily evoke imaginative identification for students, illustrate what Simon calls 'remembrance as continuity and confirmation' (Simon, 2000, p. 19). Confirming a familiar historical narrative of peaceful settlement, toiling on the land, canning produce and so on, these memories were comfortable to hear. They led to affinities between the elders and youth that teachers hoped would emerge when they designed an inquiry into 'values then and now'. One example of imaginative attachment came at the filmmaking stage. Two of the younger students donned embroidered sashes and work boots and 'Photoshopped' their own images into a series of black and white archival photographs chronicling the Doukhobors' long journey to and across Canada. Personified by these two young students in costume, Doukhobors appear to happily embark on a homesteading adventure. Other students learned to sing and play Doukhobor hymns, bake Russian pastries and incorporate traditional designs and symbols into their own artwork.

As the enquiry deepened, other, more complex and emotionally charged stories surfaced through filmed interviews. Doukhobor elders revealed the darker sides of growing up in the valley. At first, participants expressed surprise that anyone cared to ask about their memories of Residential School, since the subject was rarely raised. Karen remarked, 'What I found interesting was that they even wanted to ask us questions about being Doukhobors, about our lives, what it was like, how we felt ... because nobody ever really asked us before' (Karen, retrieved 20 January 2013 from 'The Digital Storytelling Project' http://www.ruralteachers. com). Participants began to refer to the years in the Residential School as 'the New Denver part' or, more obliquely, 'the bad times ... the sad times'. Through students' forthright questions of individuals they were coming to know and care for, stories of circumstances surrounding the residential school years took shape. Sitting in a coffee shop with students who had asked about her childhood, Kathleen vividly recalled her mother's attempts to keep her home:

> I started hiding when I was six. For two years I was hiding all the time. There were times when my Mom would just be getting up and she would say, 'Oh! The police are almost on the doorstep.' And it was under the bed or into the closet, wherever ... that morning we went into the forest – that's where I was caught – in the forest.

After a long pause she added: 'You don't come out the same. You either walk away scarred or you walk away stronger' (interview with Kathleen Makertoff, 5 October 2011, retrieved 22 January 2013 from 'Behind the Chain Link Fence' http://www.ruralteachers.com).

In moments like these, 'difficult knowledge' emerged as something that might demand a more complex ethical response from individuals who were confronted by it. Remembrance took a turn from providing 'continuity and confirmation', with the familiar narrative students knew, and instead began to disrupt their present, 'in particular unsettling the sufficiency of terms on which the present recognises the past as one of its own concerns' (Simon, 2000, p. 20). Through the painful stories of Doukhobor elders, told to youth hearing them for the first time, remembrance became a practice of 'discontinuity and unsettlement' (Simon, 2000, p. 21).

For students who had investigated historical events before, the fact that residential schools existed was not shocking, and at least one question, asked in relation to Native survivors of residential schools, had been asked before: 'How could this happen to innocent children?' Hearing first-hand accounts from those who lived through these experiences in this very community was, however, even more troubling: 'How could it happen to these *particular* children? How could it happen here, in this village, the place where we have been raised and schooled ourselves? How did residents of New Denver respond? Our grandparents? Our great-grandparents?' Perhaps most unsettling of all: 'If this is our past, what does it say about our present?'

Encounters

> Having the students come to us and ask us about us made me feel even better about who I am and where I am.
>
> (Irene Malloff, interview 9 May 2012)

The teachers carefully prepared the ground, spending considerable time gathering resources, and delving into local archives in order to approach the project responsibly and thoughtfully. Although school curriculum seems to have an astonishing 'capacity to shut out as well as shut down conflict' (Britzman, 2000, p. 54), these teachers had decided to open it up with an exploration of Doukhobor history. They were aware of the risks in taking up a controversial topic within their small community, as were the two professional filmmakers working with them. Early conversations with families, including Doukhobor families, suggested that most wholeheartedly supported the endeavour.

Teachers approached students with the promise of film production under the guidance of professionals, who would work alongside. Not surprisingly, students were excited about the prospect of working with video cameras and editing software, as well as opportunities to leave school grounds. Before meeting with Doukhobor participants, there were classes devoted to their history, to diaspora and religious persecution. Other classes were held on research ethics. Students were guided in the construction of interview questions and interview etiquette, as well as filming skills and techniques. The filmmakers taught students to create storyboards based on themes they wanted to communicate, messages they intended to convey.

Teachers were concerned about the identifications students would make to the memories of others, particularly to painful childhood experiences participants might recount. How would they regard participants whose childhood recollections go back sixty years? Would they genuinely listen to their stories? Would they be able to see Doukhobors as more than victims? Teachers wanted students to find relevance, but they also wanted students to move beyond initial attachments and interpretations to a fuller understanding of the impact of experiences. Britzman reminds us that 'fleeting identifications in themselves cannot allow for ethical thought' (Britzman, 2000, p. 35) and teachers hoped for deeper engagement than what they first saw. Initial blogs revealed that many younger students emotionally attached to stories of the residential school by imagining themselves, 'not knowing if the rest of my family was still alive', and 'being scared if I was hiding', as if a natural disaster had separated parents from children or forced them to find temporary refuge. Several expressed relief that 'this doesn't happen anymore', suggesting faith in 'a metanarrative of moral progress' (Ranck, 2000, p. 187). It was clear others were listening for uplifting messages, or silver linings in the elders' stories of social violence, constructing 'redemptive fictions as morally inert as they are hopeful' (Levine, 2000, p. 1). 'Love conquers all' became a 'core message' for many younger students.

Some older students questioned why they hadn't been taught this history before. One blog entry reflects the anger several students levelled at teachers and parents: 'It's not fair. I'm part Doukhobor and I never knew this stuff!' Others were cynical, unsurprised that curriculum excluded such stories. After poring over newspaper accounts and photographs, Grade 11 and 12 students expressed a range of emotional responses. Even in their earnestness, reactions seemed detached from the particularities of events and appeared instead as generalised indignation in the face of injustice. Many of these abstract responses came through their first attempts to identify the 'core messages' that filmmakers encouraged them to find.

With the interviews, students' relationships with the past shifted. Through hearing first-hand experiences, students' responses began to change, reflecting relationships they were building with participants. These conversations, extending over several sessions, offered listeners chances to approach others as individuals, to be attentive to their stories and continue to bear witness to painful memories. Creating films deepened engagement with participants and their memories. Proponents of media literacy point to filmmaking as a way to empower youth to tell their own and others' stories (Buckingham, 2003) and these students believed they were hearing something important. As pedagogical space in which to work through their own struggles with troubling knowledge, filming the interviews promoted sustained engagement with the stories and storytellers. As ethical response to hearing memories of others, filmmaking called for the students to hold history open, to preserve the language and tone of dialogue, and to keep photographs and documents close at hand for the sake of telling stories as faithfully as possible. Their collective sense of purpose – to share these stories with others in the community – brought an unusual level of focus and dedication to the task.

Students worked in groups of three or four to create eleven films, all under two minutes in length. Films by younger students (Grades 6–9) tended to be light-hearted in tone and focused on customs: 'Borscht', for example, focused entirely on the preparation of soup, the camera never moving from the pot on the stove, and the hands of the woman chopping beets and cabbage as she explained the recipe.

Older students confronted tensions between the obligation they felt to respond to participants, and the difficulties of understanding, much less conveying powerful loss. When a woman who had agreed to an interview about her childhood in residential school found herself unable to speak at all, the boys who had travelled to meet her were stunned by her silence and sudden exit from the room. It was perhaps the first time they realised the depth of emotion these memories contained. When days later she sent an email, it was a simple declaration that she has worked 'to forgive', and can now see the other side, a statement they found impossible to reconcile with what they had witnessed.

Some students sensed that there are still losses to mourn and questions to explore, even about their own ambiguous relationships with the past. Their ambivalent feelings about whether New Denver residents (their relatives) should or could have intervened to protest the residential school, their worry about how best to portray people's memories on screen, and their confusion about disparate perspectives, became evident as they prepared for the screening.

One film stands out as an example. It includes clips of two women interviewed in separate locations; each is white-haired and soft-spoken. The first, a Doukhobor, is drinking tea in a sunlit room as she describes hiding under her bed as a child, terrified, but also angry, wanting to run away. The scene shifts to the second woman, a former residential schoolteacher surrounded by patchwork pillows, who explains that we should do whatever we can to help children to find a place in the world: 'it was for their own good every child had to attend school'. The film returns to the first woman, who was eventually taken to New Denver. She's answering a student's question we don't hear, perhaps about regret: 'Everything that happened in your life made you the way you are now, so I don't know, do you change it?' (Agnes, interview 6 October 2011, and Kathleen Makertoff, interview 5 October 2011, retrieved 22 January 2013 from 'Behind the Chain Link Fence' http://www.ruralteachers.com).

The film screening brought over 300 people to the New Denver village hall, rare numbers for a school event in a small community. 'It was standing room only, filled with people from up and down the valley' (Terry Taylor, interview 9 May 2012) who gathered to hear children tell the stories of children, echoes of memories that went back sixty years.

Hope in learning from echoes

> When they started singing loudly again, I think that's when they saw hope.
> (student blog post on Doukhobor hymns)

In thinking about ethical risks and possible benefits of research within rural communities, I have found it useful to consider its parallels with place-conscious education in rural schools. When conceptualised and carried out as ethical practice, place-conscious research, like place-conscious education,

> is not just some feel-good, warm and cozy attempt to return to the simplicities of years past – it is a complex, and often difficult journey to bear witness to the social and ecological hardships of local communities and to gain from the wisdom that can be found within these struggles.
> (Hayes-Conroy, 2008, p. 1)

Practised critically, place-based education can be a means of reconciliation between ourselves and the places we inhabit and others who have lived, or are living there still. We can view the potential of all place-conscious research in a similar way, and no less ethical an endeavour.

Through the chapter I have begun to explore the ethical terrain researchers cross in rural communities. In my own rural experience, the ethical priorities voiced by research participants differ from those on research applications that privilege preserving anonymity, protecting confidentiality and safeguarding participants' privacy. Instead, what matters most to my participants is that I practise the ethics of listening well, retell what I hear with faithfulness, and share personal histories with integrity, all the while remaining fully conscious of their particular contexts and origins. Bringing stories to light is what counts, so concealment or erasure of detail participants consider relevant is problematic. Pseudonyms are almost always refused. Difficult knowledge may confront researchers at any turn, but genuine moral engagement with our participants most often requires that we stay and attend to their voices and stories on their own terms and that we pass on to others what we have learned (Eppert, 2000). These are lessons the students learned well.

Place-conscious research here took the form of archival studies and interviews with Doukhobor elders, intergenerational encounters that made space for fuller historical understanding to one day emerge, the hopeful start of reconciliation grounded in a 'public pedagogy of remembrance' (Simon, 2000, p. 9). For participants, having the first opening to share their stories publicly was significant: 'It's one thing for the kids, for the students to hear about it', said Karen, 'but even for the people talking about it – it's a sort of a healing' (Karen Markin, interview 9 May 2012). The earnestness and open-heartedness of their young listeners was part of what moved participants to respond so freely and frankly.

The making of films, some based on stories that students heard and troubling knowledge they encountered, opened the space further. Older students began to recognise the impossibility of fully understanding the past, of reconciling various versions of events, or disparate perspectives on experience. Some began to feel the 'disruptive touch of memories' (Simon, 2000, p. 21) that were not theirs, and to discover their own relationships to loss. Students painstakingly followed the many stages of filmmaking to communicate elders' memories with integrity and respect, suggesting they were able to 'enter a relationship of significance with the story and ... pass that story on' (Salverson, 2000, p. 60).

The film screening in a crowded hall took the project directly into the public sphere. Students became storytellers – fresh, compelling voices that brought other people's memories forward, most for the first time outside their families. Interpreted and mediated by the children, these were echoes of memories, but powerful echoes. Once in civic space, the project became an addendum to the narrative this community tells about itself. As audience members heard Doukhobor stories retold, and watched films made by their own children, their receptiveness to the experience may have represented a collective step toward 'a critical civic emotional literacy' (Kelly, 2009, p. 167). Student researchers brought troubling and suppressed episodes of local history into the light, so these memories might be felt as concerns for the present.

The screening was an invitation to return to a contentious past that many in the community wanted to believe was over, 'put in its place' and largely forgotten except by those who had personally lived the traumas and loss. Some witnesses to the event believe the invitation was accepted, and that people might become more attentive to the stories and testimonies of others, to open the present to remembrance, even when it disturbs. One teacher remarked that the students' voices echoing childhood memories of Doukhobors 'brought community together in a way that was entirely unimagined' (Terry Taylor, interview 9 May 2012). It's a hopeful note, even knowing that one school project on local history, or a gathering dedicated to bearing witness, can hardly begin to transform relationships, heal old wounds or redefine a community's sense of itself. Yet participating in these practices of remembrance – attending to these memories and listening to these echoes – may create a crack in the wall, a small, hopeful opening towards ethical learning that might eventually help us live together with a little more compassion and a deeper sense of what we owe others.

Researchers can help create these openings, these cracks in the wall. I believe we have an ethical obligation to try to do just that whenever opportunities arise. It can and should be a deliberate part of engaging with others and with history in the rural places where we work, perhaps even our contribution to the work of reconciliation. In closing, I offer an observation that I think brings together the chapter's themes: rural research, remembrance and the possibilities for ethical learning found in both. Through writing about a student research project, in a small school in a rural community, in telling the 'story of the telling of the story' (Simon et al., 2000, p. 7), I have also participated in a practice of remembrance. Listening to students bear witness to the memories of others, I have also been bearing witness to the memories of others, creating yet another echo.

Notes

1 I am grateful to the students, teachers and principal of Lucerne Elementary-Secondary School in New Denver, British Columbia, particularly Terry Taylor and filmmakers Moira Simpson and William Fitzburg for allowing me to participate in several multimedia research projects focused on local history. I deeply appreciate the cooperation of members of the Doukhobor community who granted access to their interviews. I also want to thank the British Columbia Ministry of Education for the grant that supported this project.
2 Unless otherwise cited, all interview quotes were retrieved on 31 January 2013 from the video 'The Digital Storytelling Project', http://www.ruralteachers.com

References

Balfour, R., Mitchell, C. & Molestane, R. (2008). Troubling contexts: Toward a generative theory of rurality as education research. *Journal of Rural and Community Development* 3(3): 95–107.

Britzman, D. (1998). *Lost Subjects, Contested Objects: Toward a psychoanalytic inquiry of learning.* Albany, NY: State University of New York Press.

Britzman, D. (2000). If the story cannot end. In Simon, R., Rosenberg, S. & Eppert, C. (eds), *Between Hope and Despair: Pedagogy and the remembrance of historical trauma.* Lanham, MD: Rowman and Littlefield Publishers, pp. 27–58.

Buckingham, D. (2003). *Media Education: Literacy, learning and contemporary culture.* Cambridge: Polity Press.

Cormack, P., Green, B. & Reid, J. (2008). Children's understandings of place. In Vanclay, F., Higgins, M. & Blackshaw, A. (eds), *Making Sense of Place: Exploring concepts and expressions of place through different senses and lenses.* Canberra: National Museum of Australia, pp. 57–75.

Corbett, M. (2007). *Learning to Leave: The irony of schooling in a coastal community.* Blackpoint, NS: Fernwood Publishing.

Corbett, M. (2009). Rural schooling in mobile modernity: Returning to the places I've been. *Journal of Research in Rural Education* 24(7). Retrieved 2 February 2013 from http://jrre.psu.edu/articles/24-7.pdf

Eppert, C. (2000). Relearning questions: Responding to the ethical address of past and present others. Simon, R., Rosenberg, S. & Eppert, C. (eds), *Between Hope and Despair: Pedagogy and the remembrance of historical trauma.* Lanham, MD: Rowman and Littlefield Publishers, pp. 213–230.

Gruenewald, D. (2003). The best of both worlds: A critical pedagogy of place. *Educational Researcher* 32(4): 3–12.

Gruenewald, D. (2006). Resistance, reinhabitation, and regime change. *Journal of Research in Rural Education* 21(9) (2 August). Retrieved 2 February 2013 from http://jrre.psu.edu/articles/21-9.pdf

Gruenewald, D. & Smith, G. (eds) (2008). *Place-Based Education in the Global Age.* Mahwah, NJ: Lawrence Erlbaum Associates, Inc.

Hayes-Conroy, J. (2008, February). Review of *Place-based education in the global age: Local diversity. Journal of Research in Rural Education* 23(2). Retrieved 21 January 2013 from http://www.jrre.psu.edu/articles/23-2.

Hayward, V. & Watson, E. (1919). Doukhobor farms supply all needs. *Fort Wayne Journal Gazette* (22 November). Retrieved 16 January 2013 from http://doukhobor.org/Hayward.htm

Howley, C. & Howley, A. (2010). Poverty and school achievement in rural communities: A social-class interpretation. In Schafft, K. & Jackson, A. (eds) *Rural Education for the 21st Century: Identity, place and community in a globalizing world.* University Park: Pennsylvania State University Press, pp. 34–50.

Kelly, U. (2009). *Migration and Education in a Multicultural World: Culture, Loss and Identity.* New York: Palgrave Macmillan.

Levine, A. (2000). Review of Roger Simon, Sharon Rosenberg, & Claudia Epper (eds) *Between Hope and Despair: Pedagogy and the remembrance of historical trauma.* H-Genocide, H-Net Reviews. Retrieved 12 January 2013 from www.h-net.org/reviews/showrev.php?id=9366

Orr, D. (1991) *Ecological Literacy: Education and the transition to a postmodern world.* Albany NY: SUNY Press.

Plotnikoff, V. (n.d.). Shining waters: Doukhobors in Castlegar. Retrieved 16 January 2013 from http://doukhobor.org

Putnam, Hilary. (1987). *The Many Faces of Realism.* La Salle, IL: Open Court Publishing.

Ranck, J. (2000). Beyond reconciliation: Memory and alterity in post-genocide Rwanda. In Simon, R. Rosenberg, S. & Eppert, C. (eds), *Between Hope and Despair: Pedagogy and the remembrance of historical trauma.* Lanham, MD: Rowman and Littlefield Publishers, pp. 187–211.

Roy, Gabrielle (1942). Retrieved on 5 February 2013 from http://www.civilization.ca/cmc/exhibitions/cultur/doukhobors/dou02eng.shtml

Salverson, J. (2000). Anxiety and contact in attending to a play about land mines. In Simon, R., Rosenberg, S. & Eppert, C. (eds) (2000). *Between Hope and Despair: Pedagogy and the remembrance of historical trauma.* Lanham, MD: Rowman and Littlefield Publishers, pp. 59–74.

Schafft, K. (2010). Introduction. In Schafft, K. & Jackson, A. (eds), *Rural Education for the 21st Century: Identity, place and community in a globalizing world*. University Park: Pennsylvania State University Press.

Simon, R. (2000). The Paradoxical Practice of Zakhor: Memories of what never has been my thought or my deed. In Simon, R., Rosenberg, S. & Eppert, C. (eds), *Between Hope and Despair: Pedagogy and the remembrance of historical trauma*. Lanham, MD: Rowman and Littlefield Publishers, pp. 9–26.

Simon, R., Rosenberg, S. & Eppert, C. (eds) (2000). *Between Hope and Despair: Pedagogy and the remembrance of historical trauma*. Lanham, MD: Rowman and Littlefield Publishers.

Sobel, D. (2003). *Place-Based Education*. Great Barrington, MA: The Orion Society/Myrian Institute.

Tarasoff, K. (1995). One hundred years of Doukhobors in retrospect. *Canadian Ethnic Studies* 27(3): 1–23.

White, S. & Reid, J. (2008). Placing teachers? Sustaining rural schooling through place consciousness in teacher education. *Journal of Research in Rural Education* 23(7). Retrieved 21 January 2013 from http://jrre.psu.edu/articles/23-7.pdf

White, S., Anderson, M., Kvalsund, R., Gristy, C., Corbett, M. and Hargreaves, L. (2012). Examining the Research 'Footprint' in Rural Contexts: An international discussion on methodological issues and possibilities. Symposium presented in Network 14, Communities, Families and Schooling in Educational Research, European Conference on Educational Research, 18–21 September, Cadiz, Spain.

Chapter 11

Metaphors we lose by

Re-thinking how we frame rural education

Kim Donehower

I came late to literacy studies, in graduate student terms. In the United States, academic research on literacy is divided between two disciplines. Literacy acquisition, particularly the reading abilities of young children, is the province of education departments. Large-scale ethnographic and theoretical literacy work often happens in English departments, in a small subfield of what has come to be known as composition/rhetoric studies. Comp/rhet has its roots in classroom pedagogy – in particular, teaching writing to college students. But the 'rhet' association means that compositions are also extremely interested in language use in specific cultural contexts. The location of comp/rhet in English departments forges a bond with literary and linguistic theory. Like many of my generation, I entered graduate school in English to study literature; I didn't know comp/rhet, let alone literacy studies, existed. It took years of Master's and Ph.D. coursework to find that literacy studies were my intellectual passion. This meant I began my doctoral research far more equipped with tools of linguistic and literary analysis than my newly gained qualitative methodology skills.

Anyone who researches literacy from any perspective must come to terms with how to define 'literacy'. But my positioning in English departments, and my background in literary study, means I am acutely aware of the language we use to describe literacies, and the way that language invites moral judgements on the part of our readers. Composition studies scholar Thomas Newkirk, in his essay 'The Narrative Roots of the Case Study' (1992), argues that case study researchers create 'aesthetic patterns' when they write about literacy, and that 'to create these aesthetic patterns, the writer must also assign moral weight to the actions of characters. ... The case study writer draws on ... deeply rooted story patterns that clearly signal to the reader the types of judgments to be made' (p. 135). While Newkirk is concerned with story patterns in case study research, I focus in this chapter on a different aesthetic choice qualitative literacy researchers make – that of metaphors for literacy that infuse our writing, often without our conscious awareness.

I argue that we should bring conscious attention to the metaphors that find their way into our writing about literacy and consider the ways those metaphors structure education researchers', and our readers', ideas – and moral judgements – about rural education. My argument draws on the seminal work *Metaphors We Live by,* by linguists George Lakoff and Mark Johnson (1980). Lakoff and Johnson assert that 'the human conceptual system is metaphorically structured and defined. Metaphors, as linguistic expressions, are possible precisely because there are metaphors in a person's conceptual system' (p. 6). This primacy of metaphor in humans' ability to conceptualise anything, Lakoff and Johnson argue, creates filters or, in their words, 'highlight' and 'hide' aspects of whatever is being conceptualised (p. 10). In their classic example, the metaphor 'argument is war ... is one that we live by in this culture; it structures the actions we perform in arguing' (p. 4). Alternatively, they ask us to:

> Imagine a culture where an argument is viewed as a dance, the participants are seen as performers, and the goal is to perform in a balanced and aesthetically pleasing way. In such a culture, people would view arguments differently, experience them differently, carry them out differently, and talk about them differently. But *we* would probably not view them as arguing at all.
>
> (1980, p. 5)

Attention to metaphoric framing, then, is important to us at both the analytical and representational stages of our work. Identifying the metaphors for 'rural' and 'literate' that previous researchers have operated under – and which we ourselves may have unconsciously adopted – can help us understand what else there might be to look for when we examine rural schooling. When it's time to write up our research for scholarly and public consumption, critiquing dominant metaphors for understanding rural schooling, and offering new ones, can help us communicate more clearly, and perhaps more ethically, about our subject.

My concern with this topic grows from my roots in the southern Appalachian region of the United States. My maternal family comes from a small town in the mountains of western North Carolina, where I spent many weekends and extended summer visits. It is a place deeply embedded in Appalachian culture and history; the Appalachian Trail, a famed 3,500-kilometer (2,200-mile) hiking route, runs down its main street. Historical markers dot the landscape, identifying where folklorist Cecil Sharpe collected mountain ballads and where Presbyterian mission workers started a boarding school to educate children from the more remote parts of the surrounding area. I grew up knowing that the same people who fostered my life of reading and writing, and who supported my higher education (despite their own lack of it), had been tagged for a century as America's illiterate – as hillbillies, as a 'strange and peculiar people,'[1] targeted by outsiders who wanted to collect and preserve 'authentic' mountain culture while at the same time teaching the locals the 'right' ways to be literate. Since my doctoral research in 1995, I have worked to understand how we can view rural schooling and rural literacies in communities that have been stigmatised as opposing the educational and literate values of mainstream, middle-class education – including the tradition of liberal education.

Metaphors for rural education

In the United States, 'rural' is a slippery term in the demographic sense. A 2013 article in the *Washington Post* cited 15 different ways federal institutions determine who is rural (Farenthold, 2013). Regional economist Andrew Isserman (2005) developed a useful county-by-county map of the USA, classifying areas as rural, mixed rural, mixed urban and urban, since rural/urban/suburban are not always clear categories in the USA. A town of 5,000 may have more or fewer urban amenities and attributes depending on whether it is the largest population centre for 200 kilometres (125 miles) in any direction or a scant half-hour drive across open country from a town of 10,000. 'Rural' is typically a felt term in the USA, rather than a technical one. It is associated with small populations and isolating geography, but also with conservative politics, an agricultural economy, ethnic homogeneity and an insular culture. For many in the USA, 'rural' evokes an immediate chain of associations, often negative and frequently inaccurate. This complicates research on rural education, for we researchers must write against this backdrop.

A good case study to consider the kinds of metaphors that can dominate representations of rural education is what is routinely referred to in the United States as the 'Kanawha County Textbook War'. In 1974 in Kanawha County, West Virginia – also part of Appalachia – the local school board adopted the language arts textbook series *Interactions*. Created by renowned liberal educator James Moffett, *Interactions* was, in his own words, 'a set of learning materials comprising two film series, dozens of card and board games, 800 activity cards, hundreds of recorded selections, and … 172 paperback books of reading matter' (1988, p. 4). A single school board member, Alice Moore, questioned the selection, at first solely on the basis of the 'dialectology' it embraced – what the US Conference on College Composition and Communication resolution of that same year (1974) titled *Students' Right to Their Own Language*. Once Moore and others read the books, their concerns grew to include what they saw as anti-American and anti-Christian bias. The situation escalated, and before it was over the event drew both national media attention and representatives of national groups pouring in to use the conflict for their own purposes.

The pro- and anti-textbook factions found little common ground, but both seem to agree on a pair of interlocking metaphors in their representations of the event: storms and war. James Moffett's own book about the conflict is titled *Storm in the Mountains*. Protester Don Means' (1981) book about the event has chapters titled 'The Storm Brews' and 'The Calm Before the Storm'. Original protester Alice Moore, speaking to documentarian Trey Kay (2009) in 'The Great Textbook War', uses the word 'whirlwind' more than once to describe the conflict, and another protester uses the same word. Documentarian Kay, who was a child in the Kanawha County school system when the controversy happened, and who aligns himself with the pro-textbook side, begins his documentary with the line, 'In 1974, a storm was brewing in the mountains and hollows of West

Virginia', and later asserts that 'This storm marked one of the first battles of today's culture wars.'

Here we see the slide into the war metaphor. It's easy to understand why this metaphor suggests itself. The Kanawha County controversy did escalate into violence, with fire-bombings of classrooms and cars and a fist-fight breaking out at a school board meeting and, as Lakoff and Johnson note, one of the most dominant metaphors in circulation for describing arguments is 'argument is war' (1980). Here, again, there is tremendous agreement among textbook protesters, textbook proponents and media commentators. Kay's documentary is titled *The Great Textbook War*; Means' book is called *War in Kanawha County*. In his documentary, Kay refers to the event as 'the Civil War of books'. Covering the controversy for the *Village Voice*, journalist Paul Cowan (1974) called it a 'holy war'. One of the protesters interviewed for Kay's documentary says that she 'felt like a Christian soldier'. And a number of people on all sides of the event claim it as what Kay calls 'the first battle in the culture war', sparking the Christian Right and Tea Party movements in the United States.

How do these metaphors position us educational researchers, typically operating in the tradition of, and perhaps partly aligned with, Moffett? How do they position readers and listeners of both the academic and popular representations of the conflict? First, the war metaphor creates opposing sides and invites us to take one, defining a clear Other. It also suggests that these diametrically opposed sides have clear geographical boundaries. Kay, early in his documentary, gives this curious sort of disclaimer: he says that if he were to blindfold 'you', the public radio documentary listener,

> and transport you to 'the hill,' the affluent neighborhood in Charleston where I grew up, you'd think that you were in Anywhere, Suburbia, USA: Kids playing in cul-de-sacs, dads cooking burgers on outdoor grills. Our neighbors were doctors, lawyers, businesspeople. Outside the city, twisting, bumpy roads wound through hills and hollows, past small towns and mining camps. There were general stores and filling stations; men in grease-covered overalls, and dozens of little churches filled to capacity on Sunday mornings and Wednesday evenings. There was a lot that was different between rural and urban Kanawha County.
>
> (Kay, 2009)

A moment before this section of the documentary, Kay has described the controversy as one that pitted neighbour against neighbour, hinting at the reality that Appalachian communities are far from homogeneous in their political opinions and personal commitments. But the war metaphor demands clear geographic 'sides'.

The Kanawha controversy gets represented not only as a war, but as particular kinds of war – a 'civil war', a 'holy war' and a 'culture war'. The 'civil war' comparison is Kay's, and by it he means not the general concept of a civil war, but the

American Civil War, with the implication that, at root, the controversy is about racism. In her interview with Kay, local teacher Mildred Holt says, 'I think it was about race; I don't think it was about culture. When I looked out my office window and saw the Ku Klux Klan (KKK), I knew then that it was purely racial.'

The most infamous white supremacist group in the USA, the KKK was one of the groups who had come in from outside the community to make what political hay they could of the controversy. Based on Don Means' interviews with Klan leaders, Klansmen from Georgia, Alabama, North and South Carolina, Pennsylvania, Ohio, Michigan, Texas and Oklahoma had voted to 'investigate' the textbook situation. But as Means (1981) notes, the KKK had just announced its first candidate for the US presidency and was looking for any publicity they could get. By the time the Klan showed up, the Kanawha controversy was already receiving national and international media attention and provided a ready platform. But teacher Holt sees the Klan's presence as a signal that the motivations of the local protesters are not just partly based on racism, but 'purely racial'.

In fact, protest leader Alice Moore argued that her objection to writings from Eldridge Cleaver and other black separatists in the textbooks was that the preponderance of such pieces did not fairly represent black culture. Kay's documentary immediately follows this claim of Moore's with commentary from the Reverend Ron English, a member of the local National Association for the Advancement of Colored People (NAACP) chapter, who says that he 'respects' Moore's 'strategy' as a good one to gain support from devout Christians in the black community. English does not directly say he thinks Moore is lying about her motivations here, but concludes his comments by saying simply, 'She's pretty media-savvy.' The war metaphor forces us to think in terms of 'strategies' and 'tactics'. Any public statements by either side then become indications only of strategy, and not a way to access actual feelings and motivations.

The 'holy war' label was perhaps inevitable, given that so many of the protest leaders were ministers, that many of the protesters' objections to the books were based on perceived anti-Christian bias, and that some protesters held signs saying things like 'I have a Bible. I don't need those dirty textbooks.' Journalist Cowan described the 'holy war' as being between 'people who depend on books and people who depend on The Book' (as quoted in Kay, 2009). Since the war metaphor encourages us to see two sides in binary opposition to one another, it's easy to extend the binary to the books, as being also somehow diametrically opposed. Moffett, in his interviews with protest leaders, which he transcribes at length in *Storm in the Mountains*, tries his best to get the protesters to admit that a biblical basis exists for the education Moffett advocates, but the protesters simply will not be led in this direction. Moffett tries to claim 'their book' for 'our side' in these exchanges, but the protesters can't let that happen. As Lakoff and Johnson (1980) would say, the books have become a metonym for each side in the perceived war (p. 36). Surrendering the book means surrendering the battle.

I found myself trapped in the binaries typically applied to the Kanawha County event when, as a graduate student, I participated in a discussion of Moffett's *Storm in the Mountains*. Given my background, I felt the need to speak *about* the protesters and to try to contextualise their position. My efforts were perceived, however, as speaking *for* the protesters—as taking 'their side'. Had I read Beth Daniell's thoughtful 1998 review of *Storm in the Mountains*, I could possibly have moved the conversation beyond the spectators-and-partisans-in-a-war structure that had descended on the class. Daniell notes that the protesters take a position that resists the dominant culture; however,

> this case is not ... an example of resistance to the dominant culture and its literacy that will please left-leaning scholars, since it comes from the far right ... The kind of resistance they call for is predicated on a Marxist critique of our culture. Does it count as resistance if it is based on a fundamentalist Christian perspective?
>
> (1988, p. 244)

In other words, the protesters' resistance to 'a [dominant] culture which has at best disregarded the felt needs of the local Appalachian population' (1988, p. 243) might provide a point of contact with 'left-leaning scholars' whose educational methods could be adapted to better regard some of those felt needs – particularly the need to rehabilitate an Appalachian literate identity that has so long been stigmatised by outsiders in the very ways Moffett and Kay are doing. But the 'war' metaphor was firmly – and entertainingly – in place for my classmates that day, and my own inability to point to and problematise it prevented us from having that conversation.

Today I would offer my classmates a different way to see what is at issue in the textbook controversy: not 'the books' as metonyms for 'sides' in a 'war', but for people who have different relationships with texts in general and ideas about their power and how they should be used. Carol Mason's book *Reading Appalachia from Left to Right: Conservatives and the 1974 Kanawha County Textbook Controversy* (2009) and my own research in my native part of Appalachia (Donehower, 2003) support this assertion. If you believe, from your experiences with 'The Book', that books are a powerful didactic source of values and identity, then the textbooks do become a threat to community stability. The protesters are not dismissing the textbooks as irrelevant as much as they are investing them with the potential power of 'The Book'. In contrast, textbook supporters say that they have confidence in their own parenting, that the textbooks are not a threat to family bonds and identity. I suggest that, for these textbook proponents, it's not just the textbooks that are not a threat, but books in general – this group simply does not relate to books in this way or invest the reading relationship with this kind of power. But the war metaphor, which requires metonymic symbols and standards to represent the varying sides, takes advantage of the concrete symbol of the books themselves, directing attention away from the research focus that is most needed – about people's relationships with literacy and books.

Recall that protester Alice Moore's original concern about the textbooks was their embrace of what was then being described as 'dialectology'. In a recording from that original school board meeting, Moore insists, 'I just don't think I agree with that approach at all. In fact, I'm sure I don't ... There is a correct way to speak. Now, there may be some slight variations. But, "dem" is never correct, "dat" is never correct for "that".' Given that Moore chooses dialect markers from African American Vernacular English for her examples here, it's easy, under the Civil War metaphor, to regard this statement as evidence of her racism. But it's also worth considering the long history of Appalachians being stigmatised for their dialect, and of that dialect being equated with illiteracy. Moore's concern can also be read as a desire for schools to promote class mobility for a stigmatised group of which she is a member, the kind of thing Lisa Delpit documents in 'The Silenced Dialogue: Power and Pedagogy in Teaching Other People's Children' (1988).

To consider the storm metaphor, let's first consider its relationship to the war metaphor. Based on Lakoff and Johnson's way of representing metaphors that structure concepts, we can see the relationship like this:

Argument is War
War is Storm

We can readily find instances where war is described in terms of a storm. When we liken a war to a natural event, we absolve humans of responsibility and the ability to effect change – something that, as education researchers, we should be reluctant to do. War is Storm suggests that on this planet wars just happen, and the best we can do is take precautions and try to protect ourselves until it is over. Consider protester Alice Moore's comment to Trey Kay: 'all I did was just stand where I had always stood ... I didn't cause this whirlwind, the whirlwind developed around me because I spoke up and said something. I stood where I was.' James Moffett, who went with Storm over War as his framing metaphor, ends his book's prologue by calling Kanawha County 'a model of the explosive potentialities within America' (1988, p. 9). The forces that created this storm, then, lie far from James Moffett himself.

Another relationship the storm metaphor might have to this event is this:

Appalachia (Rural) is Storm

The storm, as Moffett reminds us, is 'in the mountains' – not in the people actually involved. Kay says the storm was brewing 'in the hills and hollers' – and not, he asserts, on the orderly urban streets of nearby Charleston. Storms are localised events and, while Moffett locates it in Kanawha County as a whole, Kay isolates it to rural Kanawha County – to what most people think of when they think of 'Appalachia'. I have argued elsewhere that in the United States, 'Appalachia' is often synecdochal for 'rural'.[2]

Appalachia is Storm reinscribes many aspects of stereotypical conceptualisations of Appalachia since the 1880s. Storms are commonly described as a 'disturbance', even an 'upper-air disturbance', which links neatly with the idea that those folks living up there in those mountains are 'strange and peculiar', out of step with, and a potential threat to, the rest of society. As to the nature of the disturbance, we can look to another way the storm metaphor is deployed. The temperament of someone who appears irrational and ruled by their emotions is commonly described as 'stormy'. All this plugs neatly into the notion that the Kanawha County 'war' was a battle between rational, educated people and emotional, uneducated hillbillies. Documentarian Kay carefully notes that Alice Moore was the only member of the school board without a college education. Moffett, in a striking departure from the engaged back-and-forth he has with his research subjects in the heart of *Storm in the Mountains*, ends his book by 'diagnosing' these same people with 'agnosis', or wilful ignorance – the dismissal of rationality in favour of myth-driven emotion (1988, pp. 185–237).

This leaves us understanding the Kanawha County conflict as an inevitable clash between two distinct groups contained in distinct geographic boundaries in which the motivations on one side are purely rational and, on the other, purely emotional. This is neither an accurate nor helpful analysis for making decisions about how best to conduct literacy education. Additionally, embracing the Storm and War metaphors renders the Kanawha controversy nothing more than a spectacle for the public at large, the kind of thing to watch from afar and shake our heads at.

Metaphors for literacy (and illiteracy)

In examining and reconsidering metaphoric frames for rural education, we must also focus on metaphors for literacy. These are multiple: Sylvia Scribner (1984) documents literacy-as-adaptation, literacy-as-power and literacy-as-state-of-grace; David Barton (1994) notes illiteracy described as sickness, handicap, ignorance, incapacity, oppression, deprivation and deviance. Here I wish to examine only literacy-as-adaptation (sometimes thought of as 'functional literacy'), since it is the way of talking about literacy that often dominates discussions of rural education, especially studies such as the National Assessment of Adult Literacy in the USA that attempt to quantify literacy rates by region.

Literacy-as-adaptation, Scribner writes, 'is designed to capture concepts of literacy that emphasise its survival or pragmatic value' (1984, p. 73). However, Scribner notes, 'in spite of their apparent commonsense grounding, functional literacy approaches are neither as straightforward nor as unproblematic as they first appear ... Which literacy tasks are "necessary," and which are "optional"?' (pp. 73–74). Scribner herself puts this in the context of a rural-versus-urban issue, when she suggests, tellingly, that 'If we were to consider the level of reading and writing activities carried out in small and isolated rural communities as the standard for functional literacy, educational objectives would be unduly restricted' (p. 74).

This is Scribner's polite way of saying that rural literacies would likely be elementary to the tasks of 'adaptation' to urban lives and economies. The literacy-as-adaptation metaphor, when combined with dominant stereotypes about rural life as static and inflexible, lends itself to such downgrading of rural literacies. In the USA, this dates back at least as far as the Commission on Country Life report of 1911, which took rural schools to task for being 'in a state of arrested development and ... not yet ... in consonance with all the recently changed conditions of life' (US Commission on Country Life, 1911, pp. 121–122).

Adaptability and flexibility, on the other hand, are typically seen as the hallmarks of urban life. Economist Richard Florida, whose writings enjoy both academic and popular appeal, believes that the future will favour the creation of 'mega-regions', because cities, which Florida (2009) describes as the locus of 'invention, innovation, and creation', are somehow necessary to spark the kinds of adaptive, flexible literacies needed to sustain the American economy. As Mike Corbett notes in his critique of Florida, 'for the last 50 years at least, institutions of formal education have tended to support Florida's position', resulting in rural outmigration (2006, p. 288). If literacy-as-adaptation is a dominant metaphor for how we value school literacy, and if the cultural and economic structures to which students must adapt are conceived of as urban, it will be hard for us to see both rural literacies that provide adaptations to rural life and rural literacies that do not function in a sense of 'adaptation' at all.

Furthermore, Lakoff and Johnson (1980) ask us to consider how metaphorical structuring affects binary pairs of terms (p. 15). If we think, in Lakoff and Johnson's terms, that

Literacy is Adaptation

then illiteracy – in the sense of insufficient literacy – must be antonymic:

Illiteracy is Inability to Adapt

I choose 'inability to adapt' over 'inflexible' or 'rigid', because 'adaptation', in conjunction with human development, has about it a strong whiff of evolutionary theory – in which those who cannot adapt are destined to die out (and the overall gene pool is better for it). As others and I have written elsewhere, the notion that rural places are dying out – and that overall society would be better for it – has a long history.[3] Florida (2009) certainly adheres to this unfortunate view; the rural barely garners a mention in his vision of the future. Instead, he advances a theoretical model that privileges cities, the larger the better, in evolutionary terms:

> Big, talent-attracting places benefit from accelerated rates of 'urban metabolism,' according to a pioneering theory of urban evolution developed by a multidisciplinary team of researchers affiliated with the Santa Fe Institute. The rate at which living things convert food into energy – their metabolic rate – tends to slow as organisms increase in size. But when the Santa Fe team

examined trends in innovation, patent activity, wages, and GDP, they found that successful cities, unlike biological organisms, actually get faster as they grow. In order to grow bigger and overcome diseconomies of scale like congestion and rising housing and business costs, cities must become more efficient, innovative, and productive. The researchers dubbed the extraordinarily rapid metabolic rate that successful cities are able to achieve 'super-linear' scaling. 'By almost any measure,' they wrote, 'the larger a city's population, the greater the innovation and wealth creation per person'.

(Florida, 2009)

What we have here is nearly a form of cultural eugenics – the less urban a community is, the less suited it is to survive, and the better the overall economy will be without it. When rural education is mismeasured by urban standards, combined with the metaphoric frame of literacy-as-adaptation and insufficient-literacy-as-inability-to-adapt, the fate of the rural seems sealed. Just as with the storm metaphor above, there is nothing anyone can really to do to slow the decline of rural education and rural communities.

Trying on new metaphors

As researchers, how might we avoid these metaphoric traps, and where they lead our own analysis? How might we recast public discussion of rural education when these metaphors not only predominate, but, as we see in the case of the Kanawha County textbook controversy, are put forth by both the researchers and the researched themselves?

Careful avoidance of the most problematic metaphors is one tactic. Carol Mason's remarkable study of the Kanawha County conflict, *Reading Appalachia from Left to Right* (2009), meticulously avoids both the war and storm metaphors. She refers to the episode by the less-loaded terms 'conflict' or 'controversy', and takes up as her analytical goal questioning the assertion that 'Kanawha County was an early skirmish in the culture wars of the 1980s and thereafter' (p. 180). Freed from having to write about a war, Mason's 'goal [is] neither to inflame old sores nor to find a healing compromise' (p. 181). Instead, she is able not to isolate Kanawha County as strange and peculiar – and committed to inflexibility – as Moffett did, but to put it at the centre of a general set of 'renegotiations of American identity that left their mark on contemporary politics' (p. 181).

Like Mason, it is useful to consider the metaphors for rural and educated/ literate that dominate the sites we study, and to purposely look for what else might be there. It is also productive to document just how far these metaphors have penetrated into rural communities' beliefs about themselves, to understand how these metaphors shape their ideas about literacy, schooling and the future of rural life. In some cases, as Corbett (2007) notes, literacy-as-adaptation, with urbanity as the target for adaptation, means rural students 'learn to leave'. The war metaphor might explain the hostile reception we sometimes receive from those we might research – I can still recall the content of a stinging email I got in response to a request for an interview, even though my request was specifically because the recipient exhibited such high levels of literacy. The praise in my email was regarded solely as a tactic, and the assumption was that I had more nefarious goals in mind.

To truly rework the ways we, and others, think about rural schooling and rural literacies, our work must generate powerful alternative metaphors. This is a tall order, one that I am only beginning to undertake in my own work. As I sort through the data from my latest study site, Hammond, North Dakota, in the northern Great Plains of the USA, a possibility emerges:

Literacy is Music

In both Hammond and Haines Gap, my site in Appalachia, interviewees would often redirect conversations about literacy to ability in other subjects. In Haines Gap, it was mathematics. In Hammond, it is music. The town has a lively local music scene, despite (or perhaps because of) its geographic isolation and 500-person population. During my year of research in Hammond, I attended the community's annual musical variety show, held in the high-school auditorium, with my husband, a native New Yorker whose father is a professional musician. We were amazed at the production values and quality of the event.

A number of Hammond interviewees linked the high levels of literate activity in the community – the town hosts a number of book clubs, writing groups and reading incentive programmes for children – with its musical heritage. When I asked about the quality of English instruction at the school, a common response was, 'It's fine, but we've always had really great music teachers.' While the standard metaphors Scribner (1984) documents for literacy-as-adaptation, power and state of grace also show up in my Hammond data, it is worth considering what focusing on the literacy-as-music metaphor might bring to my analysis.

To consider Lakoff and Johnson's standards for metaphoric structuring, literacy-as-music must function in a number of ways if it is to truly shift the way I am able to conceptualise, and represent, rural literacy in Hammond. First, it should provide a coherent contrast with its oppositional pair. Lakoff and Johnson write that '[t]here is a difference between metaphors that are *coherent* (that is, "fit together") with each other and those that are *consistent*. We have found that the connections between metaphors are more likely to involve coherence than consistency' (1980, p. 44).

Determining a good fit for the opposite of music is tricky; silences artfully deployed are a part of music, and what is 'unmusical' is culturally bounded. For now, I'm going to go with 'cacophony':

Literacy is Music
Illiteracy is Cacophony

As I examine my data to see how this metaphoric pair might fit, I am struck that so much of the literacy activity I have documented in Hammond is both communal and autotelic – 'art for art's sake', having as its primary goal the continuance of the activity, without regard for its economic or instrumentalist value. The absence of this literate activity, the metaphor implies, would bring cacophony, or discordance. Perhaps part of the functioning of these literate practices is to maintain a level of harmony in the community.

The music metaphor lets me further distinguish this literacy-for-community-harmony model from a more dominant model that sees literacy as a form of cultural glue: E. D. Hirsch's notion of 'cultural literacy', which Scribner might identify as a form of literacy-as-power. Hirsch's *Cultural Literacy: What Every American Needs to Know* (1987) argues for a common knowledge base, one that offers upward mobility in the form of cultural capital. Literacy-as-harmony, however, privileges complementary, not identical, literate abilities. It allows for a more nuanced understanding of how individual literacies are supposed to work together.

Metaphoric restructuring shows promise as an analytical tool; as a representational tool when we write our research for academic and popular audiences, it has powerful potential. Lakoff and Johnson assert that '[o]ur ordinary conceptual system, in terms of which we both think *and act*, is fundamentally metaphorical in nature' (1980, p. 3, emphasis added). When it comes to literacy education, David Barton notes that 'different metaphors have different implications for how we view illiteracy, what action might be taken to change it and how we characterise the people involved' (1994, p. 12). For example, Barton notes that when illiteracy is seen as 'deprivation', the appropriate response is to 'reallocate material resources', but when illiteracy is 'deviance', 'isolation, containment, and physical coercion' are the actions to take (1994, p. 13).

I saw these models at play in my interviews with Haines Gap residents who were educated during the time of greatest outsider intervention in Appalachian education. The 'country children' from the extremely rural areas outside of town were recruited to the Presbyterian mission school, which was set up to serve the most 'deprived' in the community. As a result, these children had access to a much better library than the town children, who lacked the same material resources. This reallocation of resources, which Barton also calls 'positive discrimination' (1994, p. 13), created some tensions with the town schoolchildren as a result. At the public schools during the same time period, more of a 'deviance' model was at work, with interviewees reporting having to sit in the corner wearing a dunce cap for the inability to recite the alphabet backwards, or having one's hand tied behind one's back for writing left-handed.

These are extreme examples, but they demonstrate Lakoff and Johnson's key point – specific actions become natural and obvious solutions if they are consistent with the metaphor(s) that structure how we understand situations we wish to improve.

To return to Hammond, if literacy is music and lack of literacy is cacophony, what actions might be recommended to sustain the already high levels of literacy happening in Hammond? The idea of group 'rehearsal' comes to mind – structured practice with lots of repetition, with a desired outcome not of sameness but of complementarity. For example, book clubs and study groups should have as their goal not a common interpretation, but nuanced individual interpretations that form a coherent whole. Community writing projects should similarly respect individual differences in style and strategy, but reflect a common purpose. The autotelic nature of such activities should be promoted as much as possible.

Literacy-as-music is much more abstract than literacy-as-adaptation or power, and will likely be a hard sell. Lakoff and Johnson note that the most tenacious metaphors reflect 'values deeply embedded in our culture' (1980, p. 22), and a combination of the adaptation and power metaphors reflects United States values of social and economic upward mobility. But, as literacy scholar Deborah Brandt (1995) notes, ideas about literacy 'accumulate', and 'older and newer incarnations of literacy may be operating simultaneously at any historical moment, usually – but not always – in a complementary relationship' (p. 654). In other words, when it comes to literacy, there is always room for new metaphors to operate alongside old ones. Perhaps it is time for educational researchers to directly infuse some of these new metaphors into our discussions of rural education.

How do we go about this admittedly difficult task? First, it's worth examining the metaphors for literacy in general, and rural literacies in particular, that have most deeply affected our own work. Few people sit down to read academic research to have an aesthetic experience, but any sort of qualitative descriptive research does require aesthetic choices in how to represent literacy and rural people's relationships to literacy. If we read the research that has most influenced us for these aesthetic choices, particularly the use of metaphor, we can begin to identify our own internal metaphoric structuring for understanding 'literacy' in conjunction with 'rural'. This is different than acknowledging our theoretical stance; multiple metaphors might co-exist easily with a single theory.

Second, we must look at the aesthetic choices our research subjects use when they talk (or write) about literacy. They, too, invoke or imply metaphors in the ways they describe reading, writing and their relationships to literacy. It has long been viewed as ethical to give informants more of a voice on the page in qualitative research than they have previously had. This means not only quoting informants extensively – as Moffett did in *Storm in the Mountains* – but considering new ways of conceptualising literacy that might emerge from the metaphors informants use or imply. Sometimes we must dig deeply for these: as we saw, many of Moffett's informants used the same 'storm' and 'war' metaphors he did. But the effort will be worth it if we can profoundly alter both the moral judgements and the recommended teaching practices that have long been directed at rural communities.

Notes

1 See Donehower, K. (2007). Rhetorics and realities: The history and effects of stereotypes about rural literacies. In Donehower, K., Hogg, C., & Schell, E. E., *Rural Literacies* (pp. 37–76). Carbondale: Southern Illinois University Press.

2 See K. Donehower, C. Hogg & E. E. Schell (2007), *Rural Literacies*. Carbondale: Southern Illinois University Press; and H. Shapiro (1978), *Appalachia on Our Mind: The southern mountaineers in the American consciousness, 1870–1920*. Chapel Hill: University of North Carolina Press.
3 See, for example, J. Tobin & D. Davidson (1990), The ethics of polyvocal ethnography: Empowering vs textualizing children and teachers. *International Journal of Qualitative Studies in Education, 3*(3): 271–283.

References

Barton, D. (1994). *Literacy: An introduction to the ecology of written language*. Oxford, UK: Blackwell.

Brandt, D. (1995). Accumulating literacy: Writing and learning to write in the twentieth century. *College English, 57*(6): 649–668.

Conference on College Composition and Communication. (1974). Students' right to their own language. *College Composition and Communication, 25* (special issue).

Corbett, M. (2006). Educating the country out of the child and the child out of the country: An excursion in spectrology. *Alberta Journal of Education Research, 52*(4): 286–298.

Corbett, M. (2007). *Learning to Leave: The irony of schooling in a coastal community*. Black Point, NS: Fernwood Publishing.

Cowan, P. (1974). Holy war in West Virginia: A fight over America's future. *Village Voice, 9* December, 19–23.

Daniell, B. (1988). Literacy, politics, and resistance: Moffett's study of censorship. *Journal of Teaching Writing, 7*(2): 237–246.

Delpit, L. (1988). The silenced dialogue: Power and pedagogy in teaching other people's children. *Harvard Educational Review, 58*(3): 280–298.

Donehower, K. (2003). Literacy choices in an Appalachian community. *Journal of Appalachian Studies, 9*(2): 341–362.

Farenthold, D. (2013). What does rural mean? Uncle Sam has more than a dozen answers. *Washington Post*, 8 June. Retrieved from http://www.washingtonpost.com

Florida, R. (2009). How the crash will reshape America. *The Atlantic* (March). Retrieved from http://www.theatlantic.com/magazine/archive/2009/03/how-the-crash-will-reshape-america/307293/#

Hirsch, E. D. (1987). *Cultural Literacy: What every American needs to know*. Boston, MA: Houghton Mifflin.

Isserman, A. M. (2005). In the national interest: Defining rural and urban correctly in research and public policy. *International Regional Science Review, 28*: 465–499.

Kay, T. (2009). The great textbook war. Radio documentary. Charleston: West Virginia Public Radio.

Lakoff, G. & Johnson, M. (1980). *Metaphors We Live by*. Chicago: University of Chicago Press.

Mason, C. (2009). *Reading Appalachia from Left to Right: Conservatives and the 1974 Kanawha County textbook controversy*. Ithaca, NY: Cornell University Press.

Means, D. (1981). *War in Kanawha County: School textbook protest in West Virginia in 1974*. Bloomington, IN: iUniverse.

Moffett, J. (1988). *Storm in the Mountains: A case study of censorship, conflict, and consciousness*. Carbondale: Southern Illinois University Press.

Newkirk, T. (1992). The narrative roots of the case study. In G. Kirsch & P. A. Sullivan (eds), *Methods and Methodology in Composition Research* (pp. 130–152). Carbondale: Southern Illinois University Press.

Scribner, Sylvia. (1984). Literacy in three metaphors. *American Journal of Education*, *93*(1): 6–21.

US Commission on Country Life. (1911). *Report of the Commission on Country Life*. New York: Sturgis & Walton Company.

Chapter 12

Reciprocity as relational

Two examples of conducting research in Finnish Lapland

Maija Lanas and Pauliina Rautio

Introduction

In this chapter, we write as researchers who have both conducted studies in the Finnish rural North, focusing on how we came to see reciprocity in our studies. We discuss the ways in which we came to elaborate our understandings of ethics in research with rural – or, for that matter, any – inhabitants and locations. In our studies both of us felt uncomfortable with the common understanding of reciprocity as an 'exchange' between the researcher and the participant(s). Reciprocity is often understood as an exchange that usually refers to responding to a positive action with another positive action. In a sense it is thus about 'returning a favour'. This is considered to be an implicit social contract which increases positive interaction or, in research terms, a form of an incentive or motivation to participate in the research study. Such incentives need to be declared. A researcher might, for example, reward the participants quite literally (with a token of some kind, movie tickets or even money), or more contextually (with a village book, a copy of a publication, or photographs taken in the field/of the participants). Often the exchange is considered to take place once, usually in the beginning or at the end of the research. When conceptualising reciprocity in this way as an exchange, the participation is seen as 'bought'. In our studies in the Finnish rural North we came to think of reciprocity in research as more than a simple exchange. We began to see reciprocity as *relational* and as a *never-ending process*. We highlight how we came to this understanding through our research, both separately and together.

Finding 'true North'

For our Ph.D.s, we conducted research as part of a wider multidisciplinary research project, 'Life in Place', in Finnish Lapland, well above the Arctic Circle, in the most remote and sparsely populated area of the European Union (Muilu, 2010).[1] The landscape of the Finnish Lapland is mainly low plateau with sparse vegetation, marshes, coniferous forests and lakes and fells (rounded low mountains or high hills reaching heights of 400–800 metres/1, 312–2, 625 feet). The climate is sub-Arctic, with long and cold winters and the so-called 'polar night' and 'polar day' – a period in the winter when the sun does not rise at all and, conversely in the summer, when the sun does not set at all. The sparse population of Lapland is clustered in small villages or scattered around, house by house. In the 'Life in Place' project, narrative and ethnographic research was carried out in two such villages (populations 30 and 150) over a span of three years, from 2007 to 2010. The focus of the projects was to listen to the villagers speak about their lives, as much on their terms as possible.

In Finland, as in many other places around the globe, people are moving from rural areas into cities, partly because of diminishing services, creating a vicious circle of ever-diminishing services. The Finnish rural North, as a context for research, is saturated with stereotypical and 'othering' representations which often leave northerners feeling misrepresented (Lanas, Rautio & Syrjälä, 2012; Ridanpää, 2007; see also Eriksson, 2010 for similar findings in neighbouring Sweden). Finnish Lapland and its inhabitants are commonly considered on one hand as romanticised, wild and mythological, and on the other hand as miserable, poor and socially excluded (Lanas, 2011; Rautio, 2010). These representations are also influential in education and echo in schools in the North (Lanas, 2008).

The broader research project began with the researchers wanting to construct a new narrative and ethnographic knowledge about 'The Finnish rural North', and it ended four years later with us having understood that there is actually no such place. There is no 'Finnish rural North' as a static, representable entity. We listened to the local stories with our research group; visited the two research villages several times; hired local assistants; gathered over 50 narrative interviews; organised various group discussions in both of the villages; and took part in various events organised by the villagers. Having done all this, it became evident that anything and everything we could say about the 'Finnish rural North' would be an arrogant simplification and a disservice to our participants. Both of us found ourselves balancing feelings of failing in our research: 'What can we say about the Finnish rural North if we cannot say anything about it?'

To be able to approach rural lives as also diverse, open-ended and surprising, calls for research approaches that focus on processes, contexts and relations. Such approaches are especially important in rural settings which bear a marked stigma of being of a certain kind – whether remote and left behind (Corbett, 2008; Markey et al., 2008; Rautio, 2010) or idyllic and romanticised (Horton, 2008; Hubbard, 2005). These essentialisations are combated when researchers reflect on their own knowledge production with the participants and reflect critically on the broader theoretical, cultural, political, ideological and narrative contexts of their interaction. The research relationship, the core of which is the production of new knowledge, always takes form within a particular context, influenced by a multitude of broader power relations. Therefore, there are always underlying assumptions affecting and taking part in the knowledge we produce seemingly free of inference. In realising this during our Ph.D. studies, we turned towards non-representational theories (see e.g., Thrift, 2008) and focused on how formations were enacted, meanings inscribed and realities performed in our research as well as outside it.

An ethical orientation that is often referred to as relational ethics tends to be one which is distinct from so-called procedural ethics (Gildersleeve, 2010; Rallis & Rossman, 2010; Rossman & Rallis, 2010). Relational ethics refers to a perspective of research ethics as inherently situational, moment-to-moment decisions. It is something 'becoming', never finished, never complete, but 'done' in the everyday practices and relationships. Procedural ethics, instead, tend to focus more on following the correct ethical procedure, in which ethics are at times perceived as ticking off boxes rather than asking the difficult and continuous question, 'What is ethical practice in this instance with these people?' (Rallis & Rossman, 2010). Often the ethical concern of acknowledging local participants' perspectives in dialogical knowledge production is addressed with 'member checks' (Rallis, 2010). Relational ethics demands that these member checks are more than just a box ticked off at the end of the research, but that they are thoroughly integrated in the research process; that the research ethic itself is produced reciprocally with the participants.

Rethinking reciprocity

As we came to know the participants and the directions that our own studies were taking, we shared a strong sense that reciprocity as *taking* something, and *giving* something *back*, did not provide an adequate basis for a research that would recognize the issues of power and representation in research of the rural North. Instead, we saw our studies as spaces created together with the participants. The spaces were partly created based on our research needs, but also on the needs of the participants, with us trying to be of service to them in their lives. In these kinds of spaces, what becomes *taken* and what becomes *given back* is more complex than a simple one-off exchange, and reciprocity relies on constant negotiation in which the changing needs of both the researcher and participants are to be heard. It is then a never-ending process of seeking for appropriate, supportive and productive ways of doing research; a continuous question directed at itself: '*What does reciprocity mean in this particular research?*'

In our studies we took different paths but found similar answers. Maija conducted ethnography and narrative interviews, and focused on breaking down various representations of rural northern youth, their surroundings and their actions, and how their representations were produced. Pauliina, in turn, wrote letters with four villagers for a year, in which they reflected on beauty and thus actively and reiteratively created representations of their everyday lives. In this chapter we discuss the answers we found; what reciprocity meant in our studies. At the same time we emphasise that these answers can never be seen as more than temporally and spatially conditioned understandings. What follows is our take on reciprocity in research. This is then followed by two examples of what such a perspective may mean for research. We conclude the chapter by discussing research ethics in reciprocal research in conjunction with the emotions of insecurity and fear experienced by a researcher. Both are emotions that may either prevent or enable the researcher to conduct reciprocal and ethical research in rural sites.

Reciprocity as an ongoing relational process

What reciprocity means in a particular piece of research depends not only on the chosen methodology and methods, but also on issues that the researcher cannot influence: the particularities of the research context and the expectations and varying situations of the participants. What reciprocity initially means to the researcher might be different from what it initially means to the participants. Moreover, the demands of reciprocity may change as the research relationship progresses. As both of us asked ourselves the question 'What does reciprocity mean in this particular research?', continuously for three years, we in retrospect identified three characteristics of an ongoing reciprocal process that made sense in both our research studies:

1. *Acknowledging the ways in which information is not merely retrieved from participants.* Knowledge or 'voice' is not something that the participant gives away or emanates; rather, it is produced contextually, as thoroughly inter-twined and engaged so that the participant and researcher are 'in it together'.
2. *Reciprocity takes place through 'positive actions' during the research.* Reciprocal research requires staying open and alert to how these 'positive actions' evolve. The 'positive actions' cannot be pre-decided: the participants, engaged in their own ways, realise what kind of contribution from them is 'positive'/ ethical, and the researchers, engaged in their own ways, realise what kind of contribution from them is 'positive'/ethical.
3. *The exchange (i.e. the intra-action of researcher and participant) needs to be continually reinforced.* The reciprocal research process cannot be written off with a one-off exchange. Reciprocity is about a continuous dialogical state of being in tune with how the knowledge is produced.

When reciprocity is approached as relational the whole logic of exchange as objective goods seems absurd. Rather than exchanging goods, the participants and researchers feel that they are 'in it' together, learn from one another what kind of contribution is ethical, and reinforce their interactions with what they learn. Reciprocity as relational requires a certain amount of welcoming of the perspective of the other. This in turn requires submitting to a research process without being able to entirely anticipate the outcome.

In both of our studies the three characteristics above looked very different.

Maija: school ethnography in a reindeer herding village

For my Ph.D. research, I conducted a four-month reflexive school ethnography (Alvesson & Sköldberg, 2009; Davies, 1999) in a reindeer herding village with approximately 150 inhabitants. My partner and two children accompanied me during my stay in the village. I define reciprocity as 'being in it together', as 'positive actions' and as something 'continuously reinforced'. In this section I discuss what these meant in my research. All three overlap and have multiple sides, but I will focus on selected aspects.

In it together

Dialogical knowledge production is essentially a transformative process to both, participants as well as researchers. When conducting research in the rural North, it is not only the representations of the rural North that become questioned. First, the researcher's Self is a subject too. Second, various discourses in which 'rural' is signified and inscribed with meanings become questioned.

First, as I and my family learned about life in the rural North, we learned about ourselves and our lives, and our perceptions of ourselves, resulting in our lives becoming questioned. Sometimes this took the form of clearly articulated thoughts, such as when discussing the futures we want for our children and the offerings of the rural and the urban. Other times it was much more ambivalent. We could feel that our position had shifted in an ambiguous way without a conscious thought. For example, towards the end of the field trip I wrote in my journal that I regretted having to go back to academia. Initially the emotional outbursts in the village had frightened me, but now

> it feels warmer, somehow, when emotions are not hidden in contemporary versions of Jane Austen-style equivocations, but they are right there, to be dealt with together. I dread going back and 'maturing' my expression again (i.e. depriving it of emotion).

In this way the participants and I are *in it together*. As I learned about lives in the rural North, the participants learned about their lives, I learned about my own life and they learned something about my life.

Second, in this particular research, when the participants criticised the discourses and representations that portrayed the rural North as 'remote' or 'lacking progress', they also criticised popular conceptualisations of 'centre' which characterise something else as 'remote', and contemporary education's take on 'progress' and on situations in which 'success' can occur (Lanas, Rautio & Syrjälä, 2012). During the research process I was repeatedly surprised to learn how static the perceptions of northern villages in the academic community were. I saw this as having less to do with rural villages and more to do with how the academic community wanted to see itself (successful, progressive, vivid) in relation to the villages. In this way, we *are in it together*. The academic community can only learn about rural villages if it is willing to rethink parts of itself.

Positive actions

Even though the research relationships were made possible by the research, they were not limited by it. In other words, as I became a part of the participants' everyday lives, the participants' needs progressed and changed. They 'appropriated' me in their lives (see also Gallacher & Gallagher, 2008). The research and my existence in the village were moulded not only based on my own needs or the needs of the research but also by various participants. In this research I see *positive actions* as 'willingness to be appropriated'.

Sometimes being appropriated was simple – for example, when local children invited me to play games, to their homes or to the reindeer roundups, told me about their pets or asked me to help with a task. Other times it meant I found myself in situations for which I had no training, such as when parents shared very painful stories. For example, once I met a student's mother for the first time over a cup of coffee. She began telling me about her son, who shot himself ten years ago. She knew I was a researcher, I had my notebook open and she wasn't sensitive about anonymity. Clearly, for her it was not an issue. I, on the other hand, was deeply touched by her tears and by the things she said. I felt that if I were a real 'professional' I would know the 'right' things to say and the 'right' way to be in this situation. I was out of my depth. During those two hours I eventually decided that, although the professional in me has no idea what to do, the person does. So I listened, silently drinking my coffee and momentarily sharing her pain with her.

Sometimes being appropriated meant that I found myself in a peculiar ethical position. For example, since I lived in the village and our children played together, the parents trusted me, whereas they did not initially trust the schoolteacher (since she was a representative of the school). Therefore, as the practices in the school began improving, the parents attributed many of the positive changes in the school to my being in the school, even though the changes that took place were actually the teacher's. I struggled with being given the credit for something that was not my doing, and I repeatedly told the parents that the teacher was the one who was making the changes, but my words had no influence. Ultimately I began to see this phenomenon as not about me and credit, but as an essential part of the process. The families utilised me as a 'mediator of trust' until they had established a trusting relationship with the teacher and the school (Lanas & Kiilakoski, 2013). Five years after the fieldwork, the same teacher was still in the village school and had trusting relationships with the parents.

Finally, the research itself was constantly negotiated and renegotiated. For example, the village schoolteacher requested that I do not simply sit back, observe and merely report the struggles in the village school, but that I would try and help. The teacher asked that I do this simply by sharing perspectives with her instead of reporting them later elsewhere. This meant investing effort not only in the research but also in the field. It meant becoming engaged in the process that I observed, which brought characteristics of action research into the process.

I found that my role had to be constantly renegotiated, with each participant, with each arising situation. Otherwise the willingness to be appropriated would have led to even more blurring of the role of a researcher/therapist/assistant/activist. Whereas such blurring is not necessarily automatically harmful, it does bring additional pressure to the researcher and it may require training that the researcher may not have. This, in turn, may constitute a risk for research ethics.

Continuously reinforced

A research relationship is not static. Rather, it evolves as situations in the field change and as participants and researchers begin to know each other better. A research relationship is not something established once, but it is something constantly 'done', like relational ethics. Words such as 'respect', 'openness' and 'equality' are easy to state at the beginning of research, but actually 'doing them' and thoroughly integrating them into the research requires continuous reinforcing.

In my fieldwork I operationalised relational ethics as a set of ground rules. The ground rules were, for example:

- I showed my notebook notes to the person they were about, but never to others.
- I never commented on the actions of one participant to another.
- I did not comment unless I was asked for a comment.
- I visited all students' homes equally, when they asked me to.

I was open about these ground rules to the participants, wanting to provide them with the opportunity to call me on lapses.

An interesting aspect I discovered was that the research relationship did not end when the fieldwork ended. Since this was my first fieldwork, this came as rather a surprise to me. When I left the village with my family, with adult participants we simply agreed that we might meet again and, if we did, we would be happy about it. It was different with the students. There was a mutual heartbreak between them and me, and some students felt abandoned and angry. Relational ethics, in this situation, meant taking the anger and supporting them through it (more in Lanas, 2011). Even though I was already physically out of the field, it was ethically important that the research relationship was reciprocal as long as the relationship lasted, even distant. For half a year after the field trip, the students called me, sent me emails and text messages and wrote on my Facebook page. I had not anticipated it, but I realised it was embedded in the relationship we had built. So, when they contacted me I dropped what I was doing and was happy to hear from them. After half a year the contacts started winding down, until they stopped.

Similarly, the final reports (my Ph.D. and journal publications) were acts within the same relationship, and my reporting had to be in line with the ethics and the relationship that I had constructed during the fieldwork.

Pauliina: exchanging letters about beauty in everyday life

My Ph.D. study was carried out with four participants from a village of twenty-seven inhabitants in total. My broad research objective was to contribute new perspectives to the prevailingly negative research rhetoric, policy discourses, as well as popular imagery of life in Northern Finnish villages. The approach of the research, as well as the design of it, was built on an idea that rural places and their inhabitants do not necessarily lack resources if resources are considered also as individually and collectively produced rather than only externally given (i.e. money, work, infrastructure). The more specific objective was then to identify and discuss some of the individual and collective processes through which resources for a good-enough life are produced. To be able to approach these reiterative processes, everyday life rhythms and routines, as well as to provide space for the participants to reflect on something quite abstract – beauty in their lives – a data collection method of recurrent letter writing, or correspondence, was chosen (in more detail see Rautio, 2009).

At the time the emerging field of everyday life aesthetics was highlighting the significance of people's multisensory engagement in their everyday life environments as significant for wellbeing and meaningful place-attachment (e.g. Saito, 2007; Light & Smith, 2005; Berleant, 2010) as well as for education (Winston, 2010). Virtually no empirical research existed of actual people and their view of aesthetics in their lives, however. The four women who took part in my research were instructed to reflect on beauty in their everyday lives. The data accumulated via an exchange of letters: each participant, as well as I as the researcher, wrote one letter per month for a period of one year. We also met up several times during the year, including a lengthy group discussion in the middle and individual interviews at the end of the year. The continual acts generating reciprocity in my study, unlike in Maija's, locate more to the written representations rather than to the face-to-face meetings.

Reciprocity in my research unfolded in three ways in particular:

1   The exchange of letters was literally reciprocal for all involved: each participant wrote to the others, the researcher included, making the process of letter writing inherently motivating and rewarding in itself.
2   The lack of set questions or particular themes, apart from the overall theme of beauty, provided an open-ended process, the directions of which were up to both the researcher and the participants.
3   The research design was process-oriented, rather than outcome-oriented, directing the focus on to how phenomena are produced rather than what they are like.

Producing data relationally and reciprocally meant that I was not limited to individual views or thoughts, but could follow as well as participate in a criss-crossing and associative thought-exchange. This is particularly relevant in rural communities that are small and/or tight-knit: people craft their lives in relation to others in the same environment. That the process of writing took place within a relatively long timeframe meant that the accounts reflected were iterative and open-ended rather than static. This is to say that many ways of recounting one's life and wellbeing – also conflicting ones – were possible; everyday life stood a chance of remaining complex and rich rather than categorised.

The kind of reciprocity that allowed research data to evolve over time, in space and in relation to other people and the environment, proved significant in articulating how the participants of this research were directing their lives and regaining agency over defining their own wellbeing in an essentially relational manner. The resources that were produced and reproduced by reflecting on beauty in their lives were dependent on a variety of relations – material and immaterial, social and non-human – and pertained to a sense of continuity and belonging with one's environment. These resources were by no means clearly explicable by individual participants, but rather surfaced as a result of the whole of the collective correspondence.

The challenges of such an open-ended way of doing research have to do with motivating and engaging one's participants or co-researchers, engaging with theory and retaining an analytic 'eye', as well as justifying the research to the academy and to the wider society. In the case of my study the motivation of participants proved easy, as all of the four felt the letter writing to be inherently motivating. The engagement with theory was more difficult, as with a topic pertaining to beauty the appealing option would have been to remain on a descriptive level, accounting for elements that are experienced as beautiful and thus increase wellbeing. Engaging with theory is, however, an ethical issue in my view. Remaining at a descriptive level runs the risk of essentialising the subjects and topics of one's research. Engaging in theoretical discussions, as if on a meta-level – focusing on how phenomena are produced rather than what they are (like) – is assigning agency to the subjects researched. A focus on theorising and deconstructing processes of producing material-discursive reality retains possibilities also for transforming normalised structures of power.

A key challenge in this study was the enduring of a chronic insecurity that I as a researcher felt. Having no practical objectives or clearly explicated ideas of why this study is relevant, I often felt that the only thing missing was the little boy shouting, 'Look, the emperor has no clothes!' In addition to feeling lost, something that I've since come to cherish in research (see Lather, 2004), I also often felt that I did not get 'deep' enough into the lives of the villagers to be able to state anything of worth about their rural lives – I felt that I was failing both the participants and my academic community. This fear transformed into a still-ongoing deconstruction of the role of a researcher: rather than holding the task of understanding and representing another person's life, a reciprocal researcher attends to the interface of lives and representations. This is to say that I would cease to worry about understanding something that exists objectively from me and my research. Rather, I would focus on what our encounters produced: how were representations of good-enough life produced by all of us, in time, in space and places, in countless relations.

In an era of increasing pressure towards accountability, the highest hurdle is perhaps convincing the institutions safeguarding and funding, and therefore defining, the limits of 'proper' research (see MacLure, 2006, for example) that this open-ended approach to research is valid.

Discussion

In this chapter we have presented two studies which both, in their own way, suggest embracing uncertainty as an essential part of research. Indeed, reciprocity as described above relies on embracing uncertainty, not on avoiding it. We conclude by arguing that when constantly reflecting insecurity becomes fruitful. It can lead to a reciprocal research process in which the needs of the participants are constantly addressed.

Researchers' emotions in the field and with research participants are increasingly recognised as a part of the research process, but they are still often seen as if external to the research (Davies, 1999; Denzin & Lincoln, 1998; Lumsden, 2009; Mosselson, 2010). They are not commonly discussed openly, and engaging with emotions still often carries an air of 'unprofessionalism' in research. This is especially the case with feelings of uncertainty. As a researcher, feeling uncertain may be interpreted as a sign that researchers do not know what they are doing. Our perspective is that insecurity is a healthy part of research and that humility is good for research. Moreover, researchers' emotions, be what they may, are an integral part of the research, and reciprocity begins with acknowledging one's own emotions. When constructing ethical and reciprocal approaches, we first must recognise our own fears and insecurities in order to make sure that we do not act in their account. Research has power to create, disseminate and maintain representations.

When we look into the difficult choices we made during our researches, we see that we were often negotiating with our own fears and insecurities. As young members of an experienced research group, we felt a fear of failure. What if we failed the group? Or the participants? Or the funders? As an emotion, fear is not fruitful or empowering as such. On the contrary, it makes us freeze and seek quick solutions. The current common way of planning and reporting research encourages the idea that a researcher can and should control the outcome of the research. Pursuing control and reciprocity, however, tend to be mutually exclusive.

The key ethical insight that the reciprocity of these studies yield is grounded in the Deleuze-inspired ontology of being (existing) as becoming in relation and in intra-action with other beings and things (see especially Barad, 2007; Lenz Taguchi, 2011). That we became researchers with objectives, insights and conclusions resulted from an open-ended and unpredictable process of engaging with our research participants who in turn became research participants with reflections and thoughts about our topic at hand in relation to us. We could not research their lives as if objective observers, because the encounter affects their lives, and our lives. This is to say that we were necessarily co-researching all of our lives, resisting the assigning of any coherence or stable 'identity' to any of us, rather focusing on the processes of how we all continually (re)produce our lives as good enough (see Rautio, 2010).

We suggest replacing uncertainty of the outcome with an uncertainty of the process and an unfounded trust in the outcome. Success does not have to be an either/or question – it can also be the process of trying.

Note

1 In comparison to one of the most commonly agreed ways to delineate rural areas – a population density of fewer than 150 persons per square kilometre (330 per square mile) – Finnish Lapland is virtually empty, with a population density of only 2 persons per square kilometre (4.5 per square mile) (Statistics Finland, 2013).

References

Alvesson, M. & Sköldberg, K. (2009). *Reflexive Methodology: New Vistas for Qualitative Research*, 2nd edition. Los Angeles, CA: Sage.

Barad, K. (2007). *Meeting the Universe Halfway: Quantum Physics and the Entanglement of Matter and Meaning*. Durham, NC: Duke University Press.

Berleant, A. (2010). *Sensibility and Sense. The Aesthetic Transformation of the Human World*. Exeter: Imprint Academic.

Corbett, M. (2008). *Learning to Leave: The Irony of Schooling in a Coastal Community*. Halifax, NS: Fernwood Publishing.

Davies, C. A. (1999). *Reflexive Ethnography: A Guide to Researching Selves and Others*. London: Routledge.

Denzin, N. K. & Lincoln, Y. S. (1998). *The Landscape of Qualitative Research: Theories and Issues*. Thousand Oaks, CA: Sage.

Eriksson, M. (2010). People in Stockholm are smarter than countryside folks – Reproducing urban and rural imaginaries in film and life. *Journal of Rural Studies*, 26(2): 95–104. doi:10.1016/j.jrurstud.2009.09.005

Gallacher, L. & Gallagher, M. (2008) Methodological immaturity in childhood research? Thinking through 'participatory methods'. *Childhood*, 15(4): 499–516.

Gildersleeve, R. E. (2010). Dangerously important moment(s) in reflexive research practices with immigrant youth. *International Journal of Qualitative Studies in Education*, 23(4): 407–421.

Horton, J. (2008). Producing Postman Pat: The popular cultural construction of idyllic rurality. *Journal of Rural Studies*, 24: 389–398.

Hubbard, B. (2005). 'Inappropriate and incongruous': Opposition to asylum centres in the English countryside. *Journal of Rural Studies*, 21: 3–17.

Lanas, M. & Kiilakoski, T. (2013). Growing pains: teacher becoming a transformative agent. *Pedagogy, Culture & Society*. doi:10.1080/14681366.2012.759134

Lanas, M. (2008). Oikeus paikkaan—kuinka koulu ja pohjoinen pienkylä kohtaavat? [Right to place – How do school and a northern village meet?] in M. Lanas, H. Niinistö and J. Suoranta (eds), *Kriittisen pedagogiikan kysymyksiä 2* [*Questions of Critical Pedagogy 2*]. Tampere: The Department of Education of the University of Tampere, pp. 51–80.

Lanas, M. (2011). How can non-verbalized emotions in the field be addressed in research? *International Journal of Research & Method in Education*, 34(2): 131–145.

Lanas, M., Rautio, P. & Syrjälä, L. (2012). Beyond educating the marginals: Recognizing life in Northern rural Finland. *Scandinavian Journal of Educational Research*. doi:10.1080/00313831.2012.656283

Lather, P. (2004). *Getting Lost: Feminist Efforts Toward a Double(d) Science*. New York: State University of New York Press.

Lenz Taguchi, H. (2011). Investigating learning, participation and becoming in early childhood practices with a relational materialist approach. *Global Studies of Childhood*, 1(1): 36–49.

Light, A. & Smith, J. (eds) (2005). *The Aesthetics of Everyday Life*. New York: Columbia University Press.

Lumsden, K. (2009). 'Don't ask a woman to do another woman's job': Gendered interactions and the emotional ethnographer. *Sociology*, 43(3): 497–513.

MacLure, M. (2006). The bone in the throat: some uncertain thoughts on baroque method. *Qualitative Studies in Education*, 19(6): 729–745.

Markey, S., Halseth, G. & Manson, D. (2008). Challenging the inevitability of rural decline: Advancing the policy of place in northern British Columbia. *Journal of Rural Studies*, 24(4): 409–421.

Mosselson, J. (2010). Subjectivity and reflexivity: Locating the self in research on dislocation. *International Journal of Qualitative Studies in Education*, 23(4): 479–494.

Muilu, T. (2010). Needs for rural research in the northern Finland context. *Journal of Rural Studies*, 26: 73–80.

Rallis, S. F. & Rossman, G. B. (2010). Caring reflexivity. *International Journal of Qualitative Studies in Education*, 23(4): 495–499.

Rallis, S. F. (2010). 'That is NOT what's happening at Horizon!': Ethics and misrepresenting knowledge in text. *International Journal of Qualitative Studies in Education*, 23(4): 435–448.

Rautio, P. (2009). Finding the place of everyday beauty. Correspondence as a method of data collection. *International Journal of Qualitative Methods*, 8(2): 15–34.

Rautio, P. (2010). *Writing about Everyday Beauty in a Northern Village: An Argument for Diversity of Habitable Places*. Oulu: Oulun yliopisto.

Ridanpää, J. (2007). Laughing at northernness: Postcolonialism and metafictive irony in the imaginative geography. *Social & Cultural Geography*, 8(6): 907–928.

Rossman, G. B. & Rallis, S. F. (2010). Everyday ethics: Reflections on practice. *International Journal of Qualitative Studies in Education*, 23(4): 379–391.

Saito, Y. (2007). *Everyday Aesthetics*. Oxford: Oxford University Press.

Statistics Finland (2013). Population. http://www.stat.fi/tup/suoluk/suoluk_vaesto_en.html. Accessed 12 August 2013.

Thrift, N. (2008). *Non-Representational Theory: Space, Politics, Affect*. London: Routledge.

Winston, J. (2010). *Beauty and Education*. London, Routledge.

Chapter 13

Three Rs for rural research

Respect, responsibility and reciprocity

Michelle Anderson and Michele Lonsdale

Introduction

To work in and with local communities in regional, rural or remote areas can be among the most challenging and rewarding of research activities. A challenge for outsiders can sometimes be gaining the trust of individuals or the community as a whole. This can especially be in cases where previous 'experts' have not kept faith with those from the community and have not treated the knowledge gained or the knowledge holders with sufficient respect. A profound reward, however, is that once trust is established rich and useful insights may be gained into other ways of knowing, thinking and being.

This chapter offers some reflections on theory and practice in the context of rural research. These reflections are based on our experiences as researchers in a wide range of rural projects and settings. In particular, we explore the ethical considerations of respect, responsibility and reciprocity. These concepts can challenge reflective researchers to be the best they can be.

We begin the chapter by defining what we mean by 'rural' and then elaborate on the concepts of 'respect', 'responsibility' and 'reciprocity'. We provide brief illustrative examples of each of these principles. In each of the examples referred to, the researchers have sought to engage people as contributors rather than passive participants. Beyond this, the project examples differ in their geographic locations, purpose and how the information was gathered and used. We have deliberately chosen to share vignettes from multiple projects to illustrate the different and sometimes creative ways in which researchers must adapt to changing contexts and situations. We then share some thoughts on what being a critically self-aware researcher means to us. We conclude with some overall comments and questions to help you think about this, too.

What do we mean by rural?

'Rural' as used in this chapter covers regional, remote and very remote communities. While 'rural' is generally used to describe 'country' Australia, we are using this term to denote non-metropolitan areas, including very remote communities. In general, 'rural' here refers to communities that are:

- geographically isolated
- sparsely populated
- distant from services
- culturally diverse.

These communities may also be of low socioeconomic status, have limited access to resources and have a transient population. In remote and very remote communities there may also be extremes of climate and highly mobile populations.

These understandings of rural relate to the geographic 'place' and other aspects that can be mapped about 'the rural', but they are not the only understandings to consider. For example, writing about the experiences of new principals (head-teachers) in small schools, Helen Wildy (2010) conceptualises the rural as follows:

> *Place:* not only geography and climate, but also of culture. This includes, understanding knowledge of local traditions, history, economics and links to wider communities, as well as local politics and social orders ...
> *People:* dealing with adults in the school and the community ... building relationships with all members of the community is crucial ...
> *System:* ... provision of support across inland regions tends to be sparse, with vast distances not only between schools but also between schools and regional offices. Keeping abreast of policy shifts in a distant bureaucracy may not figure prominently ...
> *Self:* ... the challenges of developing personal resilience ... with high levels of visibility of the position [principal] ... and dealing with professional and physical isolation.
>
> (2010, pp. vi–vii)

It is important not to assume 'rurality' is static. Dalley-Trim and Alloway (2010), in their research on rural and remote students' aspirations and expectations, argue that it is misguided to think young people in these contexts experience life in the same way. Rural and remote communities in Australia can exhibit enormous diversity. Researchers need to recognise that these communities may differ in, for example, size, access to resources, social relationships and occupational options. Furthermore, when we refer to rural geographic locations we could be talking about closely populated small towns in horticultural areas; widely distributed communities in Australia's interior; coastal rural communities; isolated small camps on the fringes of outback towns, and so on. All these places tend to be small in population.

There are many rewards in undertaking research in rural communities. Often the very size of the community means it is easier for researchers to connect with people, seeing individuals less as 'objects' of research and more as contributors to the research activity. Conducting research in a rural community may also mean sharing a meal in local surrounds, living in and among members of the community, and being more attuned to the nuances and subtleties of local relationships and perspectives. It can involve learning more about the local context than might be the case when conducting research in a large urban area.

It is also important not to 'romanticise' the lived experience of the rural. Living conditions in remote and very remote areas in particular can be materially and psychologically harsh and confronting to an outsider. Researchers external to the community can be treated with scepticism and suspicion, particularly in communities where people feel their confidences or views have been previously misrepresented, overlooked or betrayed. 'Fly in, fly out' researchers who only stay for a short time in the community can also be regarded with cynicism. Sometimes, because of funding constraints, researchers are not able to stay in a community beyond a couple of days, which is barely enough time to meet and greet, let alone form a bond meaningful enough to support shared knowledge.

Sometimes, a researcher might not be able to visit the community at all and might need to be content with conversations by email or phone. In many very remote communities, even these forms of communication might not be feasible when face-to-face dialogue is the preferred form of interaction or where computer availability and proficiency might be low.

In such circumstances, important considerations about context are raised. How can you develop an understanding of context when you're not living in the community or staying for long? The principles of respect, reciprocity and responsibility become even more critical in such circumstances.

Why focus on respect, responsibility and reciprocity?

In her book, *Decolonizing Methodologies* (2012), Linda Tuhiwai Smith asks the reader to consider that:

> belief in the ideal that benefiting mankind is indeed a primary outcome of scientific research is as much a reflection of ideology as it is of academic training. It becomes so taken for granted that many researchers simply assume that they as individuals embody this ideal and are natural representatives of it when they work with other communities.
>
> (2012, p. 2)

Viewed in this way, our chapter is an attempt to encourage self-reflection in early career researchers. Without explicit self-reflection, each of us can easily slip into taking for granted our research thinking, language and practice, including in relation to ethics. In university documentation, ethics is often referred to as 'the ethics process'. Such a description suggests a technical activity rather than a process of reflection and sensitivity to those potentially affected by research. The paperwork associated with ethics approval and the fact that researchers need to gain such approval upfront can add to this way of thinking about the topic. Ethics, however, is much more than a one-off activity. In our view, it underpins and helps shape all aspects of the research activity (see also Busher, 2003).

Ethical considerations such as 'informed consent' and 'confidentiality' are important considerations for any researcher and these too can present interesting challenges in the context of rural research. For example, 'the school' in a research project may well be the *only* school in the community. Similarly, it does not matter how well a researcher tries to disguise a particular incident or the people involved in it by using pseudonyms in a report, it is more than likely that everyone in the community will know what or to whom the report is referring.

We have chosen these three ethical principles of respect, responsibility and reciprocity because they help remind us that social research is situated in social, historical, cultural and place-based contexts and perspectives. In addition, these principles have relevance to all phases of the research: from the research concept through to the sharing and dissemination of findings. Finally, we have chosen these principles because what each means in rural contexts is not necessarily well documented and understood. By putting the spotlight on these principles, we are not putting ourselves up as 'experts' on such issues. Rather, we are showing why we value these principles and how they are integral to our work as researchers.

Ethical concepts and practices

By 'respect' we mean showing that other ways of thinking and knowing are valued and treated equally. The concept of 'two-way' working together in the context of research encourages an approach that draws equally upon Western and non-Western knowledge, skills and research methodologies. In such an approach, conceptualising the research 'problem' to be addressed, the methods used to gather information, the language used to describe the research activities and the presentation and use of the information, all reflect a genuinely 'two-way' approach where both mainstream and non-mainstream cultures are integrated at every stage (see also Yunkaporta & Kirby, 2011 on Indigenous ways of knowing).

In one remote community, two researchers from the Australian Council for Educational Research (ACER) spent time with the school's Aboriginal Liaison Officer who provided a cultural context for the community and explained the social structures, clan groups and kinship links prior to any conversations taking place in the community. In this project, the researchers learned about who could marry whom in the clans and about avoidance relationships. As their stay included a weekend, the researchers were invited to share a meal of fresh fish on a beach with several families who talked about their lives past and present. These interactions gave the researchers a better understanding of local perspectives on a range of issues that have impacted on people's lives. The interactions also helped give a context to subsequent conversations about children's learning.

In our research we explicitly try to look for ways to demonstrate that we recognise and value context and place. This notion of 'two way' is in stark contrast to what Wadsworth (1984) refers to as a 'data raid, where researchers do a "smash and grab", meaning, getting in, getting the data, and getting out' (p. 218).

In another project, in order to generate 'deep learning', participants needed to feel comfortable enough with each other to be able to share their thoughts and critical feedback. To facilitate this, each school principal in the project participated in a two-day focus group workshop on the fieldwork feedback. Everyone brought along an 'artefact' that meant something important to them about their community and/or school. These objects included an artefact created by students, a school newsletter, a painting of a local landmark and photos of the environment in which one of the schools was located. Sitting in a circle, each person was invited through a process of storytelling to share the significance of his or her artefact with the others. The artefact provided a medium through which everyone could develop a sense of place, person and culture. The artefact took the attention away from the person, which helped with any nerves.

Second, the storytelling was followed by a relaxed dinner together where people could continue a conversation over a meal. Both activities were done on the evening before the focus group discussion. (For other forms and uses of storytelling in rural contexts, see Wake, 2012).

By 'responsibility' we mean conducting research that is transparent in its processes and fair in its conclusions. No finding, for example, should come as a surprise to any person in the research if there has been transparent and open engagement from the outset.

Recognising the critical importance of trusted relationships in conducting any research in rural communities, an evaluation involving two ACER researchers also included a researcher who had lived in one of the communities for many years. This researcher spoke the local language and, most importantly, was held in high esteem by the local communities. The research team met with key community members to talk about what the research would look like, who in the community should be invited to participate, how the information would be shared, captured and disseminated, and when. Sessions were facilitated by local community members, who were paid for their time and expertise. Small discussion groups encouraged stories and perspectives to be shared and captured orally, visually and in writing.

The researchers prepared several reports to go back into the communities, including short summaries written in plain English for distribution among community members. Care was taken to respect the views that were shared and to represent these in ways that accurately reflected local concerns. A thank-you 'postcard' was sent to each person who participated in the conversations in each community.

The most critical element in the success of this research project was the inclusion on the team of a researcher with pre-existing relationships of mutual trust with one of the local communities. This knowledge helped generate a strong sense of responsibility for the way in which information was collected and used.

In addition to being accurate and honest, this information must also be used in ways that are consistent with the purpose of the research and expectations of all parties. One strategy that we have used as researchers to build in a responsible approach to research is to clarify from the outset with people in a rural community that any information provided will be used in ways that are consistent with local expectation and not in ways that go against local values or principles. This can be done in different ways through conversation, email or as part of a plain language flyer of information that people directly involved in the research can share with others in their community.

In two projects, different versions of the following context were distributed within rural communities prior to each project commencing:

- the name of the program
- the purpose of the evaluation
- the individuals conducting the evaluation with a photo of, and a sentence about, each researcher who would be coming into the community
- how local community members could participate in the evaluation
- how and where conversations would be carried out (e.g. with food supplied; in a school staffroom; outside under a tree; in a community centre; in a crèche; in the Shire office, etc.)
- whether names or organisations would be disclosed
- how information would be used.

On the second page, a consent form was provided for people to sign. This covered such information as the voluntary nature of a person's engagement with the project. We also included our contact details. (*Note*: Depending on whether English is a first, second, third, fourth or even fifth language, obtaining verbal agreement to participate in a research activity may be more appropriate than expecting written consent. However, the concept of informed consent is fundamental regardless of the form it takes.)

Confidentiality

One area in which researchers need to act responsibly is in protecting confidentiality. Parties involved in a research project need to be able to trust the researcher to report on findings in such a way as to respect and protect the identities of participants. This is often a commitment given in writing as part of a consent-seeking process. However, maintaining confidentiality can be challenging when the location is a small rural community where people's identities might reasonably be guessed. Responsible research in this context means:

- establishing dignified and respectful relationships in an atmosphere of trust from the outset so that people are willing to share their perspectives
- ensuring all correspondence is managed securely and confidentially
- ensuring participants are given opportunities to amend or refine their comments early in the process (for example, by sending each person a copy of the draft notes based on their particular conversation with the researcher/s)
- writing up the research in such a way that participants are satisfied that their perspectives have been captured and reported accurately
- being clear from the start of the project whether comments will be attributed or de-identified – this will depend on the nature of the research and its intended purpose, and on sensitivities that perhaps researchers or community members may not have considered

In one project additional opportunities were provided for local community members to speak one-on-one with the researchers. This was offered after finding that there was a certain reticence in the small discussion groups that also involved work supervisors.

In another project, several participants in a rural location sought clarification from the ACER researchers regarding who would have access to the draft notes that would be written up and provided back to them. The participants opted to use their private email addresses rather than those of the organisation for whom they worked. The draft notes were sent for checking and approval. The final report de-identified all participants across the whole project while still reflecting the views that were expressed in the findings. Participants informed the researchers of their satisfaction with the process.

In yet another project, the intention to publish the information collected from the fieldwork was made clear at the start of the project. The personal and professional implications of being involved in the project were discussed with each principal, as was the likely impact of their involvement on others. This was important because, while the project focused on the principal's experience of leading a small school in a rural location, this could not be divorced from the staff, students, parents and others in the community. Each principal sought the consent of these groups and of their local school authority to participate in the project. As part of this process, whether the cases would be de-identified or not was also discussed with each principal individually. This was done to avoid anyone feeling pressured one way or the other. All agreed that the project was an opportunity to recognise and celebrate small schools and the rural communities in which these are located.

Responsible research means maintaining confidentiality, seeking informed consent to engage in the research and respecting the right of contributors to withdraw at any stage of the activity. It also means providing opportunities for individuals to be satisfied that their contributions are being represented fairly and faithfully.

By 'reciprocity' we mean engaging in a higher degree of connection with those in the research activities than would be the case in a more formal or anonymous kind of research project. Conducting research underpinned by a commitment to this principle means recognising that all parties can contribute in some way to the activity, to the relationship that enables and sustains the activity and to the outcomes of the research. A common reciprocal research approach is to engage in ethnographic participatory or action research. This approach has been used effectively with community or vulnerable groups (for example, Creswell, 2007; Hammersley & Atkinson, 2005; Liamputtong & Ezzy, 2005).

As part of an evaluation of a pilot program in a very remote community, two ACER researchers visited the community to find out how the program was going. Teachers willingly gave up precious time to share their stories. In turn, the researchers shared knowledge about literacy developments. Reciprocity was evident in other ways. For example, the principal invited the researchers to share a meal on the first night. The researchers helped staff with the preparation and serving of breakfast at the school in the mornings and with the clearing up afterwards. Some time later, staff members from this same school visited ACER's Melbourne office while they were in the city attending a conference. The staff provided an informal presentation to an ACER research team on what it was like to live and teach in a very remote community school. In acknowledgement of this contribution to organisational understanding, ACER provided a culturally appropriate gift that could be shared with the community. Reciprocity in this context was about recognising that each party had something of value to contribute, that information could be shared and relationships strengthened through recognition of what could be learned from one another.

In another project, to reaffirm that the principals were contributors to the project, participants agreed that a workshop discussion could be audio-recorded. A 'critical friend' with a deep understanding of rural living and leadership was invited into the project and workshop discussion. This person helped bring issues into the open for further discussion and debate and encouraged critical reflection. During the workshop, participants reflected on what had been learned from the project. For example: What are the areas of commonality across the literature review and our cases? What are we leaving out, why, and do these gaps matter? Overall, what are the key lessons, challenges and possibilities for leading learning in small schools in rural settings? The notes from the workshop were drafted by the ACER researcher and sent to the principals and critical friend for their comment and feedback.

Critically self-aware researchers

In this final section, we want to draw your attention to the specific issue of being a critically self-aware researcher. This is important for any research undertaken.

Think about a situation where you are doing something for the first time. Perhaps it's learning to ride a motorbike, cooking a new recipe or travelling to a place you have never been before. Or, in the context of this book, perhaps you are undertaking a piece of research for the first time in a rural community. Regardless, all senses are likely to be on high alert. You are checking and rechecking, asking questions, and in many cases seeking feedback and advice from others.

Now think about something you have done many times over. It could be something as simple as getting your breakfast in the morning, through to something more complex, like driving a car. In these cases, do you pause to reflect on a 'meta-level' the thinking and processes that make up the activity?

Earlier in this chapter, we introduced the concept of 'taken for grantedness' from Linda Tuhiwai Smith and the importance of finding ways to examine our own assumptions and pre-conceived ideas as researchers. This means being sensitive to the expertise, knowledge, skills and perspectives of others and not assuming that the researcher alone is expert.

With the explicit consent of each principal who participated in the previously mentioned research project, in-depth audio-recorded interviews were conducted to help facilitate writing with the school principals. Recording the conversations also offered a way to reflect on what was being said and *not* said, the pauses, and whether the researcher was unintentionally directing the conversation. The transcript was offered to each principal.

An interesting exercise was to listen to the questions being asked and also read them again. This allowed the researcher and the principal to reflect on why the previous question was being followed with the next question. What led to this? Was the researcher really listening to what the principal was saying, or did the follow-up question suggest that the researcher was more concerned with their own train of thought?

Being attuned to our own assumptions and ideas means valuing difference, recognising that insights are unlikely to be shared if researchers are not open to hearing them, and reflecting on the nature of the research enterprise itself. For example: Is the methodology appropriate to the audience? Do community members think about concepts like time or distance in the same way as researchers? Do they value oral or written traditions? Do they see value in the research being undertaken? Who decides such research is of value? Who will benefit from the research? How else might information be shared, other than in formal academic writing?

Talking to people outside on the ground and using crayons and butcher's paper to capture thoughts encouraged a different kind of engagement to an earlier discussion group, which was held in a classroom with a whiteboard, table and upright chairs. The later discussion was more informal and meant other family members could sit on the fringes of the group, sharing the food, listening to the 'circular' and discursive conversations and occasionally contributing. In the room, on the other hand, the set-up encouraged a more formal question-and-answer approach with less spontaneous participant involvement.

Another project culminated in the publication of a book and a jointly run national forum on the topic of the book. Each principal in the project was named as a co-author. Each contributor to the project was present on-stage and a pre-filmed reflection about their journey and the research processes was shown. Participants in this project had a strong sense of ownership all the way through the project.

The self-reflective researcher needs to be open to new or different ways of thinking and doing. Without a capacity for critical self-reflection, the other contexts and perspectives mentioned earlier, such as place, history and people, become detached from the research and the researcher. In the process, the richness and impact of the research are also in danger of being overlooked or lost.

The questions posed by Smith, below, are questions that many communities and Indigenous researchers are asking. We suggest that these are also questions that non-Indigenous researchers could be asking of themselves:

- Whose research is it?
- Who owns it?
- Whose interests does it service?
- Who will benefit from it?
- Who has designed its questions and framed its scope?
- Who will carry it out?
- Who will write it up?
- How will its results be disseminated?

(Smith, 2012, p. 10)

Thinking about these questions encourages a different starting point from that of the Western researcher going into a community, extracting knowledge, writing up this knowledge and publishing it. In this scenario the communities have little control over how their knowledge is being used. Smith's questions encourage us to think more about the context in which the research is being carried out, who 'owns' this knowledge and the extent to which knowledge is being valued or respected. Her questions also make us think about who makes decisions about the use and dissemination of research findings.

Conclusion

To embed the ethical principles and values discussed in this chapter into research thinking and practice can be a challenge. Working 'two way' requires team members to share these ethical principles. It means abandoning previously held assumptions about Western dominance in research and recognising the importance of other ways of thinking and knowing. In our experiences, this research is rewarding and inspiring and has a positive relationship with change. We conclude by offering some questions that may help you think through some of the issues raised in this chapter.

Questions

1. What images come to mind when you think of research in rural communities? Are these images likely to be shared by those in these communities? If not, how could you find out?
2. How confident are you that the research is needed and of benefit to those you are seeking to engage with? How could you find out?

3. Do you know what type of relationship contributors seek with the research and with you? If not, how could you find out?
4. Will the research be a learning opportunity for you *and* those contributing to it? If not, why not?

References

Busher, H. (2003). Ethics of research in education. In M. Coleman & A. R. J. Briggs (eds), *Research Methods in Educational Leadership and Management*, 2nd edition. London: Sage Publications.

Creswell, J. W. (2007). *Qualitative Inquiry & Research Design: Choosing Among Five Approaches*, 2nd edition. Thousand Oaks, CA: Sage Publications.

Dalley-Trim, L. & Alloway, N. (2010). Looking 'outward and onward' in the outback: Regional Australian students' aspirations and expectations for their future as framed by dominant discourses of further education and training. Online. *Australian Educational Researcher*, 37(2): 107–125.

Hammersley, M., & Atkinson, P. (1995). *Ethnography: Principles in Practice*, 2nd edition. London and New York: Routledge. Reprinted 2005.

Liamputtong, P. & Ezzy, D. (2005). *Qualitative Research Methods*, 2nd edition. South Melbourne, Victoria: Oxford University Press.

Smith, L. T. (2012). *Decolonizing Methodologies: Research and Indigenous Peoples*, 2nd edition. London: Zed Books/Radical International Publishing.

Wadsworth, Y. (1984) *Do it Yourself Social Research*. Melbourne: Victorian Council of Social Services.

Wake, D. G. (2012). Exploring rural contexts with digital storytelling. *Rural Educator*, 33(3) (Spring/Summer): 23–37.

Wildy, H. in Anderson, M., Davis, M., Douglas, P., Lloyd, D., Niven, B. and Thiele, H. (2010). *A Collective Act: Leading a small school*. Victoria: Australian Council for Educational Research, ACER Press.

Yunkaporta, T. & Kirby, M. (2011). 'Yarning up Indigenous pedagogies: A dialogue about eight Aboriginal ways of learning'. In N. Purdie, G. Milgate & H. R. Bell (eds.) *Two-way teaching and learning: Toward culturally reflective and relevant education*. Victoria: Australian Council for Educational Research, ACER Press.

Index